EASY & ELEGANT

300 Kosher International Jewish Recipes for Friends and Family

by Mindy Ginsberg

gefen גפן
publishing house בית הוצאה לאור
JERUSALEM ◆ NEW YORK

To my mother, who taught me,
and to my husband, Elliott,
and my children Yosef, Ruven, Ari and Sara
who tell me I'm the best cook in the world

My sister Carole, and daughters-in-law Revital and Sharon
are very special. Thank you for everything.

Copyright © Gefen Publishing House, Ltd.
Jerusalem 2005 / 5764

Cover Design: Art Plus, Jerusalem

Based in part on the Israeli Hebrew language work entitled
Easy, Fast and Elegant: Cooking and Baking for the Family - and Entertaining by Mindy Ginsberg
Published by Ruth Sirkis Publishers, Ltd., 131 Bialik St., Ramat Gan, Tel Aviv 61220, Israel
Photographs © 1986 Ruth Sirkis Publishers, Ltd.

5 7 9 8 6

Gefen Publishing House Ltd
6 Hatzvi Street, Jerusalem 94386, Israel
972-2-538-0247 • orders@gefenpublishing.com

Gefen Books
600 Broadway, Lynbrook, NY 11563, USA
1-516-593-1234 • orders@gefenpublishing.com

www.israelbooks.com

Printed in Israel

Send for our free catalogue

ISBN 965-229-352-0

CONTENTS

Subst/ Equiv. p 185-6

INTRODUCTION

RECIPE: A meal to remember

INGREDIENTS: Good quality and taste
A little experimentation
A feel for cooking

DIRECTIONS: Patience and love all mixed up together

RESULTS: A meal worth remembering and compliments to the chef

---

Cooking can be very creative, and "taste" is the key to great cooking. As a young girl, I was mainly interested in food simply for eating, but being exposed to my mother's good "taste" resulted in my understanding how much more could be involved with food and its preparation. I dare say that my personal experience of growing up in America and later living in Israel has helped me to create this, the *classiest, tastiest kosher cookbook ever!*

Learning how to cook took a bit of experience, patience and love. (Once, when my husband, Elliott, came home to find his birthday cake in the garbage, he was very patient with me and said he still loved me—but that's another story.) As time went on the successes and compliments kept coming, until I finally achieved a "feel" for cooking and began to enjoy experimenting and perfecting recipes according to my own taste.

What made me write a cookbook? It didn't come overnight. After years of many compliments, much appreciation, and more than enough constructive criticism from Elliott and my children—Yosef, Ruven, Ari, and Sara—relatives, friends, and others, cooking became one of my great loves. "Practice Makes Perfect": It may sound trite, but it's the absolute truth. Cooking will always take a bit of time and effort, but the results are well worth it.

Put "love" into your cooking by learning what blends together—there are endless variations. No recipe is too difficult. Some recipes may just take more time and practice. Before I made my first quiche, the thought alone seemed impossible. Now, when I am at a loss what to serve, I prepare a quiche with no effort at all. Quiches actually became a family affair.

This happened to many recipes I used to save for company. Now the difference between "easy" (family affair) dishes and "elegant" (company) dishes is in the manner of presentation and the number of courses and side dishes served at the meal. Something I would use as a side dish for company may become a main course for my family (e.g., Spinach-Noodle Casserole).

When entertaining, remember "color" and "variety." Find a colorful vegetable and be sure to include it as a side dish to the main course. If you're rushed, merely heat canned peach halves. Always have olives, carrots and celery sticks on the table as nibblers.

When I cook, all my heart goes into it and my goal is "great taste." I opened my kitchen and my heart with this book for you to enjoy the results, and I hope you'll agree: *THERE'S NO OTHER BOOK LIKE IT. GOOD LUCK!*

SALADS & DRESSINGS

The refreshing sparkle of

Whatever else you eat, a fresh, crisp salad is always delicious and refreshing. The salad dressing is even more important than the combination of vegetables used. A salad can be made with lettuce alone. Always use fresh quality vegetables unless otherwise indicated. It's tempting to use canned mushrooms, but there's nothing like the freshness of fresh.

With the wide array of possible ingredients, feel free to design your own salad. The standard tossed salad includes any combination of lettuce, cucumber, red and green pepper, tomatoes, scallions and parsley. Variations can be added to almost all salads: red cabbage, radishes, carrots, raisins, sunflower seeds, cubed Roquefort cheese, feta cheese, croutons, avocado, walnuts, pecans, etc.

Tasty, tangy dressing is the KEY to great salads. It matters little if you leave out or add an ingredient or two in the salad, but don't skimp on the dressing. (Outside of the dressing section, there are lots of dressings scattered through the salad recipes.)

Don't be afraid to experiment; salads are very flexible. Once you get into it, you'll be amazed at the creative varieties.

A few notes to keep in mind: Salads with lettuce or tomatoes should be prepared just before serving. Salads without tomatoes or lettuce should be prepared beforehand and allowed to marinate a few hours or overnight.

THOUSAND ISLAND DRESSING
A standard

Food processor comes in handy

1 egg, hard-boiled	1 scallion
1 onion	1 tbsp. lemon juice
½ green pepper	2 cloves garlic, crushed
1 tbsp. gamba	1 cup mayonnaise
1 tbsp. dill	½ cup ketchup
1 tbsp. parsley	salt and pepper to taste

Chop egg and all the vegetables and place in bowl. (Chopping can be done in food processor.) Combine lemon juice, garlic, mayonnaise, ketchup, salt and pepper; add to vegetables and mix.
Refrigerate.
P.S. Great with fresh salad, avocado, fishcakes, artichokes.

VINAIGRETTE DRESSING
Just right

Food processor comes in handy

⅔ cup olive or vegetable oil	4 cloves garlic, crushed
⅓ cup balsalmic or wine vinegar	1½ tbsp. prepared mustard
1 tbsp. water	½ tsp. paprika
2 tsp. salt	2–3 tsp. sugar
¼ tsp. pepper	1 tbsp. parsley, chopped
	2 tsp. lemon juice, optional

Process all ingredients in food processor with metal or plastic blade or shake in jar. Refrigerate.
Great with fresh tossed salad, artichokes, avocado, etc.

MAYONNAISE
Homemade is so much tastier

Takes no time

2 eggs	1 tbsp. prepared mustard
¼ cup vinegar	1 tsp. sugar
½ tsp. salt	1½ cup oil
¼ tsp. pepper	

In blender blend eggs, vinegar, salt, pepper, mustard and sugar about 10 seconds.
Add oil, very slowly, in a steady stream. Mixture will thicken by the time all the oil is poured in. Push in carefully a little at the sides until well blended (a few seconds).

TARTAR SAUCE DRESSING
Variation on a theme

2 tbsp. capers
a few green olives
1 small pickle
1 small onion

1 cup mayonnaise
½ tsp. sugar
½ tsp. salt
⅛ tsp. pepper

Chop capers, olives, pickles and onion. Add mayonnaise and sugar and mix together.
P.S. Excellent as: dip for fresh vegetables, artichokes, etc.; filling for artichoke hearts, avocados; or dressing for cold fish cakes, fried fish, etc.

TANGY MEXICAN CHILI SAUCE DRESSING
Exotic

½ cup ketchup
¼ cup lemon juice
¼ cup mild red horseradish

1 tsp. Worcestershire sauce
¼ cup chili sauce

In bowl mix all the ingredients.
P.S. Excellent on **Fish Cocktail**.
VARIATION: Mix together ½ cup chili sauce; 1 cup mild red horseradish and 2 tbsp. lemon juice.

RUSSIAN DRESSING
Another standard

1½ tbsp. lemon juice
2–3 tbsp. ketchup

½–1 tsp. Worcestershire sauce, optional
½ cup mayonnaise

In bowl mix together juice, ketchup and Worcestershire sauce. Add mayonnaise and mix until well blended. Use as dressing for salad, or dip for fresh vegetables.

COMPANY SALAD
*Simple to make
fancy to present*

Amounts depend on number of guests

Romaine lettuce
red cabbage, coarsely grated
bean sprouts
raisins

mushrooms, sliced
carrots, julienne strips
almonds, cut up
Vinaigrette Dressing, minus garlic

Marinate raisins, mushrooms and carrots in some Vinaigrette Dressing overnight.
Mix with the rest of the ingredients (except almonds) and add additional Dressing to taste.
TO SERVE: Sprinkle with almonds.

BURGHUL (BULGAR WHEAT) SALAD   *Crunchy-good*

8–10 portions
Preferable to prepare a day in advance
Food processor comes in handy

2 cups burghul (cracked wheat)
  OR whole wheat grains
8 cups water
2 scallions
1 small onion
2 cucumbers
2 carrots
1 green pepper
1 red pepper
2 tbsp. sunflower seeds
  2 tbsp. cut up pecan nuts

DRESSING
about ½ cup lemon juice
1 tsp. lemon rind, grated
½ cup salad oil
¼ cup parsley, chopped
1 tbsp. prepared mustard
2–2½ tsp. salt
1 tsp. sugar
3 cloves garlic, crushed
½ tsp. pepper

If using burghul (cracked wheat), place in large bowl; pour over boiling water, cover and set aside to soak about ½ hour. Drain and allow to dry out 1–2 hours. Return to large bowl. Dice all vegetables and add to burghul with seeds and nuts.

If using whole wheat grains, cook in water about 45 minutes. Drain and leave about ½ hour.

Place grains in large bowl. Dice all vegetables and add to grains with seed or nuts.

In food processor or jar mix Dressing ingredients; pour over salad and toss. Refrigerate at least a few hours.

AVOCADO SALAD GOURMET   *Sara's favorite*

About 4 portions
Preferable to prepare a few hours in advance

1 avocado, peeled and cubed
3 eggs, hard boiled, cut up
2 tomatoes, cut up
a few stuffed olives, sliced
1 small onion, thinly sliced
¼ cup parsley, chopped
200–250 grams (½ lb.) smoked
  meat, cut into julienne strips OR
  200 grams (7 oz.) canned tuna fish
lettuce leaves
lemon wedges

DRESSING
2 tbsp. cider vinegar
⅓ cup salad or olive oil
1 tsp. salt
¼ tsp. pepper
pinch of cayenne pepper, optional
1 tsp. sugar
1 tbsp. prepared mustard
1 tbsp. lemon juice

In large bowl place avocado, eggs, tomatoes, olives, onion and parsley.

In food processor or closed jar mix together Dressing ingredients; pour over salad and toss. Refrigerate a few hours.

Place salad on a bed of lettuce; sprinkle with smoked meat or tuna fish and decorate with lemon wedges.

P.S. Great as an appetizer or as part of a buffet.

RICH TUNA SALAD

6–8 portions
Preferable to prepare a few hours or a day in advance
If one or two salad ingredients are missing, make it anyway

DRESSING
½ cup **Vinaigrette Dressing**
¼ cup mayonnaise
3 tbsp. lemon juice
2 tbsp. prepared mustard
about 2 tsp. salt
¼ tsp. pepper

SALAD
200 grams (7 oz.) tuna fish,
   drained and flaked
1 can anchovy filets,
   (56 grams, 2 oz.)
1 cup cooked rice
a few stuffed olives
3 eggs, hard boiled
1 cup string beans, cooked

1 cup corn kernels (from cooked, fresh corn)
2 cucumbers
2 onions
pickled gamba
2 pickled cucumbers
3 tomatoes
1 red pepper
1 green pepper
2 stalks celery
2 scallions
½ avocado, diced
2 tbsp. parsley
1 tbsp. sunflower seeds
1 tbsp. walnuts, cut up

Romaine lettuce
6 small radishes

In closed jar shake Dressing ingredients.

In large bowl place tuna, anchovies, rice and olives. Cut up eggs and vegetables (except lettuce and radishes) as desired; add to tuna mixture together with sunflower seeds and walnuts.

Pour Dressing over Salad; toss and adjust seasoning. Refrigerate.

TO SERVE: Place over lettuce leaves on platter or in bowl and decorate with radish flowers.

P.S. You can even add other vegetables: e.g., fresh cauliflower, broccoli, turnip, bean sprouts, fresh mushrooms, etc.

TUNA-PASTA SALAD

6–8 portions

250 grams (8 oz.) short-cut
   macaroni, cooked and drained
200 grams (7 oz.) can of tuna
   fish, drained and flaked
2 medium cucumbers, diced
1 onion, diced
1 tbsp. parsley, chopped
1 scallion, sliced
1 gamba, diced

DRESSING
2 tbsp. olive oil
¼ cup mayonnaise
2 tbsp. lemon juice
about 2 tsp. salt
½ tsp. pepper
½ tsp. sugar
½ tsp. marjoram OR
   tarragon

In large bowl place pasta, tuna and vegetables.
Mix together Dressing ingredients; pour over salad and toss.
Garnish with lemon.

HERRING-APPLE SALAD

Herring at its best

About 8 portions
Preferable to prepare one day in advance

6 filleted halves matjes herring
3 tart apples
1 carrot
2 onions
1 can (100 grams, 4 oz.)
   tomato purée

DRESSING
½ cup white or brown sugar
¼ cup salad oil
½ cup cider or wine vinegar
½ tsp. pepper
2 tsp. prepared mustard

Cut herring into strips and place in large bowl with diced apples, carrots and onion. Add tomato purée and mix together. In closed jar or food processor mix Dressing ingredients; pour over salad and toss. Refrigerate overnight.

Serve as appetizer or part of a buffet.

GREEK SALAD IN CREAM SAUCE

Herringly good

6–8 portions
Food processor comes in handy
Better to prepare a day in advance

6 filleted halves matjes herring
1 medium cabbage, coarsely grated
1 carrot, grated
1 green pepper, thinly sliced
½ red pepper, thinly sliced
1 onion, sliced

DRESSING
¾ cup salad or olive oil
¾ cup cider or wine vinegar
½ tsp. pepper
¼ cup sugar
1 cup sour cream
½ cup water

Cut herring into strips and place in large bowl together with vegetables.

In food processor or closed jar mix Dressing ingredients; pour over salad and toss. Refrigerate overnight.

P.S. Great as appetizer or part of a buffet.

VARIATION: Salad – add stuffed olives and pickled gamba. Dressing – eliminate oil and sour cream and use ¾ cup water, ¾ cup vinegar, ¼ cup sugar and 1 teaspoon salt.

LEEK SALAD

Try it!

About 4 portions
Preferable to prepare a few hours in advance

4 leeks

MARINADE
1 tsp. prepared mustard

¼ cup vinegar
2 cloves garlic, crushed
salt and pepper to taste
⅓ cup salad oil

Soak leeks in lightly salted water about one hour to clean.

Slice entire white part of leeks and some of the green in 1 cm (½″) slices. Wash again if necessary.

In partially covered pot cook leeks in a little slightly salted water over low flame about 10 minutes; drain; rinse under cold water and place in bowl.

In closed jar shake Marinade ingredients; pour over leeks and toss.

MOROCCAN COUSCOUS SALAD
Africa-tasty

About 10 portions
Food processor comes in handy

2 cups quick cooking couscous
2 cups cold water
1 tbsp. olive oil
½ cup lemon juice
⅓ cup salad oil
¼ cup dill, chopped

¼ cup parsley, chopped
1 tsp. salt
3 cloves garlic, crushed
½ tsp. pepper
½ tsp. sugar
¼ cup Roquefort cheese, diced

Place couscous and water in saucepan with oil; bring to a boil; turn off flame and leave a few minutes. Fluff up with fork.

Add rest of ingredients, except Roquefort cheese, and toss together.

When serving, sprinkle with Roquefort cheese.

CUCUMBER SALAD
Simple elegance

4–6 portions
Food processor comes in handy
Preferable to prepare a day in advance

6 medium cucumbers, peeled
  and thinly sliced
1 tbsp. salt
2 tsp. dill, chopped
1 scallion, chopped

DRESSING
½ cup vinegar
¼ cup water
½ tsp. salt
2 tbsp. sugar

Place cucumbers in large bowl; sprinkle with one tablespoon salt and mix. Place a small flat plate on top of cucumbers, and something a bit heavy on top of plate in order to extract water from the cucumbers. Leave about one hour. Pour off excess water and repeat process for another ½ hour. Once again pour off excess water.

Add dill and scallion to cucumbers.

In closed jar shake Dressing ingredients; pour over cucumbers and toss. Cover and refrigerate.

Toss again before serving.

CABBAGE-CUCUMBER SALAD
Everyone's favorite

About 8 portions
Food processor comes in handy
Preferable to prepare a day in advance

1 medium cabbage, coarsely grated
3 cucumbers, thinly sliced
1 small onion, sliced
2 carrots, grated

DRESSING
¾ cup vinegar
⅓ cup salad oil
¼ cup sugar
¼ cup water
2–3 tsp. salt
¼ tsp. pepper
¼ cup lemon juice

In large bowl mix all the vegetables.
In food processor or closed jar mix Dressing ingredients and pour over salad and toss. Cover and refrigerate. Toss again just before serving.

CABBAGE SALAD
Refreshingly good!

About 6 portions
Food processor comes in handy
Preferable to prepare a day in advance

1 cabbage, grated	*¼ cup sugar*
1 small onion, grated	*3 tbsp. salad oil*
2 tbsp. dill, chopped	*1 tbsp. water*
	1 tsp. salt
DRESSING	*¼ tsp. pepper*
⅓ cup cider vinegar	*2 tsp. caraway seeds*

In large bowl mix together cabbage, onion and dill.
In closed jar shake Dressing ingredients; pour over salad and toss.

CAULIFLOWER-CHEESE SALAD
A nice combination

About 4 portions
Preferable to prepare one day in advance

½ small cauliflower,	*1 onion, thinly sliced into rings*
separated into flowerettes	*½ cup **Vinaigrette Dressing***
4 eggs, hard-boiled, sliced	*2 tomatoes, diced*
1 can (56 grams, 2½ oz.),	*lettuce leaves*
anchovy filets	*¼ cup Parmesan cheese*

Parboil cauliflower by placing in a pot; covering with water and cooking 5–10 minutes. Drain and cool.
In large bowl, mix cauliflowerettes, eggs, anchovies and onion rings. Add Vinaigrette Dressing and toss.
   TO SERVE: Arrange lettuce leaves on bottom of serving bowl; add tomatoes to salad; toss; place on lettuce leaves and sprinkle with Parmesan cheese.

SWEET & SOUR TOMATO SALAD
Great with summer-ripened tomatoes

3–4 portions

	DRESSING
4 ripe tomatoes, sliced	*2 tbsp. wine or cider vinegar*
1 small onion, thinly sliced	*2 tsp. water*
1 stalk celery, diced	*1 tsp. salt*
1 tbsp. dill and parsley, chopped	*¼ tsp. pepper*
1 tbsp. chives, chopped	*1 tsp. sugar*

In large bowl place tomatoes, onion, celery, dill, parsley and chives.
In closed jar mix together Dressing ingredients; pour over salad and toss.
Mix again just before serving.

PICKLED CUCUMBERS
So much better than store-bought

about 900 grams (2 lbs.)
   small, firm cucumbers
8 large cloves garlic
4 bay leaves
a few whole peppercorns
a few coriander seeds
a few mustard seeds

one hot pepper
bunch of dill
¼ cup vinegar
about 3 tbsp. coarse white salt
about 4 cups water
½ piece of bread

Rinse and clean cucumbers and place in a 2 liter (2 quart) jar.

Peel and halve the cloves of garlic and place between the cucumbers with the bay leaves. Add peppercorns, coriander, mustard seeds and hot pepper. Arrange dill in middle of jar.

When all is in place, pour in one cup of water.

Dissolve salt in one cup boiling water and pour into jar.

Mix vinegar with one cup water and pour over cucumbers.

Fill jar completely with water and place bread on top.

Be careful cucumbers are not pressed down; they should be resting loosely.

Close jar and place in a dark closet. After 3 days remove bread.

Extent of pickling desired determines the length of pickling time. It's up to you.

MARINATED MUSHROOMS
A delicate taste

Preferable to prepare a day in advance

200–250 grams (½ lb.) mushrooms,
   caps, whole or quartered

MARINADE
1 cup cider or wine vinegar
2 tbsp. water
½ cup olive oil

3 cloves garlic, crushed
1 tsp. salt
½ tsp. sugar
¼ tsp. thyme
a few peppercorns
a few whole cloves
2 bay leaves

Place mushrooms in large bowl.

In enamel or stainless steel pot, cook Marinade ingredients, covered, over low flame about 10 minutes. Pour warm Marinade over mushrooms and toss. Let cool; refrigerate overnight.

Before serving remove mushrooms with slotted spoon.

Serve separately, toss into a salad or place on an antipasto platter.

MARINATED MUSHROOMS IN WINE
Deliciously elegant

Prepare a day in advance
Food processor comes in handy

½ kilo (1 lb.) mushroom caps
1 onion, chopped
3 cloves garlic, crushed
2 tbsp. parsley, chopped
½ tsp. thyme

MARINADE
2 cups dry or semi-dry white wine
1½ cups cider or wine vinegar
½ cup olive oil
⅓ cup lemon juice
½ tsp. salt
½ tsp. pepper

In enamel or stainless steel pot place mushroom caps with onions, garlic, parsley and thyme.

In closed jar or food processor shake Marinade ingredients and pour over mushrooms.

Mix and cook over low flame about 10 minutes, stirring occasionally.

Place in bowl and refrigerate overnight.

TO SERVE: Remove mushroom caps with slotted spoon and place in serving bowl or in salad.

P.S. Use mushroom stems for sauces, soups, omelettes, etc.

MARINATED VEGETABLE SALAD   *Something different*

About 6 portions
Food processor comes in handy

1 cauliflower, separated into flowerettes	MARINADE
2 medium zucchini, sliced	3 cloves garlic, crushed
3 small tomatoes, wedged	3 tbsp. dill, chopped
150 grams (¼ lb.) mushroom caps	3 tbsp. parsley, chopped
1 onion, sliced	¼ cup salad oil
2 scallions, sliced	¼ cup olive oil
1 red pepper, diced	⅓ cup cider or wine vinegar
2 tbsp. sesame seeds	2–3 tsp. salt
100–125 grams (½ cup) Roquefort or feta cheese (optional)	1 tbsp. prepared mustard
	2 tbsp. lemon juice
2 tbsp. shelled sunflower seeds (optional)	½ tsp. pepper
	1–2 tsp. sugar

Parboil cauliflowerettes and zucchini by cooking a few minutes in a small amount of slightly salted water. Drain and cool. Place in large bowl and add rest of vegetables.

MARINADE: In food processor crush garlic, dill, and parsely; add rest of ingredients and process. Pour over vegetables and toss.

Refrigerate overnight.

MARINATED BEETS   *Colorfully tasty*

4–6 portions
Preferable to prepare a day in advance

½ kilo (1 lb.) beets	about 1 tsp. salt
1 onion, thinly sliced	⅛ tsp. pepper
	2 bay leaves
DRESSING	a few whole cloves
½ cup cider vinegar	
⅓ cup water	lettuce leaves

Place beets (with skin and part of stem) in pot. Use enough water so that beets are completely immersed; cover pot and cook 40–50 minutes until tender (depending on size); drain; rinse under cold water; peel; cut into round slices and place in large bowl. Add onion slices.

In closed jar mix together Dressing ingredients and pour over beets while still warm. Refrigerate overnight.

P.S. Before serving remove bay leaves and cloves, mix again and place on lettuce leaves.

COOKED SPINACH SALAD

Different

About 4 portions

600 grams (1 ¼ lbs.) fresh spinach

MARINADE
2 tbsp. sesame seeds
2 cloves garlic, crushed

1 tbsp. salad or olive oil
1 tbsp. cider or wine vinegar
¼ tsp. salt
1 tbsp. soy sauce
1 tbsp. sugar

Soak spinach in bowl of salted water to clean. Wash well under cold water.
In large pot over low flame cook spinach, covered, in a little slightly salted water 10–15 minutes. Drain and place in bowl.
In closed jar mix Marinade ingredients; pour over spinach and toss. Refrigerate overnight.

SPINACH-AVOCADO SALAD

Nutritious and refreshing

4-6 portions
Preferable to prepare a few hours in advance

½ kilo (1 lb.) fresh spinach
1 small avocado, cubed
1 tbsp. lemon juice
1 tomato, cut into wedges
1 onion, sliced

1 scallion, chopped
2 tbsp. parsley, chopped
¼ tsp. turmeric

Vinaigrette Dressing

Soak spinach in salted water, wash well and drain.
Cut up spinach; place in large bowl; add avocado and sprinkle over with lemon juice. Add rest of ingredients. Pour over desired amount of Vinaigrette Dressing and toss. Refrigerate at least a few hours.

FRESH SPINACH SALAD

Interestingly good

About 4 portions

¼ kilo (½ lb.) spinach, cut up
¼ cup lemon juice
2 tbsp. sunflower or olive oil
100 grams (4 oz.) salted goat's
   cheese or Roquefort
2 cucumbers, peeled and sliced
2 tomatoes, cut up
3 eggs, hard boiled, sliced
1 tbsp. mint leaves, optional

DRESSING
3 tbsp. sunflower or olive oil
2 tbsp. wine or cider vinegar
1 tsp. prepared mustard
¼ tsp. ground cinnamon
½–1 tsp. salt
¼ tsp. pepper
2 cloves garlic, crushed

In large bowl soak spinach in salted water to clean; drain and wash well. Return to bowl.

Add lemon juice and oil; toss and refrigerate about 15 minutes.

Add cheese, cucumber, tomatoes, eggs and mint.

In closed jar mix Dressing ingredients; pour over salad and toss.

LENTIL SALAD
A special treat!

6–8 portions
Start preparing two days in advance

1 cup lentils, green or orange
2 tbsp. olive oil
1 large onion, diced
3 cloves garlic, crushed
1 potato, cooked and cubed
3 medium zucchini, diced
2 leeks, sliced (optional)

2 stalks celery, diced
about 1 tsp. salt
about ¼ tsp. pepper
2 tbsp. parsley, chopped
½ tsp. sugar
½ cup lemon juice
a few parsley leaves for garnish

Sift through lentils and remove anything that doesn't resemble a lentil.

In large bowl soak lentils in 4 cups water overnight; drain.

In 2½ cups water cook lentils, covered, over low flame about one hour (until soft but still retaining shape). Add potatoes, zucchini, leeks, celery, salt and pepper and continue cooking about 20 minutes, until soft. Drain and place in bowl.

Meanwhile heat oil in frying pan and sauté onion and garlic until soft. Add to lentils, together with chopped parsley, sugar and lemon juice. Adjust seasoning and let cool.

Place in serving bowl and refrigerate overnight.

Just before serving garnish with parsley leaves.

P.S. Cubed Roquefort cheese lends an interesting flavor.

LENTIL-RICE SALAD
A whole meal in itself

About 6 portions
Start preparing two days in advance

½ cup green lentils
½ cup brown rice
2 tbsp. oil
1 onion, chopped
2 cloves garlic, crushed
1 tbsp. paprika
1 cup mushrooms, sliced
1 tbsp. parsley, chopped

1 scallion, chopped
1 green pepper, diced
1 red pepper, diced
2 tbsp. Worcestershire sauce
¼ tsp. ground cumin, optional
about 2 tsp. salt
½ tsp. pepper
2 tbsp. blanched, slivered almonds

Sift through lentils and remove anything that doesn't resemble a lentil.

In large bowl soak lentils in two cups water overnight; drain and wash under cold water.

Cook lentils and rice in 3 cups water, covered, 45–50 minutes. Drain.

In large frying pan heat oil and sauté onion, garlic and paprika a few minutes. Add rest of ingredients, except salt and pepper; continue sautéing 10 minutes more.

In large bowl place lentils and rice; add sautéed vegetables, seasoning and almonds and toss to mix.

P.S. Serve warm as side dish or cold as salad.

EGGPLANT-CAPER SALAD

An eating experience

8–10 portions
Preferable to prepare a day in advance

1–1½ cup olive oil OR
   combination of olive and salad
2 medium eggplants
3 onions, diced
3 tomatoes, cubed

¼ cup capers
¼ cup wine vinegar
2 tbsp. sugar
1 tsp. salt
¼ tsp. pepper

In large frying pan heat oil and sauté peeled and diced eggplant until browned and soft. Remove with slotted spoon and let drain.

In same pan sauté onions.

In wooden bowl place eggplant together with onion, tomatoes and capers; chop until mixture is coarsely chopped.

Transfer vegetables to medium pot; add vinegar, sugar, salt and pepper and mix. Cook, covered, over low flame about 20 minutes, stirring occasionally.

Place in serving bowl, cool and refrigerate overnight.

P.S. Great with cold cuts, cold fish cakes, etc.

CHOPPED EGGPLANT SALAD

Simple and Delicious

Food processor comes in handy

1 whole eggplant
2 eggs, hard-boiled, chopped
1 onion, chopped
sliced tomatoes, onion,
   cucumbers, turnip, etc.

DRESSING
1 tbsp. mayonnaise
3 cloves garlic, crushed
salt and pepper to taste
1 tsp. lemon juice

Preheat oven 350° F, 180° C.

Pierce eggplant with fork in various spots, place in flat baking pan and bake at medium heat 1–1½ hours until soft and wrinkled. Let cool slightly; remove pulp and let drain about 15 minutes.

In large wooden bowl chop eggplant and mix in eggs and onion.

In separate bowl prepare Dressing ingredients; add to salad and toss.

Garnish with sliced onion, tomatoes, cucumbers, turnip and other vegetables.

CHOPPED LIVER APPETIZER

The real thing!

About 4 portions

½ kilo (1 lb.) chicken livers
2 tbsp. oil
1 large onion, chopped

3 eggs, hard-boiled, sliced
salt and pepper to taste
tart apple slices

Grill chicken livers and place in wooden bowl.

In frying pan heat oil and sauté onions; add to chicken livers together with eggs, salt and pepper and chop until smooth.

To serve individually; place a ball of chopped liver on top of a cored apple slice. Decorate plate with tomatoes, cucumber, radish, onions etc. Or place a large mound of the chicken liver on a serving platter surrounded by fresh vegetables.

VEGETARIAN CHOPPED LIVER

Just as good as the real thing

About 8 portions
Food processor makes it easy

3 tbsp. oil	4 eggs, hard-boiled, cut up
3 medium onions, diced	1 tsp. salt
500 grams (1 lb.) green beans,	¼ tsp. pepper
cut up and cooked	½ tsp. paprika
½ cup canned green peas, drained	3 tbsp. sesame seeds
	1 cup walnuts, ground

GARNISH
sliced onion, tomato, cucumbers, etc.

In large frying pan heat oil and sauté onions until browned.

In wooden bowl or food processor chop green beans, onions, peas and eggs until smooth. To vegetables add seasoning, sesame seeds and walnuts and mix together.

Refrigerate a few hours or overnight.

Serve individually or on serving platter with Garnish and crackers.

P.S. Great stuffed into tomatoes. (To prepare tomatoes for stuffing, see **Meat Salad Delight**.)

VARIATION: Use 2 medium eggplants in lieu of string beans and peas. Place eggplants on aluminum foil-covered baking pan; pierce skin with fork in a few places; bake in moderate oven (350° F, 180° C) about one hour, until skin is wrinkly (this can be done in the microwave oven without aluminum foil in ¼ of the time, turning once during process); allow to cool a little; remove all the inside pulp and drain. Chop in food processor or wooden bowl.

ZUCCHINI SALAD

Quick and tasty

4–6 portions
Preferable to prepare a few hours in advance
Food processor comes in handy

6 medium zucchini, coarsely grated	¼ cup lemon juice
	2 tbsp. mayonnaise
DRESSING	1 tsp. salt
¼ tsp. pepper	½ tsp. sugar
1 tbsp. dill, chopped	

Parboil zucchini in a little slightly salted water about 2 minutes; drain and place in large bowl.
Mix together Dressing ingredients, pour over zucchini and toss.
Refrigerate.

CHEF SALAD

5–6 portions
Partly prepare a day in advance

1 head of lettuce, cut up
1 cup rice, optional
½ kilo (1 lb.) green beans,
  cut up
2 ears of corn
4 eggs, hard-boiled, cut up

3 medium tomatoes, diced
4 pickled cucumbers, sliced
about 125 grams (¼ lb.) salami

GARNISH: *asparagus tips*
Russian Dressing

Cook rice, green beans and corn separately a day in advance.

Remove corn kernels from cob (TIP: Cook corn a few days in advance and freeze. After thawing, the corn cuts more easily).

Prepare all ingredients individually.

Either serve in individual bowls in layers, topped with Russian Dressing, or place mounds of individual ingredients on a serving platter with the Dressing on the side. The latter procedure leaves the salad preparation up to each person (which is what I do).

Garnish with asparagus tips.

MEAT SALAD DELIGHT

3–4 portions

¼ kilo (½ lb.) string beans,
  cut up and cooked
2 cups lean cooked meat,
  cut into strips
2 eggs, hard-boiled, chopped
1 onion, thinly sliced
1 small beet, cooked and diced
1 fresh ear of corn, cut into kernels
2 pickled cucumbers, diced

DRESSING
⅓ cup oil
2 tbsp. cider vinegar
about 2 tsp. salt
¼ tsp. pepper
a little parsley, chopped
3 tbsp. mayonnaise

GARNISH
sliced tomato, pickled cucumber,
  radishes etc.

In large bowl place meat strips together with eggs and vegetables and mix.

In closed jar shake Dressing ingredients; pour over salad and toss. Refrigerate a few hours.

Garnish with sliced vegetables.

P.S. Great by itself or stuffed into tomatoes as appetizer or at a buffet.

NOTE: To prepare tomatoes for stuffing: Cut off top of tomato; with grapefruit knife go around inner circumference; scoop out insides with spoon; shake out excess juice; sprinkle inside of tomato with a little salt; invert onto plate and refrigerate at least ½ hour.

TANGY POTATO SALAD

The top of the heap!

6–8 portions

6 potatoes
2 carrots
1 large onion
1 cucumber
1 pickled cucumber
2 tbsp. parsley, chopped

DRESSING
⅓ cup mayonnaise
¼ cup cider vinegar
1 tbsp. prepared mustard
1½ tsp. salt
½ tsp. pepper

In large pot cook potatoes and one carrot until tender; drain; place in large bowl and cut up into pieces.
Dice raw carrot, onion, cucumber and pickle; add to potatoes with parsley and mix together.
In bowl prepare Dressing; pour over salad and toss.
P.S. Great with cold cuts or at a barbeque.

WALDORF SALAD

A delightful change

6–8 portions

2 medium apples,
   peeled and diced
2 stalks celery, diced
1 pear, peeled and diced
¼ cup raisins

½ cup walnuts, cut up
½ cup mayonnaise
½ cup sour cream or yogurt
1 tbsp. lemon juice
¼ tsp. pepper

In large bowl mix all ingredients and refrigerate.
P.S. Great as an appetizer or at a buffet.

VARIATIONS: (1) Use finely grated knob celery instead of celery stalks, or (2) Add cubed canned pineapple or cut-up orange.

STRING BEAN–ANCHOVY SALAD

A salad with a "tang"

4–5 portions
Preferable to prepare one day in advance

½ kilo (1 lb.) green beans
1 can (56 grams, 2 oz.)
   anchovy fillets, cut up
¼ cup almonds, cut up

DRESSING
1 tbsp. cider vinegar
2 tbsp. olive oil
¼ tsp. salt
⅛ tsp. pepper
2 cloves garlic, crushed

Cut green beans into small pieces. Cook, covered, in a little slightly salted water until soft. Drain and let cool. Place in wooden bowl with anchovy fillets.
In closed jar mix together Dressing ingredients; pour over green beans and toss. Refrigerate overnight. Just before serving toss again and sprinkle with almonds.

SOYBEAN SALAD

Crunchy and nutritious

Start soaking a day or two in advance
Preferable to prepare salad a few hours or a day before

½ cup red kidney beans
1 cup raw soy beans
4 cloves garlic
2 scallions
1 stalk celery
2 cucumbers
1 green and red pepper
1 onion
1 carrot
1 tbsp. parsley, chopped
1 tbsp. dill, chopped
2 tbsp. sunflower seeds
alfalfa sprouts

DRESSING
½ cup cider vinegar
½ cup mayonnaise OR ¼ cup oil
½ cup lemon juice
¼ tsp. basil
¼ tsp. pepper
1½ tsp. salt
2 tbsp. white wine
1 tbsp. prepared mustard
½ tsp. sugar

GARNISH: *1 tomato, sliced*

In large bowl soak red kidney beans in water overnight and soybeans last 3 hours. Drain. Place in large pot with a lot of water and cook about 1½ hours. Drain and place in large bowl.

Dice all the vegetables; add to beans with sunflower seeds and mix.

In closed jar or food processor prepare Dressing; pour over salad and toss. Marinate a few hours or overnight in refrigerator.

Garnish with tomato slices.

Cubed Roquefort cheese makes it a real delicacy.

CAESAR SALAD

Crisp and delicate

About 4 portions
Prepare garlic oil in advance,
  but prepare salad just before serving for that crispy taste

Romaine lettuce

DRESSING
1 clove garlic, peeled and halved
3 tbsp. olive oil

1 tbsp. lemon juice
1 tsp. prepared mustard
a few drops Worcestershire sauce
1 cup croutons
3 anchovy filets
1 egg, very soft boiled, well beaten

In large bowl place cut up lettuce.

Soak garlic in oil a few hours then discard garlic. Add lemon juice, mustard and Worcestershire sauce to oil; mix and pour over lettuce.

Add croutons and anchovy filets and toss.

Just before serving add egg and toss again.

P.S. Great with **Garlic Bread**.

VEGETABLES-IN-A-MOLD

Soooo refreshing!

About 6 portions
Food processor comes in handy

1 package lemon or lime gelatin
½ tsp. salt
1 cup boiling water
⅔ cup cold water
2 tbsp. vinegar

1 small onion, coarsely grated
½ cup cabbage, chopped
2 medium carrots, finely grated
1 stalk celery, chopped
½ green pepper, chopped

Dissolve gelatin and salt in boiling water; add cold water, vinegar and onion and mix well. Cool until gelatin is semi-jelled.

Add vegetables, mix and place in gelatin mold or serving bowl.

Refrigerate until firm.

Remove from gelatin mold or serve straight from serving bowl. To remove from mold, see **Cucumber Mold** (following).

P.S. Great side dish.

CUCUMBER MOLD

A cool green happening

About 6 portions
Food processor comes in handy

1 package lime gelatin
1 cup boiling water
1 cucumber, coarsely grated
½ cup mayonnaise

1 tbsp. vinegar
1 small onion, grated
1 tbsp. gamba, chopped

Dissolve gelatin in boiling water. Refrigerate until slightly jelled.

Meanwhile sprinkle grated cucumber with salt; place small flat plate over it with a heavy item on top of the plate (in order to extract water). Leave for about ½ hour. Spill off water.

Add all ingredients to gelatin; mix together and pour into gelatin mold or serving bowl. Refrigerate until firm. Remove from gelatin or serve directly from serving bowl.

P.S. A refreshing side dish.

TO REMOVE FROM MOLD: Go around sides of mold with a knife in order to loosen edges.
Method 1: Dip gelatin mold in a larger bowl of hot water for about 2 seconds (be careful water does not spill into mold). Place serving platter on top of mold and invert together. If gelatin does not come out, tap mold with knife gently. Refrigerate immediately.

Method 2: Invert gelatin mold onto serving platter; dip kitchen towel into very hot water; squeeze and place over gelatin mold a few seconds. Tap top of mold a few times and gelatin should come out. If necessary, repeat process. Refrigerate immediately.

CHEDDAR BALLS

A deep-fried happening

About 40 balls

⅓ cup flour
½ tsp. salt
¼ tsp. pepper
400 grams (¾ lb.) cheddar cheese,
   thinly grated

4 egg whites
breadcrumbs
oil for deep frying

In bowl sift flour, salt and pepper; add cheese and mix.

In mixer, at high speed, beat egg whites until stiff, but not dry; with wooden spoon fold into flour-cheese mixture.

Shape into small balls by hand. Roll each ball in breadcrumbs and deep fry in heated oil about ½ minute. Drain on paper toweling.

P.S. What to do with the egg yolks: 2 egg yolks = 1 egg in batter cake recipes.

CHEESE BALL

Everyone goes wild over this!

200–250 grams (1 cup) cream cheese
100–125 grams (½ cup) Roquefort
   cheese, grated
100–125 grams (½ cup) Parmesan
   cheese, grated

100–125 grams (½ cup) butter,
   room temperature
¼ cup walnuts, ground

In mixer at low speed beat the three types of cheeses and butter until smooth. Shape into a ball by hand.

In bowl place ground walnuts and roll the cheese ball in them.

Refrigerate a few hours or overnight.

Serve with crackers, raw vegetables, sliced pear, etc.

SCALLION-CHEESE DIP

Half is eaten before
it gets to the table

400–500 grams (2 cups)
   cream cheese
½ cup sour cream
2 scallions, chopped
1 tbsp. parsley, chopped

4 stuffed olives, sliced
1 tbsp. dill, chopped
½–1 tsp. garlic powder
¼ tsp. salt
1 tsp. paprika

In bowl mix all ingredients together; transfer to serving bowl and sprinkle with a little paprika.

Serve with crackers, black bread and raw vegetables (e.g. turnip, cauliflower, cucumber, radish, red pepper celery, etc.). Here are some tasty variations:

CHEESE-ANCHOVY DIP—Mix the following ingredients in blender, or stir 'till smooth: 400–500 grams (2 cups) cream cheese, 100–125 grams (½ cup) softened butter, 5 chopped anchovy fillets, 2 chopped scallions, 1 tbsp. paprika, 1 tsp. caraway seeds. Refrigerate before serving.

TANGY CHEESE DIP—Mix together in bowl: 200–250 grams (1 cup) cream cheese, a few stuffed, chopped olives, 1 small chopped onion or scallion, 1 tbsp. chopped dill, salt to taste.

Add sweet cream (about 3 tsp.) until mixture is creamy but firm. Refrigerate before serving.

There's nothing like great-tasting **SOUPS**

A smell once smelled stays forever. When I am preparing a soup, the aroma brings me back to my mother's kitchen with its warmth and intimacy.

TASTE makes the soup. I have tried to give amounts of seasoning, but there's always room for adjustment and improvement. Don't skimp on the seasoning, but of course don't overdo it either. (If soup is too salty, try putting a potato into the pot and cook it a few minutes, then discard the potato – the potato absorbs the salt).

Most soups are better when prepared a little in advance and allowed to settle, thus giving the seasoning a chance to penetrate into the ingredients. Soup can be frozen – although it will lose some of its flavor. So don't cook for the freezer; but if you have some soup left over, then freeze it for future use. Broths (clear soups) can be used as stock for sauces.

Have fun with winter hots and summer cools.

ONION SOUP

With Garlic Bread — what can be better?

About 8 portions
Cooking time: 1 ½ hours
Food processor makes it easier

50–60 grams (¼ cup) butter
5 onions, thinly sliced
2 tbsp. vegetable broth powder
7 cups water

1 tsp. sugar

1 cup dry or semi-dry white wine
1 tsp. salt
¼ tsp. pepper
sliced French bread or
Garlic Flavored Croutons
½ cup hard cheese, thinly grated

In large pot, over low flame, melt butter. Increase heat and sauté onions about 30 minutes (until onions are brown), stirring occasionally. Add broth powder, water, sugar and wine; cover and cook over low flame about 1 hour. Season with salt and pepper.

TO SERVE: Place bread slices 1 cm (½″ thick) or Garlic Flavored Croutons and grated cheese in individual bowls. Pour soup over and serve immediately.

P.S. **Garlic Bread** enhances the flavor.

MUSHROOM-BARLEY SOUP

Everyone's favorite

About 8 portions
Cooking time: 3 hours
Food processor makes it easier

15 grams (½ oz.) dried
   mushrooms
½ cup pearl barley
8 cups water
about 2 tsp. salt
½ tsp. pepper
2 tsp. paprika
30 grams (1 oz., 2 tbsp.) butter

2 onions, chopped
1–2 potatoes, diced or grated
2–3 carrots, grated
250 grams (¼ lb.) fresh mushrooms
1 tbsp. flour
½ cup milk
¼ cup dry or semi-dry white wine

In small bowl soak dried mushrooms in ¼ cup cold water about 10 minutes.

In large pot place dried mushrooms together with water, pearl barley, salt and pepper; cover and cook over low flame 1½ hours.

Meanwhile, in frying pan, melt butter over low flame; increase heat and sauté onion with paprika until browned. Set aside.

To soup add potatoes, carrots and fresh mushrooms and continue cooking 1 hour more.

Add sautéed onions and cook an additional ½ hour. Allow some time for soup to settle.

Just before serving, mix flour with milk and add together with wine. Heat through.

P.S. Sprinkle over **Garlic Flavored Croutons** and serve with **Garlic Bread**.

I usually double this recipe.

MUSHROOM SOUP

An elegant touch

About 8 portions
Cooking and settling time: 1 ½ hours
Food processor comes in handy

50–60 grams (¼ cup) butter
 or margarine
2 large onions, chopped
2 cloves garlic, crushed
½ kilo (1 lb.) mushrooms, sliced
2 stalks celery, diced
2 tbsp. parsley, chopped
about 2 tsp. salt
½ tsp. pepper

1 tbsp. paprika
2 bay leaves
7 cups water
2 tbsp. vegetable broth powder
1 tsp. Worcestershire sauce
1 cup dry or semi-dry white wine

GARNISH
grated hard cheese
Croutons *(see Soup Accompaniments)*

In large pot melt butter or margarine over low flame. Increase heat and sauté onion and garlic about 5 minutes. Add mushrooms, celery and parsley; continue sautéing 6–7 minutes.

Add salt, pepper, paprika, bay leaves, broth and Worcestershire sauce; cover and cook over low flame one hour.

Remove from flame; add wine and let stand 20–30 minutes.

Remove bay leaves. Blend in blender until smooth. Heat and serve.

Sprinkle individual portions with Garnish.

P.S. I always serve the soup with **Garlic Bread**.

MINESTRONE SOUP

Two bowls of this and you have a meal!

About 8 portions
Cooking time: about 2 hours
Food processor comes in handy
Prepare dried beans a day in advance

¼ cup dried white beans
2 tbsp. olive oil
2 medium onions, chopped
8 cups beef or vegetable broth
1 cup green beans, cut up
½ cup spinach, cut up
2 tbsp. tomato purée

2 carrots, grated
2 small zucchini, diced
2 medium potatoes, diced
¼ small cabbage, grated
2 tsp. salt
½ tsp. pepper
1 tsp. paprika
1 cup pasta (shortcut macaroni)

In bowl soak beans overnight in enough water for expansion.

In large pot heat oil and sauté onion 10 minutes. Add broth and rest of ingredients, except pasta; cover and cook over low flame about 1½ hours until beans are soft.

Add pasta and continue cooking another 20 minutes. Adjust seasoning.

P.S. If using vegetable broth, sprinkle individual portions with cheese.

LENTIL-SPINACH SOUP

Another great winter soup

About 8 portions
Cooking time: 1¾ hours
Prepare lentils a day in advance

1 cup orange lentils
8 cups water
¼ cup oil
2 onions, chopped
3 cloves garlic, crushed
2 tsp. paprika
2 tbsp. dill, chopped

½ kilo (1 lb.) spinach, cut up
2 tbsp. tomato purée
2 tsp. salt
½ tsp. pepper
pinch of cayenne pepper (optional)
Garlic Flavored Croutons

Sift through lentils and remove anything that doesn't resemble a lentil.

Soak lentils in about 4 cups water overnight. Drain and place in large pot. Add 8 cups water; cover and cook over low flame about 1½ hours.

Meanwhile in large frying pan heat oil and sauté onion, garlic and paprika five minutes. Add spinach and continue sautéing a few more minutes. Cover and cook over low flame about five minutes.

Add to lentils with tomato purée and seasoning; cook an additional few minutes. Let cool somewhat.

Blend soup in blender. Return to pot and heat.

Serve with Garlic Flavored Croutons.

VEGETABLE SOUP

Nothing like it

About 8 portions
Cooking time: 2½ hours
Food processor comes in handy

2 tbsp. butter or margarine
2 onions, diced
3 cloves garlic, crushed
2 tsp. paprika
½ cup pearl barley
½ cup dried split peas
¼ cup lentils
about 9 cups water
½ small cauliflowerettes
2 stalks celery, diced

¼ small cabbage, coarsely grated
½ red pepper, diced
1 cup pumpkin, grated
1 tbsp. dill, cut up
1 tbsp. parsley, cut up
2 tsp. salt
¾ tsp. pepper
1 tsp. paprika
2 tomatoes, peeled and blended
¼ cup dry or semi-dry white wine

In large frying pan melt butter or margarine over low flame. Increase heat and sauté onion and garlic with a little paprika 7–8 minutes. Set aside.

In large pot mix pearl barley, split peas and lentils. Add water; cover and cook over low flame about 1 hour.

Add vegetables, seasoning and tomatoes and continue cooking another hour.

Add sautéed onions and cook an additional 20 minutes.

Add wine and adjust seasoning.

P.S As always, **Garlic Bread** enhances the flavor.

SKINNING TOMATOES: In a large pot, bring to boil enough water to immerse all the tomatoes. Add tomatoes, remove pot from flame, let stand 1–2 minutes and drain. Rinse under cold water; pierce skin gently with knife and remove.

LENTIL SOUP

About 8 portions
Cooking time: 1 ¼ hours
Prepare lentils a day in advance
or cook in the 8 cups water ¾ hour before adding vegetables
Food processor comes in handy; I prefer it blended.

2 cups orange lentils	about 2 tsp. salt
2 tbsp. butter	½ tsp. pepper
2 onions, chopped	¼ cup dry red wine
2 cloves garlic, crushed	1 tomato, chopped
8 cups water	1 tbsp. lemon juice
2 carrots, diced	1 tbsp. brown sugar
2 stalks celery, diced	2 tsp. wine vinegar
2 tbsp. fresh dill	¼ tsp. dried basil
2 tbsp. paprika	

Sift through lentils and remove anything that doesn't resemble a lentil.

Clean lentils and soak in large bowl with 6–7 cups cold water overnight, or cook in the 8 cups water on same day ¾ hour before adding vegetables.

In frying pan, over low flame, melt butter. Increase heat and sauté onions and garlic.

Drain lentils; place in large pot; add water, sautéed onions, carrots, celery and dill. Cover and cook over low flame about 50 minutes.

Add rest of ingredients and cook another 25 minutes.

Allow to cool somewhat and blend in blender until smooth.

Heat and serve.

P.S. Even better when served with **Garlic Flavored Croutons** and **Garlic Bread**.

RICH CHICKEN SOUP

About 10 portions
Cooking time: 3–4 hours

1 chicken, cut in half	2 medium zucchini
giblets, if available	250 grams (½ lb.) pumpkin
¼ kilo (½ lb.) soup meat OR	1 tbsp. salt
dark turkey	pepper, to taste
1 cup cabbage, strips	1 tbsp. havaege, optional
¼ cup pearl barley	nob and stalks of celery
5 small onions	2 parsley roots
1 large carrot	small bunch of parsley
	small bunch of dill

In large pot place chicken, giblets and soup meat. Cover completely with water and bring to boil. Add rest of ingredients; cover and cook over medium-low flame 3–4 hours.

Remove parsley, dill, celery and parsley roots. Remove chicken and meat. Serve soup with rest of vegetables and giblets.

Serve with **Egg Drops, Matzo Balls, Crunchy Noodle Kugel**, plain noodles or rice.

P.S. Clear soup may be used as broth for sauces. Use cooked chicken for other recipes, or serve fresh as a nosh. (If you don't know, 'haveage' is a Mideastern spice.)

HUNGARIAN GOULASH SOUP

Paprika
does it all the time

About 10 portions
Cooking time: about 3½ hours

250 grams (½ lb.) lean beef
¼ cup oil
6 medium onions, diced
250 grams (½ lb.) smoked
    meat or frankfurters
2 tsp. salt

½ tsp. pepper
3 tbsp. paprika
1 tsp. caraway seeds
10 cups water
2 potatoes, diced
Dumplings (see Soup Accompaniments)

Cut beef into cubes.

In large pot heat oil and sauté onions about 6 minutes. Add beef cubes, smoked meat, salt, pepper and paprika and sauté lightly. Add caraway seeds and water; cover and cook over low flame about 3 hours.

Add potatoes and continue cooking 20 minutes. If soup appears too thick, add a little water.

COLD YOGURT SOUP

The coolness of a summer delight

6–8 portions
No cooking time

2 cups yogurt
2 cups tomato juice
1 tsp. honey
½ tsp. basil
½ tsp. salt
¼ tsp. pepper

1 cucumber, diced
1 scallion, sliced
1 tbsp. parsley, chopped
1 tbsp. dill, chopped
1 cup mushrooms, sliced

In large bowl mix together yogurt, tomato juice, honey, basil, salt and pepper.

In separate bowl mix together vegetables.

To serve: Place vegetables in individual soup bowls or sherbet glasses and cover with the Soup.

P.S. Serve with crackers or black bread

BORSCHT (Cold Beet Soup)

Colorful, cool summertime

Cooking time: about 20 minutes
Allow a few hours to cool
Food processor comes in handy

800 grams (1½ lbs.) beets,
    finely grated or chopped
about 5½ cups water
1¼ cups lemon juice
½ cup sugar
2 tsp. salt
4 eggs

sour cream

SUGGESTED GARNISHES
diced cucumber
sliced hard boiled eggs
cooked potatoes, cut up

Place beets in large pot. Add water just enough to cover beets; cover and cook over low flame about 20 minutes.

Remove from flame and allow to cool.

In blender, blend lemon juice, sugar, salt and eggs and some of the beets. Pour into cooked beets and mix well. Adjust seasoning.

Refrigerate a few hours.

TO SERVE: Place a spoon of sour cream on top and garnish.

P.S. I usually serve it in large mugs. (There are those who prefer more beets than soup.)

Soup Accompaniments

DUMPLINGS
They make soup into something else!

Food processor comes in handy

1¼ cup flour	*1 egg*
½ tsp. salt	*about 2 tbsp. water*
⅛ tsp. pepper	

In bowl sift flour salt and pepper. Add egg and enough water to form soft, not sticky, dough. Process can be done in food processor with metal blade.

On floured board roll out dough about 0.5 cm (¼″) thick. Cut with knife into small pieces of desired shapes and drop into soup last 15 minutes of cooking.

KNAIDLACH (Matzo Balls)
The best — soft and firm

4 eggs	*½ tsp. salt*
½ cup soda water	*¼ tsp. pepper*
⅓ cup oil	*¼ tsp. ginger*
	1–1¼ cup matzo meal

In medium bowl beat eggs well. Add soda water, oil, salt, pepper and ginger; mix together. Add matzo meal slowly and stir to form a loose-firm mixture.

Refrigerate about 20 minutes.

In large pot boil enough, slightly salted, water so that knaidlach will be completely immersed.

With wet hands form desired size balls and drop into boiling water. Cover and cook over medium-low flame about 30 minutes. Remove with slotted spoon. Set aside.

About 10–15 minutes before serving, drop knaidlach into soup and cook 10–15 minutes.

EGG DROPS

2 eggs
¼ tsp. salt
⅛ tsp. pepper

about ⅔ cup matzo meal
about ½ cup water

In medium bowl beat eggs with salt and pepper.
Add matzo meal and enough water to form loose-firm batter.
Refrigerate about 20 minutes.
Drop spoonfuls of batter into boiling soup and cook about 10 minutes.
Place in soup before serving.
P.S. If batter is too soft (egg drops fall apart), add a little more matzo meal.

CHOLENT DUMPLINGS

Tasty!

Food processor comes in handy

1 cup flour
½ tsp. baking powder
½ tsp. salt
⅛ tsp. pepper

100–125 grams (½ cup) margarine,
   room temperature
1 tbsp. parsley, chopped
about 1 tbsp. cold water

In large bowl sift flour, baking powder, salt and pepper. Add margarine and mix together until crumbly. Add parsley and enough water to form soft dough. Process can be done in food processor. If dough is too wet add a little flour, or if too dry add a drop of water.

Form ball (or several small balls) and place in **Cholent** during cooking.

GARLIC-FLAVORED CROUTONS

*They make soup
into a treat!*

50–60 grams (¼ cup) butter or
   margarine
4 cloves garlic, crushed
⅛ tsp. pepper

¼ tsp. salt
¼ tsp. paprika
4–6 slices bread, cubed

Preheat oven 350° F, 180° C.
In medium pot melt butter or margarine over low flame. Add garlic and seasoning; remove from flame. Add bread cubes and mix together.
Spread bread cubes on shallow baking pan and bake in medium oven about 20 minutes, turning and stirring occasionally.
Sprinkle croutons over individual soup bowls and serve rest in separate bowl for extra helpings.
P.S. Freeze leftovers for future use.

Everyone loves # PASTA & RICE

I find rice to be one of the most versatile foods, and brown rice has more taste and of course, all the nutrition. Just remember brown rice takes a little extra water and longer cooking time.

Warm rice dishes can become tomorrow's cold salads.

Who doesn't go crazy over PASTA?

RICE-LENTIL CASSEROLE
A great smoky winter dish

8–10 portions
Cooking time: about 1 ½ hours
Start a day in advance
Food processor comes in handy

1 cup lentils
4½ cups water
½ cup brown rice
1 cup **Tomato Sauce**
2 tsp. salt
½ tsp. pepper

¼ tsp. marjoram
50–60 grams (¼ cup) margarine
2–3 cloves garlic, crushed
3 onions, chopped
250 grams (½ lb.) smoked meat,
cut into strips

Sift through lentils and remove everything that doesn't resemble a lentil.

Soak lentils overnight in 4 cups cold water and drain.

Preheat oven 350° F, 180° C, ten minutes before using.

In large pot cook lentils in 4½ cups water, covered, over low flame about ½ hour. Add rice, Tomato Sauce and seasoning; mix and continue cooking covered another ½ hour.

Meanwhile, in large frying pan, heat margarine and lightly sauté garlic, and onions. Add to lentils together with smoked meat and stir.

Place mixture in suitable deep baking dish, cover and bake in moderate oven 20 minutes.

RICE-LENTIL PILAF
This became a family affair

About 8 portions
Sautéing and baking time: about 1 ¾ hours
Start a few hours in advance
Food processor comes in handy

1 cup brown rice
1 cup lentils
2 tbsp. raisins
oil for frying
5 cloves garlic, crushed
1 large onion, diced
2 tbsp. parsley, cut up
1 carrot, sliced
¼ kilo (½ lb.) mushrooms, sliced, optional

2 tsp. salt
⅛ tsp. pepper
½ tsp. turmeric
½ tsp. ginger
2 tbsp. cumin
¼ tsp. ground cloves, optional
2 tbsp. brandy
¼ cup blanched almonds, halved
2 tbsp. pine nuts
1 tbsp. butter of margarine

Sift through lentils and remove everyting that doesn't resemble a lentil. Wash lentils a few times until water is clear.

In bowl soak lentils in boiled water at least ½ hour. Drain. Preheat oven 350° F, 180° C.

In large frying pan heat oil and sauté garlic, onion, parsley, carrot and mushrooms about 8 minutes, stirring occasionally. In small bowl mix together all of the seasoning.

Arrange sautéed vegetables in 2½ quart, (2¼ liter) deep casserole.

Spread rice, lentils, raisins and seasoning over vegetables; add 3 cups boiling water and brandy; cover and bake 1 hour.

In small saucepan sauté blanched almonds and pine nuts in butter or margarine a few minutes, stirring continuously (beware of burning). Sprinkle over pilaf, mix well and serve.

CHINESE RICE WITH MUSHROOMS

A delight

About 6 portions
Cooking time: 15 minutes
Food processor comes in handy

4 tbsp. oil	3 cups cooked white or brown rice
2 eggs, beaten	1 tbsp. soy sauce
1 onion, chopped	1–1½ tsp. salt
3 cloves garlic, crushed	¼ tsp. pepper
250 grams (½ lb.) mushrooms, sliced	2 tbsp. pine nuts

In frying pan heat 1 tablespoon oil and fry eggs to form flat omelette. Remove from pan and cut into thin strips and set aside.

In frying pan melt 2 tablespoon oil and sauté onion and garlic about 4 minutes.

Add mushrooms and continue sautéing 8–10 minutes more, stirring occasionally.

Add rest of oil, rice, omelette strips, soy sauce, seasoning and pine nuts and heat through, stirring continuously.

RICE-MUSHROOM MIX

Make it a weekly happening

6–8 portions
Sautéing and baking time: about 1½ hours
Food processor comes in handy

¼ cup plus 2 tbsp. oil	1 tsp. paprika
1 large onion, chopped	¼ cup onion soup powder
3 cloves garlic, crushed	½ tsp. salt
1½ cups rice	¼ tsp. pepper
250 grams (½ lb.) mushrooms, sliced	1 tbsp. margarine

Preheat oven 350° F, 180° C.

In large frying pan heat ¼ cup oil and sauté onion and garlic about 3 minutes. Add rice and continue sautéing, stirring continuously, over medium flame, until rice browns.

In separate pan heat 3 tablespoons oil and sauté mushrooms and paprika. Add to rice with onion soup powder, salt and pepper. Mix together and spread in a 3–3½ quart greased baking pan. Dot with margarine.

Add about 4 cups boiling water; cover and bake in moderate oven about 1¼ hours, until rice is soft and water is absorbed. (White rice takes less time than brown.)

If rice is not soft add some more boiling water and bake longer.

RICE-VEGETABLE MIX

Today's side dish is tomorrow's salad

4–6 portions
Sautéing time: 10–15 minutes
Food processor comes in handy

1 cup brown rice	*1 cup mushrooms, sliced*
3 tbsp. oil	*about 2 tsp. salt*
1 large onion, chopped	*½ tsp. pepper*
3 cloves garlic, crushed	*¼ tsp. turmeric*
1 turnip, grated	*1 tomato, diced*
2 zucchini, diced	*1 scallion, chopped*
1 stalk celery, diced	*2 tbsp. parsley, cut up*

Cook rice and set aside.

In large frying pan heat oil and sauté onion and garlic a few minutes.

Add turnip, zucchini, celery, mushrooms and seasoning and continue sautéing 7–8 minutes more, stirring occasionally.

Add tomato, scallion, parsley and rice and sauté a few more minutes.

SWEET RICE

It's so easy and sooo good!

4–5 portions
Cooking time: 10 minutes

2 tbsp. margarine	*1 tsp. grated orange rind*
2 stalks celery, diced	*½ cup golden raisins*
1 tbsp. concentrated pure	*1½ cups cooked rice*
orange juice	*½ tsp. salt*

In large frying pan melt margarine and sauté celery about 7 minutes, stirring occasionally.

Add rest of ingredients and mix well. Heat and serve.

P.S. Great with duck. See Poultry section for recipe for **Glazed Orange Duck.**

SPAGHETTI–CHEESE CASSEROLE

Kids can prepare
this themselves

About 4 portions
Baking time: 20 minutes

200–250 grams (7–8 oz.)	*½ cup feta or cottage cheese*
spaghetti	*2 cups **Tomato Sauce***
2 tbsp. oil	*¼ tsp. basil*
3 cloves garlic, crushed	*2 tsp. salt*
2 scallions, chopped	*¼ tsp. pepper*
1¼ cups hard cheese, grated	*3 tbsp. parsley, chopped*
¼ cup Parmesan cheese, grated	*1 tbsp. butter*

Cook and drain spaghetti.

Preheat oven 350° F, 180° C.

In small frying pan heat oil and over low flame gently sauté garlic about 2 minutes. Add scallion and sauté a few minutes more. Add to Tomato Sauce with seasoning and parsley.

Spread a little tomato sauce on bottom of greased casserole dish. Make two layers of spaghetti-sauce-cheese.

P.S. For hard cheeses I use a combination of Swiss and cheddar.

VARIATION: Leave out all the cheeses and prepare as directed.

SPEEDY SPAGHETTI ITALIANO
A quick delight

250 grams (8 oz.) spaghetti	1 tsp. salt
2–3 tbsp. olive oil	¼ tsp. pepper
4 cloves garlic, crushed	1–2 tbsp. fresh dill

Cook spaghetti until "al dente"; drain and place in pot or bowl.

In saucepan heat oil and sauté garlic; add salt and pepper and mix into spaghetti.

CREAMY NOODLE RING
Melts in your mouth

About 8 portions
Baking time: 1 ¼ – 1 ½ hours

200–250 grams (7–8 oz.) medium noodles	about 2 tsp. salt
2 eggs, slightly beaten	¼ tsp. pepper
2 cups cottage cheese	80 grams (⅓ cup) butter, melted
2 cups sour cream	**Mushroom Cream Sauce**

Preheat oven 300° F, 150° C.

Cook and drain noodles.

In large bowl mix together all the ingredients except Sauce.

Place into buttered large ring mold and bake in slow oven about 1¾ hours (top should be crispy golden brown).

To remove from pan, go around sides and inner ring with knife. Place serving platter over pan and turn pan over carefully with the platter.

Fill center with Mushroom Cream Sauce.

P.S. Casserole can be baked in large buttered rectangular flat baking pan; adjust timing. Serve Mushroom Cream Sauce separately.

VARIATION: For Cornflake Topping use flat rectangular pan. Mix together ½ cup cornflake crumbs (cornflakes can be blended in blender), 2 tablespoons sesame seeds and 1 tablespoon melted butter. Sprinkle over casserole in pan before baking.

NOODLE-SPINACH CASSEROLE   *A whole meal in itself*

About 8 portions
Baking time: about 50 minutes
Allow time for settling

200–250 grams (7–8 oz.)
   medium noodles
400 grams (1 lb.) chopped,
   frozen spinach
2 tbsp. butter
2 onions, diced
2 tbsp. breadcrumbs or wheat germ

2 cups cottage cheese
2 eggs, slightly beaten
2 tbsp. sour cream
about 2 tsp. salt
½ tsp. pepper
1½ cup hard cheese, grated

Preheat oven 350° F, 180° C.

Cook and drain noodles.

Thaw out spinach; drain and dry out in frying pan over medium-low flame; pouring off excess water from time to time. (Process can be done in microwave oven.)

In large frying pan, over low flame, melt butter and sauté onions, stirring occasionally.

In large bowl mix together noodles, spinach, sautéed onion, cottage cheese, eggs, sour cream, salt and pepper.

Spread mixture in large flat baking pan and bake in moderate oven ½ hour. Meanwhile in bowl mix together grated cheese and breadcrumbs or wheat germ.

Remove casserole from oven, sprinkle with cheese mixture; return to oven and bake an additional 15 minutes.

Allow at least 15 minutes for settling.

Serve alone with a great salad or as side dish with fish.

P.S. For hard cheeses, I use a combination of Swiss and cheddar.

SPINACH LASAGNA   *Try it!*

About 6 portions
Baking time: 45 minutes

9 lasagna noodles
400 grams (1 lb.) spinach,
   cooked and chopped
2 scallions, cut up
1 cup ricotta or cottage cheese
1 egg

¼ tsp. dried dill
¼ tsp. basil
about 1½ tsp. salt
½ tsp. pepper
*2 cups **Tomato Sauce***
2 cups hard cheese, grated

Cook, drain and pat dry noodles.

Preheat oven 350° F, 180° C.

In bowl, mix together spinach, scallions, ricotta or cottage cheese, egg and seasoning.

Spread a little Tomato Sauce in bottom of large rectangular baking pan.

Make 4 layers: noodles–sauce–spinach–hard cheese. Bake, covered, in moderate oven 30 minutes.

Uncover and bake another 15 minutes.

CABBAGE-NOODLE MIX

I can eat a potful of this!

4–6 portions
Cooking time: 30 minutes
Food processor makes it easier

50–60 grams (¼ cup) butter
1 medium cabbage, grated
200 grams (7 oz.) noodles

about 2 tsp. salt
½ tsp. pepper
½ tsp. caraway seeds

In large frying pan, over low flame, heat butter or margarine. Increase heat and sauté cabbage about ½ hour. Meanwhile cook and drain noodles. Add to cabbage together with salt, pepper and caraway seeds and mix.

VARIATIONS: (1) Instead of cabbage, sauté 700 grams (1½ lb.) broccoli with 1 onion, diced and 3 cloves garlic, crushed. Omit caraway seeds.

(2) For a whole meal: Mix ½ kilo (1 lb.) chopped meat with 2 cloves crushed garlic, 1 chopped small onion, 1 egg, 2 tablespoons prepared mustard, breadcrumbs. Brown mixture over medium flame. Add cabbage and continue as directed.

KASHA-MUSHROOM MIX

Delicious and nutritious

About 6 portions
Total Cooking time: about 45 minutes
Food processor comes in handy

1 cup kasha (buckwheat groats)
1 egg, slightly beaten
1¾ cups boiling water
2 tbsp. butter or margarine
3 tbsp. oil

2 onions, diced
3–4 cloves garlic, crushed
250 grams (½ lb.) mushrooms, sliced
about 1 tsp. salt
½ tsp. pepper
1 tsp. paprika

In medium bowl mix kasha with beaten egg.

Heat large frying pan; pour in kasha mixture and brown over medium heat, stirring constantly, until kernels of kasha separate and dry out.

Transfer to medium pot. Add boiling water, ½ tsp. salt and butter or margarine; mix; cover and cook over low flame about 20 minutes until water is absorbed.

Meanwhile in same frying pan heat oil and sauté onions and garlic about 5 minutes. Add mushrooms, rest of salt, pepper and paprika and sauté another 5 minutes.

Add sautéed onion and mushroom to kasha and mix. Adjust seasoning. If mixture is a bit dry add a little more butter or margarine.

VARIATION: Add 125 grams (4 oz.) cooked medium bow-tie noodles. Adjust seasoning.

CRUNCHY NOODLE KUGEL

Delicious all by itself

About 8 portions
Baking time: about 1 ¼ hours

200 grams (7 oz.)	*3 eggs, slightly beaten*
medium noodles	*about 2 tsp. salt*
¼ cup oil	*¼ tsp. pepper*

Preheat oven 350° F, 180° C.

Cook and drain noodles. Place in large bowl; add oil, eggs, salt and pepper and mix together.

Spread mixture into greased deep dish 25 cm (10″) round pie plate and bake about 1¼ hours, until top is brown and crunchy.

P.S. Great as side dish or in **Rich Chicken Soup.**

Take time out for homemade **SAUCES**

It's the Sauce that gives the delicate tang.

Sauces should not be too thick or too thin — experience makes perfect.

When liquid is called for, water, broth (meat, chicken, vegetable) or milk can be used.

Additional sauces not given here are interspersed in other recipes throughout the book.

MUSHROOM-WINE SAUCE

Smooth as silk

2 tbsp. oil
2 medium onions, diced
3 cloves garlic, crushed
250–300 grams (½ lb.)
  mushrooms, sliced
1 tsp. salt

½ tsp. paprika
a little parsley, chopped
2 tbsp. mushroom sauce powder
1½ tbsp. flour
2 cups liquid (your choice)
¼ – ½ cup dry or semi-dry white wine

In large pan heat oil and sauté onion and garlic about 7 minutes, stirring occasionally. Add mushrooms together with spices; cover and cook over low flame about 7 minutes more, stirring occasionally.

Remove from flame; add parsley, mushroom sauce powder and flour and mix until smooth.

Return to flame. Slowly pour chosen liquid and wine into pan, bring to a boil over medium low flame and cook, stirring continuously, a few minutes until sauce thickens.

P.S. Serve on toast, in pastry shells or on **Broccoli Roll**.

VARIATION: Add broiled chicken livers to ready-made sauce. Heat and serve.

MUSHROOM SAUCE

A standard

2 tbsp. butter or margarine
1 onion, chopped
2 cloves garlic, crushed
1 stalk celery, diced
2 tbsp. parsley, chopped
250 grams (½ lb.) mushrooms,
  sliced

1 tsp. salt
¼ tsp. pepper
½ tsp. dried basil
1½ tbsp. flour
1 cup liquid (water, milk, broth, etc.)
1 tbsp. lemon juice
¼ cup dry or semi-dry white wine

In large pan melt butter or margarine and sauté onion, garlic, celery and parsley a few minutes, stirring occasionally. Add mushrooms and continue cooking 6–8 minutes more, stirring occasionally.

Add seasoning and flour and stir well. Add liquid, lemon juice and wine and cook about 5 minutes more, stirring continuously, until Sauce thickens.

P.S. For fish add 2 tablespoons capers with the mushrooms.

MUSHROOM-CREAM SAUCE

Creamily good!

Food processor makes it easier

50–60 grams (¼ cup) butter, melted
2 tbsp. flour
½ tsp. salt

⅛ tsp. pepper
250 grams (½ lb.) mushrooms, sliced
1 cup sweet cream

In saucepan melt butter over low flame; sprinkle and coat mushrooms with flour and add to butter. Cover and cook about 5 minutes, stirring occasionally.

Add sweet cream and cook 5 minutes more, stirring occasionally. Season to taste.

P.S. Excellent on cooked vegetables and **Rich Noodle Pudding**.

WHITE SAUCE

An all-purpose sauce

THIN
1 tbsp. butter or margarine
1 tbsp. flour
½ tsp. salt
⅛ tsp. pepper
1 cup milk or broth

MEDIUM
2 tbsp. butter or margarine
2 tbsp. flour

½ tsp. salt
⅛ tsp. pepper
1 cup milk or broth

THICK
3 tbsp. butter or margarine
3 tbsp. flour
½ tsp. salt
⅛ tsp. pepper
1 cup milk or broth

In sauce pan, over low flame, melt butter or margarine.

Remove from flame and immediately add flour, salt and pepper and stir until smooth.

Return to medium-low flame, add liquid slowly and cook, stirring continuously until sauce thickens to desired consistency.

P.S. If left standing, sauce will thicken a little more.

VARIATION: Cheese Sauce — add ¼ cup grated hard cheese to the finished sauce and stir over low flame until cheese melts.

DUCK SAUCE

A tangy orange sauce

1 container pure, concentrated
   orange juice
⅓ cup apricot jam
2 tsp. soy sauce

¼ tsp. ground ginger
¼ tsp. Tabasco sauce, optional
salt and pepper to taste

In small saucepan combine all the ingredients and heat over low flame a few minutes.

Serve lukewarm or at room temperature.

P.S. Excellent with spare ribs, duck, egg rolls (and even plain chicken).

QUICK TOMATO SAUCE

*Helpful and
Healthful*

100 grams (3 oz.) tomato purée
½ cup water
1 tbsp. parsley, cut up
½ tsp. salt

½ tsp. pepper
2 cloves garlic, crushed
½ tsp. sugar

Place all ingredients in closed jar or food processor and mix.

P.S. Can be used as substitute for Tomato Sauce (on the following page) in such dishes as **Stuffed Cabbage** and **Sweet & Sour Meatballs**.

TOMATO SAUCE   *There's nothing like fresh tomato sauce; it's easy*

3–4 tbsp. olive oil
1 large onion, diced
4 cloves garlic, crushed
1 kilo (2 lbs.) tomatoes, cut up
1 small green pepper, cut up

a little parsley, chopped
a few bay leaves
1 tsp. basil
1 tsp. salt
¼ tsp. pepper
1 tsp. sugar

In pot heat oil and sauté onion and garlic about 10 minutes.
Add rest of ingredients; cover and cook, over low flame, about ¾ hour, stirring occasionally.
Let cool; remove bay leaves and blend in blender until smooth.
P.S. Great for **Pizzazy Pizza, Spaghetti Casserole, Eggplant Parmesan**, etc.

SWEET & SOUR TOMATO SAUCE   *Goes well with tongue*

1 onion, diced
⅓ cup lemon juice
¼ cup brown sugar

1 cup **Tomato Sauce**
¼–½ cup water
¼ cup raisins

In medium saucepan cook, covered, over low flame, onion, lemon juice and sugar about 15 minutes, stirring occasionally.
   Add Tomato Sauce, water and raisins and continue cooking another 20 minutes, stirring occasionally.
   P.S. Excellent as a sauce for cooked pickled tongue. Place sliced tongue in sauce and heat. Serve with rice or **Noodle Kugel**.

LEMON-FISH SAUCE   *Change a simple fish into a gourmet dish!*

100–125 grams (½ cup) butter
½ cup almonds, blanched
   and slivered
2 tbsp. lemon juice

1 tsp. Worcestershire sauce
1 tbsp. parsley, chopped
1 tbsp. dill, chopped
salt and pepper to taste

In small pot, over low flame, melt butter. When brown add almonds and sauté a few minutes, stirring continuously (beware of burning).
   Add rest of ingredients and mix until well blended. Remove from flame.
   At serving time heat and serve immediately.

The freshness of VEGETABLES

Of course, the easiest thing is to boil vegetables — but where's the fun, creativity and taste? With vegetables, there are unlimited possibilities. But remember, whatever you try, always use FRESH, quality vegetables.

In recipes requiring hard cheese, I find the best combination is Swiss, cheddar and Parmesan or a mild-flavored cheese. To grate cheeses use the fine grater attachment of the mixer or food processor. Frozen cheese grates more easily; keep grated cheese in the freezer for ready use.

Stir Fry — It's amazing the variety of vegetables suitable for stir frying — almost all of them. Besides the usual, try adding radishes, turnips, carrots, etc.

Vegetables for Entertaining: Side dishes for Entree (main course) — choose a colorful vegetable (green, red, purple) — for an added touch heat canned peach halves and serve. Besides the vegetable recipes, quiches and pies are great side dishes.

43

STRING BEAN–CHEESE BAKE
A delicious variation

About 6 portions
Baking time: 15–20 minutes

800 grams (1½ lbs.) string
   beans, cut into thirds,
   cooked and drained
2 tbsp. oil
2 tbsp. cider or wine vinegar
1 onion, diced
1 tsp. salt
¼ tsp. pepper

⅛ tsp. marjoram
3 cloves garlic, crushed
3 tbsp. bread crumbs or wheat germ
½ cup cheddar cheese, grated
2 tbsp. Parmesan cheese, grated
1 tbsp. butter, melted
2 tsp. paprika
a few almonds, coarsely chopped

Preheat oven 350° F, 180° C.

In large bowl mix together string beans, oil, vinegar, onion, seasoning and garlic. Place in flat ungreased baking pan.

In small bowl mix breadcrumbs and grated cheeses; add melted butter and sprinkle over string beans.

Top with a little paprika and bake in moderate oven 15–20 minutes. Sprinkle with almonds.

P.S. If anything is left over, rewarm or eat cold the next day.

STRING BEAN–CHEESE MIX – In large pot heat oil and lightly sauté onion, garlic and 1 small green pepper. Add string beans and continue sautéing a few more minutes. Add ¼ cup boiling water and salt, pepper, 1 tsp. basil, and ¼ tsp. paprika. Mix, cover, and cook over low flame until sting beans are soft. Drain and return to pot, add ¼ cup grated Parmesan cheese and mix. Place on serving platter and cover with rest of cheese.

CHINESE STRING BEANS
Very, very good

About 4 portions
Cooking time: 20 minutes

2 tbsp. oil
1 onion, thinly sliced
3 cloves garlic, crushed
½ kilo (1 lb.) string beans,
   cut into thirds
2 tbsp. soy sauce

1 cup vegetable broth
2 tsp. lemon juice
½ tsp. salt
⅛ tsp. pepper
¼ cup almonds, blanched and
   slivered

In medium pot heat oil and sauté onion and garlic. Add string beans and continue sautéing about 5 minutes. Add soy sauce, vegetable broth, lemon juice and seasoning; cover and cook over low flame 8–10 minutes. Remove with slotted spoon; place on serving platter and sprinkle with almonds.

STRING BEANS WITH ALMONDS
A delicate taste
to a familiar dish

About 4 portions
Cooking time: about 25 minutes

½ kilo (1 lb.) string beans
3 tbsp. oil
½ cup almonds, blanched
   and slivered

2 tbsp. lemon juice
½ tsp. salt
¼ tsp. pepper

Cut string beans into julienne strips (in half lengthwise and crosswise).

In large frying pan heat 2 tablespoons oil and sauté string beans 5–7 minutes; remove from pan with slotted spoon and place in pot.

Add ¼ cup water and ½ tsp. salt. Mix; cover and cook over low flame about 15 minutes.

Meanwhile in small frying pan heat 1 tablespoon oil and lightly sauté almonds a few minutes, stirring continuously (beware of burning).

Drain cooked string beans and return to pot. Add almonds, lemon juice, salt and pepper.

Heat and serve.

RATATOUILLE

A stir-fry happening

About 4 portions
Cooking time: about 35 minutes
Food processor comes in handy

1 small eggplant, cubed	¼ tsp. oregano
1 tsp. salt	½ tsp. sugar
¼ cup olive oil	2 medium zucchini, thinly sliced
2 onions, cut in wedges	1 large tomato, cut in wedges
3–4 cloves garlic, crushed	a little parsley, cut up
1 green pepper, in strips	a few stuffed olives or
1 tsp. salt	pitted green olives
½ tsp. pepper	2 tbsp. shelled sunflower seeds
½ tsp. basil	

Place eggplant cubes in strainer; sprinkle with one tablespoon salt and leave about 20 minutes. Rinse under cold water and dry on toweling.

In large frying pan heat oil and sauté onions and garlic about 5 minutes.

Add green pepper, eggplant, seasoning and sugar and sauté about 10 minutes, stirring occasionally.

Add zucchini and tomatoes; mix; cover and cook over low flame about 10 minutes, stirring occasionally. Uncover and continue cooking over medium-low flame another 8–10 minutes, stirring occasionally. Add parsley, olives and sunflower seeds and stir together.

Remove vegetables with slotted spoon and place in serving bowl.

Garnish with sprigs of parsley.

MUSHROOMS IN WINE

Elegance

About 4 portions
Baking time: ½ hour

½ kilo (1 lb.) mushroom caps	1 tbsp. parsley, cut up
3 tbsp. olive oil	3 cloves garlic, crushed
1 cup **Tomato Sauce**	½ tsp. salt
1 cup dry white wine	¼ tsp. pepper

Preheat oven 350° F, 180° C.
Place mushroom caps in baking dish.
In bowl mix together rest of ingredients and pour over mushrooms, cover and bake in medium oven ½ hour.
P.S. Use mushroom stems for sauces, soups, omelettes, etc.

CRUMB-TOPPED TOMATOES

Colorful taste

6 portions
Broiling time: 10–15 minutes

6 tomatoes
½ cup bread or cornflakes
   crumbs
¼ tsp. garlic powder

1 tsp. salt
¼ tsp. pepper
butter or margarine

Cut tomatoes in half crosswise and place them side by side close together on a greased broiling pan.
In bowl mix together crumbs with seasoning and place about 2 tablespoons of mixture on each tomato half.
Dot with butter or margarine and broil, far from flame, 10–15 minutes.

SPINACH-STUFFED TOMATOES

*A great way
to eat spinach*

About 6 portions
Baking time: 20–30 minutes

6 tomatoes
½ kilo (1 lb.) spinach, cooked,
   drained and chopped
50–60 grams (¼ cup) butter
   or margarine
3 tbsp. pine nuts or cut up almonds

3 cloves garlic, crushed
1 tsp. salt
¼ tsp. pepper
¼ tsp. marjoram
pinch of rosemary
3 tbsp. cornflakes crumbs

Preheat oven 350° F, 180° C.
Cut off top of each tomato and scoop out pulp with knife or spoon.
Sprinkle cavity with salt; turn over and leave for about 15 minutes.
Melt butter or margarine in frying pan over low flame; increase heat and gently sauté pine nuts or almonds with garlic a few minutes, stirring continuously (beware of burning). Remove from flame.
In bowl mix spinach, sautéed nuts and seasoning.
Fill tomatoes; place side by side close together on greased shallow baking pan; sprinkle with cornflakes crumbs and bake in moderate oven 20–30 minutes.

VARIATION: Sprinkle with grated cheese upon removing from oven.

ONIONS IN VINEGAR

Try this!

4–6 portions
Food processor comes in handy

50–60 grams (¼ cup) butter
   or margarine
4 large onions, thinly sliced
4 cloves garlic, crushed

3 tbsp. flour, seasoned with salt
   and pepper
2 tbsp. vinegar

In large frying pan heat butter or margarine over low flame; increase heat and sauté onions and garlic until golden brown, stirring occasionally.

Sprinkle with seasoned flour and sauté a few more minutes, stirring continuously.

Remove from flame and mix in vinegar.

P.S. As part of buffet or with smoked meat.

SAVORY BAKED ONIONS
Everyone loves onions this way

About 5 portions
Baking time: 1 hour

5 medium onions	¼ tsp. pepper
50–60 grams (¼ cup) butter, room temperature	1¼ tsp. marjoram
½ tsp. salt	½ tsp. caraway seeds

Preheat oven 325° F, 165° C.

Peel and halve onions crosswise. Place in baking pan open side up.

In small bowl mix together butter or margarine, salt, pepper, marjoram and caraway seeds and spread over each onion half.

Bake in moderate-low oven 1 hour, turning over after 30 minutes.

CRACKER JACK ONION PIE
What flavor!

About 6 portions
Sautéing and baking time: about 50 minutes
Food processor comes in handy

DOUGH
1 cup flour
2 tsp. baking powder
¼ tsp. salt
1 tsp. sugar
50–60 grams (¼ cup) butter
½ cup milk

FILLING
5 big onions, sliced
3 cloves garlic, crushed
50 grams (¼ cup) butter
1 tsp. salt
¼ tsp. pepper
½ tsp. paprika
1 egg
½ cup sour cream
½ cup hard cheese, grated
3 tbsp. crushed cornflakes

DOUGH: In large bowl sift flour, baking powder, salt and sugar. Cut in butter until crumbly. Add milk and form soft, not sticky, Dough (adjust amount of flour).

On floured board, roll out Dough thin about 0.3 cm (⅛″), big enough for a 23 cm (9″) pyrex pie plate overlapping on sides. Fold in edges and flute as desired. Set aside.

Preheat oven 350° F, 180° C.

FILLING: In large frying pan, over low heat, melt butter. Increase heat and sauté onion and garlic a few minutes. Add seasoning and continue sautéing about 8 minutes, stirring occasionally. Add egg, sour cream, cheese and seasoning and mix together.

Spread over pie crust; sprinkle with crushed cornflakes and bake in moderate oven 40 minutes.

P.S. For hard cheeses I use a combination of Swiss and cheddar.

FRIED ONION RINGS

Always a treat

onion rings
equal amount of water and milk,
or milk substitute

flour
oil for deep frying
salt

Soak onion rings in water-milk solution about ½ hour; drain and dry on paper towel.
Dip each ring in flour and deep fry in heated oil; drain on paper towel.
Sprinkle with salt.
P.S. With fish or steak, it's great.

SWEET & SOUR RED CABBAGE *A standard in our house*

6–8 portions
Cooking time: About 40 minutes
Food processor makes it easier

3 tbsp. butter, margarine or oil
1 onion, chopped
3 cloves garlic, crushed
1 medium (½ kilo, 1 lb.) red
cabbage, coarsely grated

¼ cup brown sugar
⅓ cup vinegar
1–2 tbsp. lemon juice
1 tsp. salt
¼ tsp. pepper

In large pot heat butter, margarine or oil and lightly sauté onion and garlic about 10 minutes.
Add rest of ingredients; mix; cover and cook over low flame about 30 minutes, stirring occasionally until cabbage is soft.
P.S. Warm as side dish or cold as salad with cottage cheese.

ARTICHOKE DELIGHT *A conversation piece*

6 portions
Cooking time: 35–45 minutes

6 artichokes
¼ cup lemon juice
2 tsp. salt
¼ tsp. pepper

2 bay leaves
1 tbsp. oil
Vinaigrette or **Tartar Sauce**
Dressing

When buying artichokes choose all green ones with closed leaves.
Cut off stems and about ½ cm (¼″) from top. Snip off ends of leaves with scissors.
In large bowl soak artichokes in water to which was added salt and lemon juice; leave about 15 minutes. Rinse under cold water.
Place artichokes in large pot; cover with water; bring to boil; add 2 teaspoons salt, pepper, bay leaves and oil; partially cover and cook over medium flame 35–45 minutes. Cooking time will vary according to the size of artichokes. Artichokes are ready when bottom leaves come off easily.
Remove artichokes with slotted spoon and drain on shallow dish, stem side up. Serve at room temperature with desired Dressing. If you don't know how to eat them ask someone to show you; it's worth it.

ARTICHOKE HEARTS GOURMET

Talk of the town

6 portions
Cooking time: 50 minutes

6 artichokes
2 tsp. flour
3 cups cold water
2 tbsp. lemon juice
½ tsp. salt
⅛ tsp. pepper

GARNISH
lettuce leaves
sliced tomatoes and onions
asparagus tips
Vinaigrette or **Tartar Sauce**
Dressing

TO PREPARE: Remove leaves by pulling each one down and twisting off. As you approach the center it will become more difficult. Cut the last ones straight off with a sharp knife. Trim around with scissors, but do not remove choke (hairy center). This is removed after cooking.

TO COOK: Do not use aluminum or iron pot (this will cause blackening). In pot large enough to hold all of the artichoke hearts stir the flour into ¼ cup cold water until smooth. Add rest of water, lemon juice, salt and pepper; bring to boil, stirring continuously. Lower flame and cook 5 minutes.

Place artichoke hearts in pot (artichokes should be completely immersed throughout cooking period). Adjust water, bring to boil, lower flame, partly cover and cook 40–45 minutes. If necessary add a little water during cooking.

With slotted spoon remove artichoke hearts.

Let cool and with spoon or knife remove center choke.

Serve at room temperature on lettuce leaf with desired Dressing placed in center of each heart. Surround with sliced tomato, onion and asparagus tips. Place additional Dressing in bowl for extra helpings.

P.S. My father-in-law always complains about not being able to use the leaves. Actually, there isn't too much waste and this delicacy is definitely worth it.

CAULIFLOWER GOURMET

A gourmet dish with a tang

About 4 portions
Baking time: about ½ hour

1 medium cauliflower
1 cup **Tomato Sauce**
2 tbsp. parsley, cut up
1 tsp. salt
¼ tsp. pepper
¼ tsp. ground cloves

1 tbsp. capers
6 green or black olives, chopped
¼ cup hard cheese, grated
2 tbsp. breadcrumbs
1 tbsp. sesame seeds
1 tbsp. olive oil

Cut cauliflower into flowerettes and cook. Drain and set aside.

Preheat oven 350° F, 180° C.

In medium bowl mix together Tomato Sauce, parsley, seasoning, capers and olives. Pour ¼ of the Sauce mixture in a flat baking pan.

Mix cauliflower with remaining sauce in bowl. Arrange cauliflower in baking pan, over existing sauce.

In small bowl mix together grated cheese, breadcrumbs and sesame seeds and sprinkle over cauliflower. Sprinkle with olive oil.

Bake in moderate oven about ½ hour.

P.S. For hard cheeses I use a combination of Swiss and cheddar.

CRUMBLY CAULIFLOWER

Crumbly delicious!

About 4 portions
Baking time: 20–25 minutes

1 medium cauliflower	½ tsp. salt
1 egg	⅛ tsp. pepper
½ cup cornflakes crumbs	¼ tsp. garlic powder

Cook cauliflower in slightly salted water until almost done.

Remove carefully (keeping it whole) and let cool somewhat.

Preheat oven 350° F, 180° C.

In medium bowl beat egg.

In separate bowl mix cornflakes crumbs with seasoning. Dip cauliflower in egg so that all parts are covered, then roll in seasoned cornflakes crumbs making it crumby all over.

Place cauliflower in greased medium baking pan and bake in moderate oven 20–25 minutes.

P.S. Cauliflower can also be cut up into flowerettes and then coated and baked.

CAULIFLOWER-MUSHROOM BAKE

Different

About 4 portions
Cooking and baking time: about 40 minutes

1 medium cauliflowerettes	2 tbsp. flour
50–60 grams (¼ cup) butter	1 cup milk
½ tsp. paprika	1 cup mushrooms, sliced
¼ cup hard cheese, grated	2 tbsp. parsley, cut up
	½ tsp. salt
SAUCE	¼ tsp. pepper
2 tbsp. butter	¼ cup breadcrumbs

Cook cauliflowerettes about 15 minutes and drain.

In large frying pan, over low flame, melt ¼ cup butter.

Increase heat and sauté cauliflower a few minutes.

Arrange in greased flat baking pan.

Preheat oven 375° F, 190° C.

SAUCE: In medium saucepan melt the remaining butter over low flame; remove from flame; add flour and mix until smooth. Return to flame; add milk slowly and cook over medium-low flame, stirring continuously, until Sauce becomes thick. Add mushrooms, parsley, salt, pepper and 2 tablespoons grated cheese and mix.

Pour Sauce over cauliflower; sprinkle with breadcrumbs, rest of cheese and paprika and bake in moderate-high oven about 20 minutes.

MUSTARD-GLAZED CARROTS

A sumptuous flavor

6–8 portions
Cooking time: about 25 minutes
Food processor comes in handy

1 kilo (2 lbs.) carrots, sliced	¼ cup brown sugar
50–60 grams (¼ cup) butter	¼ cup parsley, cut up
3 tbsp. prepared mustard	⅛ tsp. pepper

Cook carrots until partially done. Drain and return to pot. In small pot cook butter, mustard, sugar, parsley and pepper over low flame a few minutes, stirring constantly until mixture becomes syrupy.

Pour over carrots and cook over low flame a few minutes, stirring continuously.

TO SERVE: Sprinkle with parsley.

VEGETABLE OMELETTE
Eggs never tasted so good

About 3 portions
Sautéing and cooking time: about 25 minutes
Food processor makes it easier

3 tbsp. plus 1 tbsp. butter	*½ cup mushrooms, sliced*
1 onion, chopped	*2 tbsp. parsley, chopped*
3 cloves garlic, crushed	*5 eggs*
1 small green pepper, diced	*1 tsp. salt*
2 stalks celery, diced	*¼ tsp. pepper*
2 scallions, chopped	*¼ tsp. marjoram*

In large frying pan, over low flame, melt butter; increase heat and lightly sauté onion and garlic. Add green pepper, celery, scallions, mushrooms and parsley and sauté over medium flame a few minutes. With slotted spoon transfer vegetables to medium bowl.

In large bowl beat eggs with whisk; add sautéed vegetables and seasoning and mix.

In frying pan, over low flame, melt and heat 1 tablespoon butter; add egg mixture and fry 12–15 minutes, until desired firmness.

Fold over and place on serving platter. Serve immediately.

VARIATION: Add ½ cup grated Parmesan cheese to egg mixture before frying.

SWEET & SOUR CABBAGE–APPLE MIX
Just the right texture

About 8 portions
Sautéing and cooking time: 2 hours and 10 minutes
Food processor comes in handy

1 head green or red	*2 tart apples, peeled and diced*
cabbage, or ½ of each	*2–2½ tsp. salt*
3 tbsp. oil	*¼ tsp. pepper*
1 large onion, diced	*¼ cup brown sugar*
1½ tbsp. flour	*⅓ cup lemon juice*
½–1 cup water	*3 tbsp. white raisins*

Grate cabbage and set aside.

In large pot heat oil and sauté onion about 10 minutes; sprinkle with flour and continue sautéing, stirring continuously a few more minutes.

Add cabbage and water; bring to boil; add remaining ingredients and cook over low heat about 2 hours, stirring occasionally.

P.S. Great with sour cream.

RED CABBAGE–POTATO BAKE

A great combo

About 6 portions
Baking time: 1 hour and 20 minutes
Food processor comes in handy

¾ kilo (1½ lbs.) red cabbage
2 onions, cut into rings
2 tbsp. white raisins
½ cup soup stock
1¼ cups dry red wine
1 tsp. sugar
1 tsp. salt

¼ – ½ tsp. pepper
½ cup salami strips
about 3 tbsp. margarine
6 small potatoes,
   whole or halved
1 tbsp. parsley
1 tsp. paprika

Preheat oven 350° F, 180° C.

Grate cabbage; place in bowl; mix together with onion rings and raisins and set aside.

In saucepan, over medium heat, bring to boil stock and wine; boil about 2 minutes and remove from flame. Add sugar, salt and pepper; mix; pour over cabbage and toss.

Spread into greased large shallow baking pan; cover and bake 1 hour. Uncover; arrange salami strips on top; dot with one tablespoon margarine and continue baking another 20 minutes. Meanwhile cook potatoes until tender. Drain.

In same pot melt 2 tablespoons margarine over low flame with chopped parsley, salt and pepper and toss. Add potatoes and toss.

Place potatoes over salami; sprinkle with paprika and serve.

P.S. Maybe double the amount of salami, since, in my house, almost all of the salami is gone before it gets to the table.

POTATO-CHEESE BAKE

A layered delight

About 6 portions
Baking time: 1½ hours
Food processor comes in handy

4 medium potatoes
2 onions
¾ cup hard cheese, grated
¾ cup milk

1 egg
salt and pepper
½ tsp. paprika
2 tbsp. sesame or caraway seeds

Thinly slice potatoes and onions.

Preheat oven 350° F, 180° C.

In deep greased baking pan form three layers of potatoes, salt and pepper, onion rings and cheeses. (Sprinkle ½ teaspoon salt and ⅛ teaspoon pepper over each layer.)

In blender blend milk, egg, ¼ teaspoon salt and ⅛ teaspoon pepper and pour carefully over top layer.

Cover and bake in moderate oven 45 minutes.

Sprinkle with paprika and sesame or caraway seeds.

Uncover and continue baking another 45 minutes.

P.S. For hard cheeses I use a combination of Swiss and cheddar.

ITALIAN EGGPLANT CASSEROLE

A tasty,
family treat

About 4 portions
Cooking and baking time: 1 hour
Allow time for settling

1 large eggplant	½ tsp. oregano
1 onion, chopped	½ cup breadcrumbs
2 eggs, slightly beaten	2 tbsp. parsley, chopped
30 grams (2 tbsp.) butter, melted	2 large tomatoes, thinly sliced
1 tsp. salt	½ cup hard cheese, grated
¼ tsp. pepper	1 tsp. paprika

Peel and slice or dice eggplant.

Preheat oven 375° F, 190° C.

Cook eggplant in a little salted water 10–15 minutes. Drain and mash. Transfer to large bowl; add onion, eggs, butter, seasoning, breadcrumbs and parsley and mix.

Grease baking pan with butter and place half of tomato slices on bottom.

Spread eggplant mixture over tomatoes and cover with remaining tomato slices.

Sprinkle grated cheese over tomatoes.

Sprinkle with paprika and bake in moderate-high oven 45 minutes.

Allow to settle about 15 minutes before serving.

P.S. For hard cheeses I use a combination of Swiss and cheddar.

EGGPLANT-MUSHROOM BAKE

Eggplant with taste

About 4 portions
Cooking and baking time: 1 ¼ hours

1 eggplant, peeled and cubed	¼ tsp. pepper
¼ cup oil	1 tsp. paprika
1 onion, diced	½ tsp. oregano
3 cloves garlic, crushed	4 tbsp. mushroom soup powder
1 cup mushrooms, sliced	1 cup hard cheese, grated
1 small green pepper, diced	¼ cup Parmesan cheese, grated
2 small zucchini, grated	2 eggs, slightly beaten
salt to taste	½ cup bread or cornflakes crumbs
1 tbsp. parsley, cut up	

Preheat oven 350° F, 180° C ten minutes before using.

In medium pot place eggplant cubes and cook in a little salted water over low flame until soft (about ½ hour). Meanwhile, in large frying pan, heat oil and sauté onion, garlic, mushrooms, green pepper, zucchini and parsley 5–7 minutes, stirring occasionally. Add seasoning and mix.

Add sautéed vegetables to eggplant together with soup powder, cheeses, eggs and crumbs and mix.

Transfer to greased baking pan and bake in moderate oven 45 minutes.

P.S. For hard cheeses I use a combination of Swiss and cheddar.

MUSHROOM-STUFFED EGGPLANT
Excellent

4 portions
Sautéing and baking time: about 1 hour
Food processor comes in handy

2 medium eggplants
100–125 grams (½ cup) butter
500 grams (1 lb.) mushrooms, sliced
1 green pepper, chopped
1 onion, chopped
4 cloves garlic, crushed
1 tsp. paprika

1 tsp. salt
¼ tsp. pepper
½ cup flour
½ cup sweet cream
1 marinated gamba, diced
¼ cup Parmesan cheese, grated

Preheat oven 350° F, 180° C.

Cut eggplants in half lengthwise; remove pulp and cut into small cubes (reserving skin).

In large frying pan, over low flame, heat butter; increase heat and sauté eggplant cubes, mushrooms, green pepper, onion, garlic and seasoning about 15 minutes, stirring occasionally.

Remove from flame; add flour and mix.

Add sweet cream and gamba and mix together.

Fill eggplant skins and place on greased baking dish close together.

Sprinkle with grated cheese and paprika and bake in moderate oven 40–45 minutes.

EGGPLANT PARMESAN
Yosef's favorite

About 6 portions
Frying and baking time: about 1 hour
Use food processor if preparing flour batter
Allow time for settling

2 eggplants
3 eggs
⅓ cup flour OR
   about 1 cup breadcrumbs
½ tsp. salt
¼ tsp. pepper
olive oil

1 cup hard cheese, grated
½ cup Parmesan cheese, grated
Tomato Sauce
⅓ cup cottage cheese
½ tsp. paprika

Peel and slice eggplants into medium slices and place in colander. Sprinkle with salt and leave ½–1 hour. Rinse under cold water and dry on toweling.

FRYING EGGPLANT SLICES:

(1) Flour Batter – beat eggs, flour, salt and pepper (best done in the processor) and pour into flat bowl. In large frying pan heat oil, dip and cover eggplant slices with batter and fry over medium flame on both sides until golden brown. Drain on paper toweling.

(2) Breadcrumbs – Beat eggs in flat bowl; mix breadcrumbs, salt and pepper in separate bowl. Dip eggplant slices in egg and then in seasoned breadcrumbs. Proceed to fry as in Flour Batter.

In separate bowl mix grated cheeses.

Preheat oven 350° F, 180° C.

In large flat baking dish arrange casserole in layers as follows: Cover bottom with ½ of eggplant slices, pour over ½ of Tomato Sauce; sprinkle with ½ of grated cheese and dot with cottage cheese. Arrange another layer of eggplant slices; pour over rest of Tomato Sauce; sprinkle with remaining grated cheese and paprika and bake in moderate oven about ½ hour.

Allow to settle about 20 minutes before serving. It's possible to leave in oven ½ hour or more to settle.

P.S. Delicious even when reheated. For hard cheeses I use a combination of Swiss and cheddar.

GIVETCH
All in one pot

About 10 portions
Sautéing and cooking time: 1 ½ hours
Food processor comes in handy

3 tbsp. oil	2 green peppers, diced
2 large onions, diced	¼ cup pearl barley
4–5 cloves garlic, crushed	⅓ cup cider vinegar
1 tsp. paprika	¼ cup sugar
1 eggplant, peeled and cubed	2 tsp. salt
½ kilo (1 lb.) zucchini, diced	¼ tsp. pepper
½ kilo (1 lb.) soft tomatoes, diced	

In large pot heat oil and sauté onions, garlic and paprika about 10 minutes, stirring occasionally.

Add rest of ingredients; mix; cover and cook over low flame about 1 hour, stirring occasionally.

P.S. Excellent warm as side dish or cold as salad with cottage cheese.

SAUERKRAUT CASSEROLE
WOW! With hot dog on roll

3–4 portions
Baking time: 25 minutes

2 cups sauerkraut	2 tbsp. brown sugar
1 large green pepper, diced	½ tsp. caraway seeds

Preheat oven 400° F, 200° C.

In large bowl mix all the ingredients.

Place in greased baking pan and bake in moderate-hot oven 25 minutes.

The versatility of **POULTRY**

Before starting make sure you have enough fresh garlic, prepared mustard and white wine on hand for most of the recipes.

Poultry can substitute for meat in many recipes: e.g., beef stew, pepper steak, meat balls, stir fry, stuffed cabbage, etc.

AMERICAN BARBECUE-STYLE CHICKEN   *Wow!*

About 6 portions
Baking time: 1 ½ hours

2 small chickens	2 stalks celery, cut up
oil for frying	½ cup lemon juice
2 onions, chopped	1½ cup **Tomato Sauce**
4 cloves garlic, crushed	1 cup water
1 tbsp. paprika	½ cup dry or semi-dry white wine
1 tbsp. prepared mustard	¼ cup brown sugar
3 tbsp. Worcestershire sauce	about ½ tsp. salt
	¼ tsp. pepper

Cut the chickens in eighths and pat dry.

Preheat oven 325° F, 175° C.

In large frying pan heat oil and brown chicken pieces on all sides. Transfer to large baking pan, arranging them side by side close together. Set aside.

In same frying pan sauté onion, garlic and paprika about 7 minutes. Add rest of ingredients; cover and cook over low flame about 20 minutes, stirring occasionally.

Pour Tomato Sauce over chicken pieces and bake in medium-low oven about 1 ½ hours, basting occasionally.

SUGGESTED SIDE DISHES: **Noodle Kugel** and **Broccoli Kugel**.

FRENCH CHICKEN   *For a change!*

About 3 portions
Browning and baking time: about 2 hours

1 small chicken	3 cloves garlic, crushed
1 cup plus 1 tbsp. flour	1 tbsp. paprika
1 tsp. paprika	250 grams (½ lb.) mushrooms, sliced
1 tsp. dried parsley	3 medium tomatoes, diced
¼ cup plus 2 tbsp. oil	1 cup broth
2 onions, thinly sliced	½ cup sherry or dry red wine

Cut chicken into eighths and pat dry.

In medium bowl mix together one cup flour, paprika and parsley. Dip and coat chicken on all sides. In large frying pan heat ¼ cup oil and brown chicken pieces on all sides. Transfer to baking dish, placing chicken pieces side by side close together, skin side up.

Preheat oven 350° F, 180° C.

SAUCE: In same frying pan heat 2 tablespoons oil. Sauté onion, garlic and paprika about 7 minutes. Add mushrooms, tomatoes and one tablespoon flour. Mix until blended. Add broth slowly, stirring constantly. Add wine and cook over low flame about 5 minutes, stirring continuously.

Pour the sauce over chicken pieces; cover and bake in moderate oven about 1 ½ hours, basting occasionally.

SUGGESTED SIDE DISHES: **Rice-Lentil Pilaf** and heated canned peach halves.

CHICKEN ON THE BARBECUE

Unbelievably moist & delicious

6–8 portions
Marinating time: 4 hours
Barbecuing time: about 1 hour
Food processor comes in handy

2 chickens, halved

MARINADE
1 large onion, chopped
4 cloves garlic, chopped
2 tbsp. prepared mustard
1 tsp. dried dill

1 tsp. thyme
1 tsp. marjoram
½ cup oil
1 tbsp. Worcestershire sauce
2 tsp. soy sauce
2 tsp. lemon juice

Prepare Marinade. Rub over chickens and leave to marinate about 4 hours (reapply again after 2 hours).

Grease barbecue grill – preheat at Medium for 10 minutes. Remove chicken from Marinade *(reserving liquid)* and place chicken on barbecue grill. Cover grill; lower heat to medium-low and barbecue chicken about 1 hour, basting frequently with Marinade and turning twice.

SUGGESTED SIDE DISHES: Rice with sautéed, blanched, slivered almonds and pine nuts.

ORANGE CHICKEN

Ari always wants variety

About 6 portions
Roasting time: 1 ½ hours
Food processor comes in handy

½ cup flour
3 tbsp. dried parsley
¼ tsp. pepper
2 small chickens
¼ cup oil
2 large onions, diced
5 cloves garlic, crushed

ORANGE SAUCE
1 cup orange juice
2 tbsp. soy sauce
½ tsp. ground ginger
2 tbsp. prepared mustard
½ cup dry or semi-dry white wine
2 tbsp. honey

Cut chicken into eighths and pat dry.

Preheat oven 350° F, 180° C.

In flat bowl or plastic bag mix together flour, dried parsley and pepper. Coat chicken pieces all over and in large frying pan brown chicken on both sides in heated oil. Remove from pan.

In same pan sauté onion and garlic and place on bottom of roasting pan (large enough to fit chicken pieces on top of onions).

In jar or food processor mix together Orange Sauce ingredients and pour over chicken. Cover and bake one hour; uncover and continue baking another ½ hour or until soft. Baste every 20 minutes during roasting time.

SUGGESTED SIDE DISH: **Rice-Lentil Pilaf.**

CHICKEN MARENGO

A whole meal in itself!

About 6 portions
Cooking time: about 1 hour
Food processor comes in handy

2 small chickens
4 tbsp. oil
2 onions, diced
3 cloves garlic, crushed
350 grams (¾ lb.) mushrooms,
   sliced
3 tbsp. parsley, cut up

6 tomatoes, cut in wedges
2 tsp. paprika
about 2 tsp. salt
½ tsp. pepper
½ cup dry or semi-dry white wine
2 tbsp. brandy
1 cup rice, cooked

Cut chickens into eighths and pat dry.

In large frying pan heat oil and brown chicken pieces on all sides.

Cover pan, lower flame and cook about 10 minutes. Remove chicken and set aside.

In same pan sauté onion, garlic, mushrooms, parsley and seasoning about 7 minutes, stirring occasionally.
Add tomatoes, wine and brandy; mix and continue cooking, stirring continuously for 6–7 minutes.

Return chicken to pan, cover and cook about ½ hour, until chicken is soft.

Serve on a bed of rice.

CHICKEN CHOW MEIN

What to do with cooked chicken

About 4 portions
Cooking time: about 15 minutes
Food processor comes in handy

3 cups cooked chicken
2 tbsp. oil
1 large onion, sliced
3 cloves garlic, crushed
3 stalks celery, sliced
1 cup mushrooms, sliced
½ turnip, grated
salt to taste

½ tsp. pepper
2 tsp. paprika
2 cups chicken broth
1 tbsp. soy sauce
1½ tbsp. cornflour
1 scallion, sliced
1 cup rice, cooked
Chow Mein noodles

Cut chicken into strips.

In large frying pan heat oil and sauté onion and garlic a few minutes. Add celery, mushrooms, turnip and seasoning. Sauté another 5 minutes. Add chicken, one cup chicken broth and soy sauce and cook, uncovered about 5 minutes, stirring occasionally.

Mix cornflour with rest of cool broth; add to pan and cook, stirring continuously, until mixture thickens. Add scallions and remove from flame.

Serve on a bed of rice topped with Chow Mein noodles.

BASIC ROAST CHICKEN

My unusual usual

About 6 portions
Roasting time: about 2 hours

1 large onion, sliced
2 small chickens
3 cloves garlic, crushed
¼ tsp. pepper
1 tbsp. prepared mustard
1 tbsp. paprika

3 tbsp. orange or apricot jam
a little white wine or wine vinegar

BASTING SAUCE
¾ cup orange juice
¾ cup dry or semi-dry white wine

Preheat oven 375° F, 190° C, *i.e.* moderately high.

Place sliced onion in roasting pan and add a little water. With a little white wine or wine vinegar make a paste out of garlic, mustard, paprika and jam; brush all over chickens; tie up legs and wings with thread (if desired) and place, breast side down, on top of onions.

Mix together Basting Sauce.

Roast chicken in preheated oven. After 30 minutes of roasting, pour Basting Sauce over chickens. After another ½ hour, turn chickens over, then baste every ½ hour with Sauce in pan until chickens are done. Chicken should be cooked a total time of about 2 hours.

Baste once more before serving.

P.S. Chickens can be cut in half and roasted; in which case, chickens are skin-side up throughout and roasting time is 1½ hours.

BREADED BAKED CHICKEN

Ari's favorite—
it's like a magnet

About 6 portions
Baking time: about 1 hour

2 small chickens
2 eggs, beaten
2 tsp. oil
about 1¾ cups cornflakes, crumbs

2 tbsp. garlic powder
¼ tsp. salt
¼ tsp. pepper
2 tbsp. sesame seeds

Cut chickens into eighths. Clean and dry.

Preheat oven 350° F, 180° C.

Cover large baking pan with aluminum foil. Pan should be big enough to arrange chicken pieces side by side (use two pans if necessary).

In flat bowl mix together eggs and oil.

In a separate bowl place cornflake crumbs, add garlic powder, salt, pepper and sesame seeds and mix together.

Dip chicken pieces in egg (covering all sides) and then roll in cornflake-crumb mixture until completely coated.

Arrange pieces on aluminum foil-covered baking pan and bake in moderate oven about 1 hour.

P.S. Chicken can be prepared in pan a few hours in advance before baking (refrigerate until ready to bake).

SUGGESTED SIDE DISHES: **Cabbage Roll** and corn on the cob.

SHERRY CHICKEN

About 6 portions
Marinating time: 1 hour
Cooking time: about 1 ½ hours

2 tbsp. soy sauce   *2 small chickens, cut into eighths*
½ cup sherry   *10 grams (⅓ oz.) dried mushrooms*
¼ tsp. pepper   *2 tbsp. oil*
½ tsp. ginger   *1 cup chicken broth*
3 cloves garlic, crushed   *1 ½ tbsp. cornflour*
1 tbsp. prepared mustard   *1 tbsp. sugar*

Mix together one tablespoon soy sauce, sherry, pepper, ginger, garlic, and mustard.

Brush chicken pieces with mixture and leave in pan to marinate about 1 hour.

After ½ hour of marinating add mushrooms to pan, making sure they are immersed in the sauce. Continue marinating remaining ½ hour.

In large frying pan heat oil and brown chicken pieces on all sides. Add mushrooms with sauce and ½ cup chicken broth; cover and cook over low flame about 1 hour. Remove chicken pieces from pan.

In small bowl mix together cornflour, rest of cool broth, 1 tablespoon soy sauce and sugar. Add to sauce in frying pan. Cook, stirring continuously, until thickened. Return chicken pieces to pan and continue cooking another 5 minutes.

TO SERVE: Place chicken pieces on platter and cover with the sauce.

SUGGESTED SIDE DISHES: **Cabbage-Noodle Mix** and **Mushrooms in Wine**.

ITALIAN CHICKEN

6–8 portions
Cooking time: 1 ½ hours

½ cup flour   *2 small chickens*
2 tsp. oregano   *¼ cup oil*
1 tbsp. dried parsley   *350 grams (¾ lb.) mushrooms, sliced*
½ tsp. pepper   *½ cup dry or semi-dry white wine*

Cut up chicken into eighths and pat dry.

Preheat oven 350° F, 180° C.

In paper or plastic bag shake together flour, oregano, parsley and pepper.

Shake each piece of chicken in mixture, making sure all sides are coated.

In large frying pan heat oil and brown chicken pieces on both sides. Transfer to large flat roasting pan so that pieces are close together, skin side up.

In same frying pan slightly sauté mushrooms; add wine; mix and pour over chicken pieces.

Roast in moderate oven 1–1¼ hours (until chicken is soft), cover for ½ hour during roasting.

TO SERVE: Arrange chicken pieces on platter and pour the sauce over.

SUGGESTED SIDE DISH: **Speedy Spaghetti Italiano**.

ALGERIAN APRICOT CHICKEN

Exotic dish
everyone loves

Number of portions depends on who's eating!
Roasting time: about 1 ½ hours
Food processor comes in handy

SAUCE

1 large onion, sliced
4 cloves garlic, crushed
1 tbsp. prepared mustard
1 tbsp. paprika
a little dry white wine
2 small chickens, quartered
a few dried apricots

⅓ cup orange juice
⅓ cup coca cola
⅓ cup ketchup
⅓ cup apricot jam
2 tbsp. water
2 tbsp. soy sauce
1 tbsp. prepared mustard
2 tbsp. lemon juice

Preheat oven 350° F, 180° C.

Place sliced onion in roasting pan large enough to place chicken quarters side by side. Add a little water.

Make a paste out of garlic, mustard and paprika with a little wine. Spread over chicken pieces and place in roasting pan.

Pour boiling water over apricots. Set aside.

In food processor mix together Sauce ingredients.

Roast chicken in moderate oven. After 20 minutes, drain apricots and place over chicken. Pour Sauce over chicken and continue roasting about 1¼ hours more, basting every 20 minutes.

SUGGESTED SIDE DISHES: **Broccoli Roll in Mushroom Sauce**, **Cucumber Mold** or just-heated peach halves.

P.S. Everyone ends up licking their fingers, so prepare rose water for washing up.

ORIENTAL CHICKEN

East meets West

About 6 portions
Marinating time: 2 ½ hours
Baking time: 1 ¾ hours

2 small chickens, quartered

1 tbsp. honey
½ cup water

SAUCE
1 onion chopped
4 cloves garlic, crushed

2 tbsp. soy sauce
1 tbsp. prepared mustard

In large baking pan place quartered chicken side by side skin side down.

In bowl mix together Sauce ingredients and pour over chicken making sure that all sides of chicken are coated. Marinate about 2½ hours, turning twice during that time.

Preheat oven 350° F, 180° C.

Cover pan and bake 45 minutes; uncover; turn chicken pieces over (skin side up) and continue baking uncovered about one hour more, basting occasionally.

SUGGESTED SIDE DISHES: **Rice & Mushrooms** or **String Beans with Almonds**.

PLUM CHICKEN

A plum of a dish

About 6 portions
Baking time: about 1½ hours
Food processor comes in handy

A few apricots and prunes
1 tbsp. prepared mustard
4 cloves garlic, crushed
2 tbsp. paprika
½ tsp. pepper
a little white wine
2 small chickens, quartered

PLUM SAUCE
2 cups (540 grams) canned plums,
  pitted (reserve syrup)
50–60 grams (¼ cup) margarine
1 onion, chopped
⅓ cup lemon juice
¼ cup brown sugar
2 tbsp. ketchup
2 tsp. Worcestershire sauce

In bowl pour boiling water over apricots and prunes and leave ½ hour.

Preheat oven 350° F, 180° C.

Make a paste with mustard, garlic, paprika, pepper and wine. Spread on chicken pieces and place in large baking pan side by side, skin side up.

Drain plums (reserving syrup). In small saucepan melt margarine and sauté onion 5–7 minutes. Transfer to food processor; add plums, lemon juice, brown sugar, ketchup and Worcestershire sauce and process until smooth.

Add enough plum syrup to form semi-liquidy sauce. Set aside.

Drain prunes and apricots and set aside.

Bake chicken pieces in moderate oven about 1½ hours. After 20 minutes of baking, spread prunes and apricots over chicken and pour Plum Sauce over all. Continue roasting, basting every 20 minutes until done. Baste once more.

SUGGESTED SIDE DISHES: **Kasha-Mushroom Mix** and **Vegetables-in-a-Mold.**

CHINESE CHICKEN WITH RICE

It's cooked-chicken time

4–6 portions
Cooking time: about 25 minutes

3 tbsp. oil
1 cup cooked chicken, diced
2 cup cooked rice
1 tsp. salt
¼ tsp. pepper
2 tsp. paprika
1 onion, sliced

1 green pepper, diced
1 gamba, diced
3 tbsp. soy sauce
2 eggs, slightly beaten
½ cup bean sprouts
2 scallions, cut up
2 tbsp. almonds, blanched and slivered

In large frying pan heat oil and brown chicken. Add rice and seasoning; continue cooking about 10 minutes. Add onion, green pepper and gamba; cook about 8 minutes, stirring occasionally. Add soy sauce and eggs; cook one minute more. Add bean sprouts and scallions and mix.

Before serving, sprinkle with almonds.

CHICKEN-MUSHROOM LOAF

Cooked chicken never tasted so good

About 6 portions
Baking time: about 1 hour
Food processor comes in handy

1 tbsp. margarine
1 large onion, chopped
½ cup mushrooms, sliced
1 pimento, chopped
1½ cups soft breadcrumbs
  (about 4 slices)
2 eggs, slightly beaten

3 cups cooked chicken, diced
2 tbsp. parsley, cut up
¼ cup dry or semi-dry white wine
1 tsp. salt
½ tsp. pepper
1 tsp. paprika
Mushroom-Wine Sauce

Preheat oven 350° F, 180° C.

In large frying pan melt margarine and sauté onion a few minutes. Add mushrooms and pimento. Continue sautéing another 10 minutes. Remove from flame.

Add rest of ingredients except Mushroom-Wine Sauce and mix together. Place in greased loaf pan; place pan in large pan of water and bake in moderate oven about 1 hour (until firm, but not dry).

Serve with Mushroom-Wine Sauce.

NUTTY SHNITZEL STRIPS

It's fun in the wok

About 5 portions
Cooking time: about 20 minutes

1 kilo (2 lbs) chicken breasts
250 grams (½ lb.) mushrooms
2–3 tbsp. margarine or oil
⅓ cup fresh brown breadcrumbs
1 cup walnuts, coarsely chopped
¼ tsp. turmeric

½ tsp. paprika
salt to taste
½ tsp. pepper
½ cup dry or semi-dry white wine
2 tbsp. brandy
¼ cup walnuts, cut up

Bone chicken breasts and pound very thin. Cut into thin strips (cutting away stringy portions) and set aside.

Heat margarine or oil and sauté mushrooms about 8 minutes, stirring occasionally (until softened). Add chicken and stir fry about 5 minutes. Add coarsely chopped walnuts and seasoning and stir fry about 1 minute. Add wine and brandy and stir fry about 5 minutes.

P.S. To serve, top with cut-up walnuts.

SUMPTUOUS TURKEY BREAST

Scrumptious!

Approximately 8 portions
Roasting time: 1 ½ hours
Settling time: 15-20 minutes

6 lbs (3 kilo) whole turkey breast	*½ tsp. pepper*
2 tbsp. peach jam	*1 tbsp. oil*
2 tbsp. apricot jam	*1 onion, sliced*
4 cloves garlic, minced	*3 cloves garlic halved*
1 tbsp. paprika	*½ cup dry or semi-dry white wine*

Preheat oven 450° F (230° C)

Clean, rinse and pat dry turkey breast

Make a paste from jams, garlic, paprika, pepper and oil and spread over outside and inside of turkey breast.

Spread sliced onion and garlic halves on bottom of suitable roasting pan and place turkey breast on top (top side up).

Cover pan tightly with aluminum foil and roast in hot oven 45 minutes.

Lower heat to 425°F (220°C); uncover pan and continue roasting another 45 minutes. After 10 minutes pour wine over turkey breast and baste every 10 minutes.

Remove from oven; cover tightly and leave 15-20 minutes.

Serve hot or at room temperature.

P.S. A general rule for roasting time: 15 minutes per pound.

CHICKEN LIVER-FILLED PASTRIES

Gobbled up in no time

5–6 portions
Baking time: about 40 minutes
Food processor comes in handy

*1 recipe **Plain Pastry***

FILLING	*½ kilo (1 lb.) chicken livers*
3 tbsp. margarine or oil	*about 1 tsp. salt*
3 onions, diced	*¼ tsp. pepper*
3 cloves garlic, crushed	*1 egg, slightly beaten*
250 grams (½ lb.) mushrooms, sliced	**Mushroom Sauce**

Preheat oven 350° F, 180° C.

In large frying pan heat 2 tablespoons margarine or oil and sauté onion and garlic a few minutes. Add mushrooms and continue sautéing another 5–6 minutes, stirring occasionally. Transfer to wooden chopping bowl.

Sear chicken livers under broiler or over flame.

Add 1 tablespoon margarine or oil to frying pan; heat and sauté chicken livers a few minutes.

Transfer to chopping bowl; add seasoning and chop everything until smooth.

Divide pastry dough into two parts.

Roll out each half to medium thickness, about 0.5 cm (¼″); cut into circles about 7 cm (3″) round and place about 1 tablespoon chicken liver mixture in center of each circle.

Brush circumference of circles with beaten egg; fold in half (to form semi-circles) and press edges together.

Place pastries on greased cookie sheet and bake in moderate oven about 40 minutes.

Serve warm with Mushroom Sauce.

CHICKEN LIVERS IN WINE

A delectable taste

4–6 portions
Cooking time: about 20 minutes

½ kilo (1 lb.) chicken livers
2 tbsp. margarine
250 grams (½ lb.) mushrooms,
   sliced
2 tbsp. parsley

1½ tsp. flour

½ cup chicken broth
½ cup dry red wine
1 tsp. salt
½ tsp. pepper
4–6 slices toasted white bread
   or cooked rice
½ cup chicken broth

Sear chicken livers under broiler or over open flame.

In large frying pan heat margarine and sauté chicken livers about 3 minutes. Add mushroom, parsley and flour; mix and continue sautéing a few minutes. Add broth, wine and seasoning; cover and cook over low heat about 15 minutes, stirring occasionally.

Serve on toast or bed of rice.

BASIC ROAST TURKEY

Moist and meaty

10–12 portions
Roasting time: about 4 hours

1 small fresh turkey
   (10–12 lbs.; 4½–5 kilo)
3 onions, sliced
3 stalks celery, sliced
5 cloves garlic, crushed
1 tsp. pepper

2 tbsp. prepared mustard
2 tbsp. paprika
¼ cup orange or apricot jam
a little dry or semi-dry white wine
1½ cups dry or semi-dry white wine
1½ cups orange juice

Preheat oven 350° F, 180° C.

Clean, rinse and pat dry turkey.

In large roasting pan spread onion and celery.

In bowl place garlic, pepper, mustard, paprika and jam; make paste with a little white wine and brush all over turkey. Place, breast side up, in roasting pan.

Combine orange juice and white wine; set aside.

Cover turkey tightly with aluminum foil (secure aluminum foil around rim of pan) and roast. After ½ hour roasting, turn turkey over in pan. Cook another hour, remove aluminum foil, return turkey to breast-side-up position; pour over juice and wine mixture. Roast about another 2 hours, basting every ½ hour with pan gravy.

Test for doneness by moving drumstick up and down; it should twist easily at the joint. Remove from oven, cover, and allow to stand about ½ hour in pan.

TO CARVE: Place turkey on serving platter. Prepare second platter for pieces and slices. Cut off drumsticks and wings at joint. Slice white meat starting at center breast bone, cutting down one side; repeat on other side. Carve dark meat.

FOR STUFFED TURKEY: Add one hour to roasting time.

P.S. Delicious served cold the next day.

STUFFED CORNISH HENS

One of a kind

About 6 portions
Roasting time: about 1 ½ hours
Food processor comes in handy

6 Cornish hens

FILLING
1 cup cooked brown rice
2 tbsp. margarine or oil
1 onion
3 cloves garlic, crushed
2 cups mushrooms
2 stalks celery
2 scallions
1 tbsp. parsley
2 tbsp. pine nuts or
   chopped almonds

½ tsp. turmeric
about 1 tsp. salt
½ tsp. pepper
½ tsp. marjoram

1 large onion, sliced
5 cloves garlic, crushed
3 tbsp. prepared mustard
1 tbsp. paprika
melted margarine
½ cup dry or semi-dry white wine
½ cup orange juice
⅓ cup apricot jam

Preheat oven 400° F, 200° C.
Clean and pat dry Cornish Hens.
In large bowl place rice and set aside.
Chop all vegetables in Filling separately.

In large frying pan heat margarine or oil and sauté onion and garlic a few minutes. Add mushrooms and continue sautéing 7–8 minutes. Add onion, mushroom mixture to rice together with celery, scallions, parsley, pine nuts (or almonds) and seasoning; mix together and let cool slightly.

Line roasting pan (large enough for 6 Cornish hens) with aluminum foil and place sliced onions on bottom. Add about ¾ cup water.

Fill each hen with about ½ cup Filling and close up with either thread, toothpicks or small skewers. Make a paste from the garlic, mustard and paprika with a little white wine and brush over hens. Tie up wings and legs and place in roasting pan, breast side up. Roast in medium-hot oven.

After ½ hour of roasting, brush hen with melted margarine and pour over white wine. Turn hens over and continue roasting another 20 minutes.

Meanwhile in small saucepan, heat orange juice and apricot jam and cook over low flame about 5 minutes.

Turn hens over again (breast side up) and cover with sauce. Continue roasting.

After 20 minutes, baste hens with pan gravy and continue roasting another 20 minutes or until soft. Baste once again.

Remove thread, toothpicks or skewers before serving.
SUGGESTED SIDE DISHES: **Cabbage-Apple Mix** and **Vanilla-Carrot Pudding**.

Poultry   69

GLAZED ORANGE (PEKING) DUCK *Always a treat*

2–4 portions
Roasting time: about 2¼ hours

1 duck (about 2½ kilo, 5 lbs.)
2 tsp. lemon juice
2 stalks celery, cut up
1 orange, cut into rings
1 large onion, sliced

GLAZE
¼ cup concentrated orange juice
¼ cup honey
½ cup dry red wine

2 tbsp. orange or apricot jam

Preheat oven 450° F, 230° C.

Remove any stray feathers from duck and clean insides. Rinse and dry.

Brush inside of duck with lemon juice and place celery, 2 orange rings and onion rings inside cavity (to remove unpleasant odors).

Tie up wings and legs with string.

Arrange rest of orange and onion rings on bottom of roasting pan; place rack on top and add one cup of water.

GLAZE: In small saucepan mix together concentrated orange juice, honey and wine and heat slightly. Brush a little Glaze on duck and place, breast side up, on rack. Pierce skin with fork in a few places to allow fat to drain.

COOKING: Roast duck in hot oven ½ hour. Lower heat to 350° F (180° C), and brush duck with ⅓ of Glaze. *Always baste with fresh glaze* (do not use gravy in pan.)

After ½ hour turn duck over; once again pierce skin with fork and brush with second third of Glaze.

After another ½ hour turn duck back (breast side up); pierce skin and brush with remaining Glaze.

After another ½ hour brush with slightly heated orange or apricot jam. Continue roasting last 15 minutes.

Before serving the duck, remove vegetables from cavity; cut duck in half or quarters with poultry shears.

Serve with **Duck Sauce**.

SUGGESTED SIDE DISHES: **Sweet Rice**, **Egg Rolls** and **Mustard-Glazed Carrots** (see Index).

Delicious, healthful **FISH**

Fresh fish is always better than frozen or dried. When buying fish, watch for signs of freshness. If buying whole fish, check that the eyes are clear and glossy—not dull or filmy. Look for the same clear, glossy texture when buying pieces of cut fish. Fresh fish should not look dull in any way.

And, if you must freeze your fish, try freezing it in water.

Fish gives many nutritional advantages to any diet. It's low in fat and high in protein. The fats many fish contain, omega-3 fats, have been thought to play a role in reducing cholesterol. In addition, fish contains high concentrations of vitamins and essential minerals that are more difficult to find in other foods. Because of all these qualities, some think of fish as a "diet" food. Fish, however, holds many more possibilities than just as a vehicle for losing weight.

You'll see from these recipes that fish is versatile and fun. It can easily be a healthy part of your diet.

COLD TROUT APPETIZER

Trout at its best!

4–6 portions
Cooking time: 5–minutes
Prepare a few hours or a day in advance

4 trout	1 carrot
¼ cup lemon juice	1 tsp. paprika
1 large onion, sliced	1 tsp. salt
1 stalk of celery	¼ tsp. pepper
a few sprigs of parsley and dill	**Tartar Sauce Dressing**

Rinse trout and marinate in flat pan in lemon juice for about ½ hour, turning once. Rinse again.

Place onion, celery, parsley, dill, carrot and seasonig with a little water in a large flat pot and cook, covered, for 5 minutes. Add trout and continue cooking about 10 minutes.

OR, as an alternate cooking method, boil enough salted water (pepper added if desired) so trout will be submerged. Add trout and cook over medium-high flame 5 minutes. Whatever method you use, *be careful not to overcook the fish.*

Carefully remove trout from pot with wide metal spatula; allow to cool for easier handling. Skin and bone each fish. Place in lipped dish. Refrigerate.

Serve with Tartar Sauce Dressing, plain mayonnaise, or a mayonnaise-mustard combination.

SUGGESTION: Garnish individual plates with frest colorful vegetables, asparagus tips or artichoke hearts filled with tartar sauce. (For Tartar Sauce Dressing see page 5 – Salads and Dressings.)

FISH COCKTAIL

Elegant, delicious appetizer

4 portions
Cooking time: about 15 minutes
Prepare fish a few hours in advance

1 onion, sliced	SAUCE
2 stalks celery	½ cup ketchup
small bunch of parsley	¼ cup lemon juice
1 tsp. salt	¼ cup mild horseradish
¼ tsp. pepper	1 tsp. Worchestershire sauce
600 grams (1 ¼ lbs.) fish fillets,	OR
(sole or flounder)	½ cup horseradish
parsley for garnishing	½ cup chilli sauce

In large pot place, onion, celery, parsley, salt and pepper. Arrange fish over vegetables; add ½ cup water and cook, covered over low flame about 15 minutes, until fish is soft. Remove fish with slotted spatual and allow to cool slightly. Remove any soft skin that may be on the fish and flake.

Place in bowl and refrigerate a few hours.

In separate bowl mix together Sauce ingredients.

TO SERVE: Place flaked fish in 4 stemmed sherbet cups; garnish with a little parsley; pour 2 – 3 tablespoons Sauce over each one. Place additional Sauce in center of table for extra helpings.

SWEET & SOUR FISH

Cooling off a hot day

Cooking time: 45 minutes

1 large onion, sliced	⅓ cup lemon juice
6 slices carp or salmon	2 tbsp. sugar
1 carrot, sliced	a few whole cloves and allspice
2 tsp. salt	3 bay leaves
½ tsp. pepper	

In large pot cook onion in a little water about 5 minutes.

Add fish slices, carrot, salt and pepper. Cook 15 minutes.

Add lemon juice and sugar and cook another 15 minutes.

Add cloves, allspice and bay leaves. Cook an additional 10 minutes. Let cool.

Remove fish carefully with metal spatula and place in lipped serving platter. Pour sauce over fish and refrigerate.

P.S. Serve as appetizer with **Cucumber Salad.** (see index)

ROLLED FISH FILLETS

A choice of filings, but the taste remains

5–6 portions
Sautéing and baking time: about 1¼ hours

FILLING	
1 tbsp. butter	800 grams (1½ lbs.) fish fillets
1 onion, chopped	salt
3 cloves garlic, crushed	thick onion slices
2 tbsp. parsley, chopped	2 cups sour cream
1 tsp. salt	2 cups **Tomato Sauce**
½ tsp. pepper	¼ cup dry or semi-dry white wine
1 tsp. paprika	½ tsp. basil
8 large mushroom caps	

If fish has soft skin, remove before rolling.

Preheat oven 350° F, 180° C.

FILLING: In sauce pan, over low flame, melt butter; increase heat and sauté onion, garlic parsley and seasoning 7–8 minutes.

Sprinkly slat over fish fillets. Place some of the sautéed mixture in center of each fish fillet; place mushroom cap on top and roll up. A toothpick may be used to hold roll together; or place in baling pan open side down.

Place a thick slice of onion on top of each fish roll.

In medium bowl mix together sour cream, Tomato Sauce, wine and basil; pour over fish rolls and bake in moderate oven 1 hour.

SUGGESTED SIDE DISHES: **Cabbage Roll,** or desired **Quiche.**

ADDITIONAL FILLINGS: Cooked mashed and seasoned potato, cooked cauliflower mixed with sautéed onion, or pieces of salmon.

BAKED FISH FILLETS

White wine is the secret

About 5 portions
Baking time: about 30 minutes

600 grams (1¼ lbs.) fish
   fillets
lemon juice
2 tbsp. butter
3 cloves garlic, crushed
2 onions, diced
1 cup mushrooms, sliced

1 tsp. salt
½ tsp. pepper
1 tsp. paprika
2 tomatoes, diced
2 tbsp. parsley, chopped
¼ cup dry or semi-dry white wine
slivered almonds

Preheat oven (350°, 180°C) ten minutes before using.

Rinse fish under cold water. Marinate in lemon juice about one hour in refrigerator, turning over after ½ hour.

Rinse again and pat dry.

In large saucepan heat butter and sauté garlic, and onions a few minutes. Add mushrooms, salt , pepper and paprika and sauté about 10 minutes more, stirring occasionally. Add tomatoes, parsley and wine and heat through. Place fish in greased flat baking pan pour onion mixture over fillets, cover and bake in moderate oven about 30 minutes.

TO SERVE: sprinkle with slivered almonds.

SUGGESTED SIDE DISHES: **Creamy Noodle Ring** and **Spinach Pie.**

MUSTARD-BAKED TROUT

Melts in your mouth

6 portions
Baking time: about 20 minutes

6 small trout

STUFFING
1 onion, chopped
3 cloves garlic, crushed
250 grams (½ lb.) mushrooms,
   chopped
3 tbsp. butter

250 grams (½ lb.)
   cooked, chopped spinach
1 tsp. paprika
1 tsp. salt
½ tsp. pepper
1 onion, sliced
½ cup lemon juice
salt and pepper to taste
1 tbsp. prepared mustard
1 cup dry or semi-dry white wine

Preheat over 400° F, 200° C.

Clean, rinse and pat dry trout.

STUFFING: Sauté onion and garlic in heated butter a few minutes; add mushrooms and paprika and sauté about 10 minutes. In bowl mix together sautéed vegetables with spinach, salt and pepper.

COOKING: Grease suitable-size baking pan with butter so that trout lie side by side. Spread sliced onion on bottom. Rub inside and outside of trout with lemon juice and stuff. Spread mustard over entire outside of fish; sprinkle with salt and pepper; place in baking pan; pour wine into pan. Bake in hot oven about 20 minutes.

P.S. Serve with large wedges of lemon and blanched, halved almonds which have been sautéed in butter.

BAKED FISH WITH VEGETABLES

A one-pan meal

About 4 portions
Baking time: 1 hour

1½ kilo (3 lbs.) whole fish
  (buri or white fish)
lemon juice
3 potatoes, cut up and
  partially cooked
1 large onion, sliced
2 tomatoes, sliced
1 green pepper, sliced
5 cloves garlic, crushed
1 tsp. salt

½ tsp. pepper
1 tbsp. paprika
2 tbsp. lemon juice
½ cup dry or semi-dry white wine
lemon slices, halved
1 cup mushrooms,
  whole or halved
2 tbsp. butter
¼ cup almonds, blanched
  and slivered

Rub fish with lemon juice; sprinkle with salt and let stand about two hours (turning over after one hour). Preheat oven 375° F, 190° C.

Cover large flat baking pan with aluminum foil (large enough to cover fish).

Spread onion, tomatoes and green pepper on bottom and sprinkle with 1 teaspoon salt, ½ teaspoon pepper and 2 teaspoons paprika.

Rinse fish under cold water and pat dry.

In small saucepan melt butter; remove from flame; add garlic, seasoning, 2 tablespoons lemon juice and wine and stir. Spread fish with mixture and place on top of vegetables. Cut 6 slits along top of fish and place ½ slice of lemon in each slit.

Arrange potatoes and mushrooms around fish and sprinkle with remaining salt, pepper and paprika. Close aluminum foil so that fish is completely covered.

Bake in moderate-high heat about 45 minutes. Open aluminum foil and finish baking at high heat (550° F, 260° C) 15 minutes.

In small saucepan over low flame heat butter and sauté almonds a few minutes (beware of burning).

Sprinkle fish with almonds and serve with lemon wedges.

P.S. Choice of side dishes: **Spinach** or **Broccoli Pie** and **Scallion Quiche**, or just serve with a salad.

GEFILTE FISH (COOKED FISH BALLS)

Hit of the town

About 16 portions
Cooking time: about 2¾ hours
Eat warm or prepare a day in advance
If the fish store will bone, skin and grind the fish, then it's no effort at all

3 kilo (6 lbs.) carp (2 fish)
5 large onions
1 tbsp. salt
1 tsp. pepper
⅓ · ½ cup sugar
3 · 4 slices bread

4 eggs
¼ cup wheat germ
¼ · ⅓ cup raw oatmeal
about 2 tbsp. salt
about 2 tsp. pepper
roe (fish eggs), optional

Fish must be boned, skinned and heads removed to be cooked separately.

In large pot place slices from one onion, arrange heads, bones and skin over onions; cover with water; season with 1 tablespoon salt, 1 teaspoon pepper and all of sugar. Cover and cook over low flame about 45 minutes. Taste soup — it should have a good taste — adjust seasoning, if necessary.

Meanwhile, grind "fish meat" together with 1 carrot, 3 onions and bread. In mixer at medium-low speed, beat fish mixture, adding eggs, wheat germ, oatmeal, salt and pepper (don't be stingy on the seasoning). If fish is loose add more wheat germ or raw oatmeal. Refrigerate about ½ hour. Mixture should be firm but not too stiff.

Slice last onion into a large, clean pot. Place strainer over pot and pour in fish stock (from bones). Bring to boil; form fish balls from fish mixture with wet hands and place into boiling water. Lower flame. It may be necessary to leave over medium flame until it starts to cook. Lower flame more and cook 1½–2 hours.

After 15 minutes of cooking place 2 carrots on top (if too big cut into several pieces). Carrots can also be placed on bottom of pot before placing fish balls. Add roe and continue cooking.

Let cool slightly.

Carefully remove fish balls and place in large flat-lipped pan or platter. Reserve stock in jar. Cut up carrots and place on each ball.

Serve warm or cold with horseradish or mayonnaise.

VARIATION: Buy an extra fish, sliced. Use some of the fish mixture to fill the center of the slices, and with a metal spatula carefully place the filled fish slices on bottom of pot before adding the fish balls.

FISHCAKES

Out of the pan into the mouth

4–6 portions
Cooking and frying time: about 1 hour
Food processor comes in handy

1 onion, sliced	*¼ – ½ cup raw oatmeal*
400 grams (1 lb.) fish fillets	*2 tbsp. wheat germ*
2 potatoes, quartered	*about 2 tsp. salt*
1 carrot, cut up	*½ tsp. pepper*
250 grams (½ lb.) pumpkin, diced	*oil for frying*
2 eggs	**Tartar Sauce Dressing**

In large pot place onion slices with ½ cup water and 2 teaspoons salt; add fish, potatoes, carrot and pumpkin and cook until soft (about ½ hour). Drain and mash. Mashing can be done in food processor (except for potatoes), but let cool before processing.

Place mixture in large bowl; add eggs, oatmeal, wheat germ, salt and pepper and mix until well blended. Add enough oatmeal to form firm mixture. If time allows, refrigerate about 1 hour.

In large frying pan heat oil; form flat fishcakes and fry over medium flame on both sides. Drain on paper toweling.

Serve hot or cold with Tartar Sauce Dressing or plain cottage cheese.
SUGEGSTED SIDE DISH: **Soy Bean Salad**.

VARIATION: Use cooked cauliflower instead of fish and call them Cauliflower Pancakes.

FISH-FILLED PASTRIES

Great flying saucers

About 25 pastries
Sautéing time: about 25 minutes

1 recipe **Plain Pastry**

FILLING
1 tbsp. butter
1 onion, chopped
3 cloves garlic, crushed
400 grams (1 lb.) fish fillets,
  cooked and chopped
2 small tomatoes, chopped
2 tbsp. parsley, chopped
½ cup broth

¼ cup dry or semi-dry white wine
¼ cup flour
about 1 tsp. salt
½ tsp. pepper
⅛ tsp. thyme
stuffed olives, chopped
1 egg beaten (for brushing)
2 tbsp. sesame seeds

oil (if frying)
Mushroom or **Mushroom-Wine Sauce**
  (if baking)

Divide dough in half (for easier handling) and roll out each piece to medium thickness – 0.3 cm (¼″). Cut into rounds about 7 cm (3″).

If baking, preheat oven 350° F, 180° C.

In large frying pan over low flame melt butter; increase heat and sauté onion and garlic about 5 minutes, stirring occasionally. Add mushrooms, fish, tomatoes and parsley and continue sautéing 5 minutes more, stirring continuously. Mix remaining broth with flour until smooth and add to pan together with salt, pepper and thyme. Stir over flame until mixture thickens, about 5 minutes.

Remove from flame; add olives and mix. Cool slightly.

Place 1 tablespoon of mixture on bottom half of pastry circle; close to form half moon; press together with fingers dipped in egg or water and bake or fry. Bake in moderate heat about 25 minutes or fry in oil on both sides until browned.

P.S. If baked, serve with Mushroom or Mushroom-Wine Sauce.

ALMOND FISHCAKES

Almonds do it all the time

4–6 portions

800 grams (1½ lbs. fish)
  fillets, ground up
1¼ cups almonds,
  blanched and ground
2 scallions, chopped
about ½ tsp. salt

¼ tsp. pepper
1 tbsp. soy sauce
1 tbsp. cornflour combined
  with 2 tbsp. cold water
1½ tsp. oil plus oil for frying
Tartar Sauce Dressing

In large bowl mix together fish fillets, almonds, scallions, salt, pepper, soy sauce, cornflour mixture and 1½ tablespoons oil.

In large frying pan heat oil; form flat fishcakes and fry on both sides.

Serve hot or cold with Tartar Sauce Dressing.

Bring out the flavor of **MEATS**

Four ingredients I use quite extensively with meats are fresh garlic, prepared mustard, wine and parsley.

If you're trying to cut down on eating red meat, you can try these recipes with turkey parts (cut up or chopped). I frequently substitute turkey for red meat. You'll still have great-tasting dishes. Try it and you'll see what I mean.

BEEF-IN-WINE CASSEROLE

It's the ultimate

About 4 portions
Cooking time: about 2 hours

2 tbsp. flour
¼ tsp. salt
¼ tsp. pepper
1 kilo (2 lbs.) lean beef and/or
   dark turkey meat, cubed
3 tbsp. margarine or oil
1 large onion, diced
5 cloves garlic, crushed

1 large carrot, diced
1 cup dry red wine
2 tbsp. parsley, cut up
a few bay leaves
¼ tsp. thyme, optional
¼ cup ketchup
4 small onions, in wedges
250 grams (½ lb.) mushrooms, sliced
   or quartered

Preheat oven to 350° F, 180° C.

Mix together flour, salt and pepper and coat meat cubes.

In large frying pan heat 2 tablespoons margarine or oil and brown meat on all sides. Add diced onion, garlic, carrot, salt and pepper. Continue sautéing a few minutes more, stirring occasionally.

Add wine, parsley, bay leaves, thyme and ketchup; mix together. Place in suitable baking pan, cover and bake in moderate oven about 1½ hours (for turkey meat about 1 hour).

Meanwhile sauté the four wedged onions in 1 tablespoon margarine or oil a few minutes; add mushrooms and sauté another 5 minutes.

Add to beef; mix in and bake another ½ hour.

P.S. Excellent when served on a bed of rice.

SUGGESTED SIDE DISHES: **String Beans with Almonds** and **Cucumber Mold**.

CHOLENT

Great on a winter's day

Slow-cooking meat-potato-bean-stew
6–8 portions
Cooking time: 1½ hours and overnight

½ cup dry white or red beans
2 tbsp. margarine or oil
2 large onions, chopped
meat bones
1 kilo (2 lbs.) cooking meat, cubed
⅓–½ cup pearl barley

¼ cup buckwheat groats (kasha)
5–6 potatoes, cubed
about 1 tbsp. salt
1 tsp. pepper
1 tsp. ginger
1 tbsp. paprika
Cholent Dumplings (optional)

In large bowl soak beans in water a few hours. Drain.

In large pot heat margarine or oil; sauté onions and meat. Add bones, beans, barley, buckwheat groats and potatoes; cover with water; add another 2–3 cups water. (Breathing space: Ingredients should not take up more than ⅔ of pot capacity.)

Bring to boil; add spices; cover and cook 1½ hours. Add Cholent Dumplings last half hour of cooking.

Leave overnight in low-heated oven (225° F, 110° C).

Serve immediately upon removing from oven.

P.S. Rice and lentils can also be added.

CHINESE PEPPER STEAK

Everyone loves Chinese,
so try it!

About 4 portions
Cooking time; about 30 minutes

750 grams (1½ lbs.) lean
   meat, or bottom turkey meat
3 tbsp. oil
2 onions, diced
4 cloves garlic, crushed
2 tsp. paprika
¼–½ cup ketchup
½ cup dry red wine
¼ cup brandy

about 1 tsp. salt
¼ tsp. pepper
¼ cup soy sauce
1 tbsp. prepared mustard
2 green peppers, thinly sliced
2 tbsp. cornstarch
¼ cup cold water
2 tomatoes, skinned and cut up
1 cup rice, cooked
blanched and slivered
   almonds and sunflower seeds

Cut meat into thin strips.

In large frying pan heat oil and brown meat. Push meat to the side or remove, add onion, garlic and paprika and sauté about 7 minutes. Return meat to pan.

Add wine, ketchup, soy sauce, brandy, mustard, salt and pepper and mix. Cook uncovered a few minutes, stirring occasionally; cover and cook over low flame a few minutes, stirring occasionally, until meat is soft. Add green peppers, mix, cover and cook a few more minutes.

Mix cornstarch with water, add to pan and cook over medium-low flame, stirring continuously, until mixture thickens. Add tomatoes and heat.

Serve on a bed of rice. Sprinkle with slivered almonds and sunflower seeds.

Try serving with: **Eggrolls, Cabbage Roll,** or **Mustard-Glazed Carrots.**

VARIATION: Add one cup sliced mushrooms and sauté with onions.

BARBECUED SPARE RIBS

Fantastic on the barbecue
or in the oven

About 4 portions
Cooking time (sauce): 20 minutes
Marinating time: overnight
Baking time: 2–2½ hours in oven; 15–20 minutes on BBQ

1 kilo (2 lbs.) spare ribs or
   lean meat, cubed

SAUCE
¼ cup oil
1 onion, chopped
3 cloves garlic
¾ cup ketchup
¾ cup water

⅓ cup lemon juice
¼ cup soy sauce
2 tbsp. prepared mustard
½ tsp. salt
¼ tsp. pepper
3 tbsp. sugar
1 tbsp. paprika

1 cup rice, cooked

Place meat in large bowl; set aside.

In medium pot heat oil and sauté onion and garlic about 10 minutes; add rest of Sauce ingredients and mix; cover and cook over low flame about 15 minutes, stirring occasionally.

Pour Sauce over meat; mix and refrigerate overnight.

Place on skewers alternately with onion, tomato and green pepper wedges and barbeque 15–20 minutes.

TO BAKE: Transfer meat mixture to large flat baking pan and bake in moderate oven (350° F, 180° C) about 2½ hours, turning every 20 minutes. (Turkey meat baking time is about 1½ hours).

SUGGESTED SIDE DISHES: **Egg Rolls** and **String Beans with Almonds**.

CORNED BEEF WITH CABBAGE
A fun meal

About 6 portions
Cooking time: 3½ hours
Prepare Corned Beef one day in advance

1½ kilo (3 lbs.) corned beef
1 onion, sliced
a few cloves, peppercorns,
   allspice and bay leaves
3 cloves garlic
½ green pepper, sliced

1 stalk celery, diced
1 medium carrot, sliced
2 medium potatoes, quartered
1 onion, quartered
1 small cabbage, cut into strips

In large pot place corned beef; cover with water, add sliced onion, spices, garlic, green pepper, celery and carrot; cover and cook 2–3 hours until tender.

Remove meat from pot, reserving ¾ of the broth. Cool and refrigerate meat and broth separately.

One hour before serving heat broth; add potatoes, quartered onion and cabbage; cover and cook about ½ hour.

With very sharp knife slice meat (against grain); place carefully in pot with vegetables and heat.

Remove meat slices carefully, arrange on serving platter surrounded with vegetables.

P.S. Make cold corned beef sandwiches with leftovers.

GLAZED CORNED BEEF
This is something else!

cooked corned beef
cloves
1 cup ginger ale
3 tbsp. brown sugar

canned pineapple slices,
   reserved syrup (from pineapple slices)
maraschino cherries

Preheat oven 350° F., 180° C.

Pour ginger ale into flat baking pan; place beef on rack in pan; score beef horizontally and vertically; place cloves at intersections; cover with canned pineapple slices and cherries; sprinkle over with brown sugar.

Bake in moderate oven 35–45 minutes, basting every 10 minutes with canned pineapple syrup.

TO SLICE: Use very sharp knife and slice against the grain.

SUGGESTED SIDE DISHES: **Vanilla Carrot Pudding** and **Cabbage Roll**.

SWEET & SOUR TONGUE
Unbelievably good

About 8 portions
Cooking time: Tongue — 3 hours
Sauce — about ½ hour
Prepare tongue a few hours in advance

1½ kilo (3 lbs.) tongue,
   pickled
2 bay leaves
a few allspice
2 tbsp. vinegar

SWEET & SOUR SAUCE
4 tbsp. oil
1 onion, chopped
3 cloves garlic, crushed

2 tbsp. flour
2 cups tongue liquid
2 tbsp. walnuts, ground
pinch of ground cloves
⅛ tsp. cinnamon
2 tbsp. raisins
½ cup lemon juice
¼ cup honey or brown sugar
¼ cup dry red wine
cooked rice or pasta

(If tongue is very salty, change water after it boils up). In large pot place tongue; cover with water; add bay leaves, allspice and vinegar; cover and cook 3 hours. Remove tongue. Reserve 2 cups of liquid. Remove skin from tongue while still warm. Let cool before slicing (easier to slice).

SAUCE: In medium saucepan heat 2 tablespoons oil and sauté onion and garlic about 7 minutes; set aside.

In separate medium pot heat 2 tablespoons oil; remove from flame; add flour and mix together until smooth; return to flame and over low flame add tongue liquid slowly, stirring continuously.

Continue cooking, stirring, until Sauce thickens a bit.

Add rest of Sauce ingredients; cover and cook over low flame about 10 minutes, stirring occasionally.

Transfer finished Sweet & Sour Sauce to suitably sized pot to include tongue slices.

Arrange tongue slices in Sauce; heat and serve on rice or pasta.

VARIATION: Serve with **Sweet & Sour Tomato Sauce**.

SWEET & SOUR MEATBALLS
My husband Elliot's favorite

About 4 portions
Cooking time: 2½–3 hours
Food processor helps

1½ kilo (3 lbs.) chopped meat
   or turkey meat (white and dark)
3 slices bread
2 eggs, slightly beaten
about ¼ cup wheat germ*
about ½ cup oatmeal*
¼ cup parsley, chopped
1 tsp. pepper
2 onions: 1 chopped, 1 diced
8 cloves garlic, crushed
1 tbsp. paprika

2 tbsp. prepared mustard
3 tbsp. oil
2 tomatoes, sliced
1 cup **Tomato Sauce** or tomato paste
salt, pepper and paprika, to taste
⅓ cup lemon juice
¼ cup dry red wine
¼ cup brown sugar
2 tbsp. light raisins

cooked rice or pasta

Easy and Elegant

Place meat in large bowl.

In separate bowl soak bread slices in warm water until softened. Squeeze out water and chop in food processor; add to meat together with eggs, wheat germ, oatmeal, parsley, pepper, chopped onion, half amount of garlic and mustard; mix together and set aside. (*Turkey meat needs more wheat germ and oatmeal than does red meat to attain firmness. Adjust seasoning accordingly.)

In large pot heat oil; sauté diced onion, rest of garlic and paprika about 10 minutes. Add sliced tomato, Tomato Sauce (or canned tomato paste) and seasoning and mix together. Bring to boil over medium heat. Shape meat into small balls and place in pot. Cover and cook over low flame 2½ hours altogether (turkey meat = 2 hours).

After 15 minutes of cooking add lemon juice, wine, brown sugar and raisins. After one hour of cooking carefully separate meat balls. Finish cooking.

Serve with rice or pasta.

SUGGESTED SIDE DISH: **Mustard-Glazed Carrots**.

MEAT LOAF POTATO ROLL
All rolled up in one

6–8 portions
Baking time: 50 minutes
Food processor makes it easy

1 kilo (2 lbs.) chopped meat or	*2 tbsp. parsley, chopped*
turkey meat (white and dark)	*1 tbsp. prepared mustard*
¼ cup oil	*about ¼ cup oatmeal**
2 onions, chopped	*about ¼ cup wheat germ**
3 cloves garlic, crushed	*¼ tsp. pepper*
2 slices bread	*¼ tsp. basil*
3 eggs, slightly beaten	*2 large potatoes*
1 scallion, chopped	*salt and pepper to taste*
	about 3 tbsp. dry breadcrumbs

Preheat oven 350° F, 180° C.

In large bowl place chopped meat.

In large frying pan heat oil; sauté onions and garlic about 10 minutes. Soak bread slices in warm water until softened; squeeze out water and chop in food processor; add to chopped meat together with ½ of sautéed onion mixture, two eggs, scallion, parsley, mustard, oatmeal, wheat germ, pepper and basil and mix together well. (*Turkey meat needs more of both wheat germ and oatmeal than does red meat to attain firmness. Adjust seasoning accordingly.)

Mash cooked potatoes together with salt, pepper, one egg and rest of sautéed onions.

Sprinkle breadcrumbs on waxed paper; spread chopped meat mixture on breadcrumbs and spread mashed potato on meat. Carefully roll up like jelly roll (without waxed paper).

Place carefully on greased flat baking pan and bake in moderate oven about 50 minutes.

SUGGESTED SIDE DISH: **Sweet & Sour Red Cabbage**.

GREEK MOUSSAKA GOURMET

Delectable

About 6 portions
Frying and baking time: about 1 hour

2 eggplants	½ tsp. cinnamon
oil for frying	3 cloves garlic, crushed
1 kilo (2 lbs.) ground red meat OR	½ tbsp. lemon juice
turkey meat (white and dark)	salt and pepper to taste
1 large onion, chopped	2 tomatoes, sliced
½ cup plus 2 tbsp. **Tomato Sauce**	3 eggs, slightly beaten
¼ cup dry red wine	¼ cup dry red wine
¼ cup parsley, chopped	breadcrumbs

Slice eggplants into about 1 cm (⅓″) slices; sprinkle with salt and leave about 1 hour. Rinse under cold water and pat dry.

Preheat oven 375° F, 190° C.

In large frying pan heat oil; fry eggplant slices on both sides; drain on paper toweling. In same pan heat a little more oil and brown meat and onions, stirring occasionally so that meat separates. Add to meat two tablespoons Tomato Sauce, wine, cinnamon, garlic, lemon juice, salt and pepper. Continue frying, stirring continuously, until most of the liquid is absorbed.

In large flat baking pan arrange a few eggplant slices. Spread meat mixture over eggplant and cover with remaining eggplant slices. Arrange tomato slices on top. Mix eggs with ½ cup Tomato Sauce and wine and carefully pour over casserole. Sprinkle with breadcrumbs.

Bake in moderate-high oven about 35 minutes. Allow time to settle.

P.S. Great as appetizer or side dish.

MEAT-STUFFED ZUCCHINI

Unbelievably good!

About 6 portions
Cooking time: about 45 minutes
Food processor comes in handy

6 medium zucchini	salt to taste
2 tbsp. oil	¼ tsp. pepper
1 tbsp. pine nuts or blanched	1 onion, sliced
sliced almonds	1 tomato, sliced
½ kilo (1 lb.) chopped meat OR	
turkey meat (white and dark)	SWEET & SOUR SAUCE
1 cup rice, partially cooked	½ cup **Tomato Sauce**
2 tsp. lemon juice	1 tbsp. sugar
1 small onion, chopped	2 cloves garlic, crushed
2 tbsp. parsley, chopped	2 tsp. Worcestershire sauce
2 tbsp. ketchup	1 tbsp. prepared mustard
1 tbsp. prepared mustard	salt to taste
¼ tsp. basil	¼ tsp. pepper
3 cloves garlic, crushed	¼ cup dry red wine
¼ tsp. cinnamon	

Cook zucchini in a little salted water about 10 minutes. Drain. Cut in half lengthwise, scoop out pulp and sprinkle cavity with salt.

In small saucepan heat oil and fry pine nuts or almonds a few minutes, stirring continuously. Drain. *(The nuts burn easily; be careful.)*

In large bowl mix together meat, rice, lemon juice, onion, parsley, garlic, mustard, ketchup, spices and nuts. Fill zucchini cavities.

In small pot cook Sauce ingredients over low flame a few minutes, stirring occasionally.

Arrange onion and tomato slices in large frying pan. Place stuffed zucchini over them (if any stuffing is left, form meat balls and place in pan with zucchini).

Stir Sauce and pour over everything; cover and cook, over low flame, about 35 minutes, basting occasionally.

P.S. Great as appetizer or side dish.

STUFFED CABBAGE

A real treat

10–12 portions
Cooking and baking time: 3½ hours

2 medium cabbages, good for stuffing

FILLING	SAUCE
1 cup rice	*2 onions, sliced*
1 kilo (2 lbs.) chopped meat or	*3 large tomatoes, sliced*
turkey meat (white and dark)	*salt, pepper and paprika to taste,*
3 eggs, slightly beaten	*a few prunes and apricots*
1 large onion, chopped	*½ cup raisins*
and sautéed	*2 cups tomato juice*
5 cloves garlic, crushed	*½ cup dry red wine*
2 tbsp. lemon juice	*4 cups **Tomato Sauce***
¼ tsp. cinnamon	*⅓ cup brown sugar*
1 tsp. salt	*¾–1 cup lemon juice*
¼ tsp. pepper	

TO SOFTEN CABBAGES: Method 1: Place cabbages in freezer a few days before using. Remove from freezer and allow to defrost on drain overnight. Remove core and separate leaves. Method 2: Remove cabbage leaves and place in rapidly boiling water 10–15 minutes.

FILLING: Partially cook rice in boiling water about 10 minutes. Drain.

In large bowl place meat; add rest of Filling ingredients and mix together.

Place a mound of meat in center of each cabbage leaf; fold in sides and roll up. Prepare all the rolls.

Place ¾ onion slices in bottom of large pot. Grate remaining cabbage coarsely and spread over onion. Place ⅓ of the tomato slices on the grated cabbage. Season with salt, pepper and paprika.

Place one layer of cabbage rolls on tomatoes. Make layer of rest of onion slices, ½ of tomato slices, prunes, apricots, raisins, one cup tomato juice and 1½ cups Tomato Sauce. Make another layer of cabbage rolls. Cover with rest of tomato slices and add one cup tomato juice, wine and 1½ cups Tomato Sauce.

Cover and bring to boil over medium flame. Lower flame and cook 1½ hours. After 30 minutes of cooking add brown sugar and lemon juice and continue cooking.

Preheat oven 325° F, 170° C.

Pour last cup of Tomato Sauce over cabbage rolls and bake in low oven 2 hours.

TO SERVE: Remove top layer and first serve bottom layer so that vegetables, fruit and Sauce on bottom of pot will be available.

P.S. If serving only part of the stuffed cabbages, reserve some fruit and sauce. If necessary, when rewarming add tomato juice.

SUGGESTED SIDE DISH: **Mustard-Glazed Carrots**.

RICE NOODLE-MEAT MIX
What a combination!

About 6 portions
Cooking time: 40 minutes
Food processor comes in handy

⅓ cup oil
1 tbsp. pine nuts
1 kilo (2 lbs.) chopped meat,
   or turkey meat (white and dark)
1 onion, chopped
2 cloves garlic, crushed
1 egg
2 scallions, chopped
handful of parsley, chopped
2 tbsp. prepared mustard
2 tbsp. ketchup
½ cup breadcrumbs
1 tbsp. caraway seeds
2 tbsp. sesame seeds

250 grams (½ lb.) rice noodles
4 onions in wedges
4 cloves garlic, crushed
¼ medium cabbage, shredded
2 carrots, julienned
1 red and green pepper in strips
½ tsp. pepper
2 tsp. paprika
¼ tsp. marjoram
about ¼ cup soy sauce
2 tbsp. sunflower seeds or coarsely
   chopped walnuts

In small frying pan heat one tablespoon oil and fry pine nuts a few minutes; set aside. *Nuts burn easily — be careful not to burn them.*

In large bowl mix chopped meat with onion, garlic, egg, scallions, parsley, mustard and ketchup. Set aside.

In bowl soak rice noodles in cold water about 20 minutes. Drain.

Meanwhile in wok heat remaining oil and stir fry onions, garlic, cabbage, carrots and peppers and seasoning about 10 minutes, stirring occasionally. Remove from wok with slotted spoon. Form meat balls from chopped meat and sauté, stirring occasionally until cooked. Add drained rice-noodles and soy sauce and sauté, stirring continuously, another 5 minutes.

Add vegetables, seeds and pine nuts and mix together.

MEAT-FILLED PASTRIES
Boiled or fried: well worth waiting for!

About 12 pastries
Cooking time: about 15 minutes
Food processor comes in handy

PASTRY DOUGH
1¼ cup flour
pinch of salt
2 tbsp. water
1 egg, slightly beaten

FILLING
2 tbsp. oil
250 grams (½ lb) chopped meat
3 cloves garlic, crushed
1 onion, chopped
1 tbsp. parsley, chopped
¼ tsp. pepper

1 egg, slightly beaten
oil for frying

Pastry dough: In large bowl sift flour and salt; add water and egg and knead until smooth (dough should be soft, but not sticky). Process can be done in food processor.

FILLING: In large frying pan heat 2 tablespoons oil and brown meat, garlic, onion and parsley; stirring occasionally, and separating meat. Add seasoning and mix together.

Remove with slotted spoon; place in wooden bowl and chop slightly. Let cool somewhat.

On floured board roll out pastry dough to medium thickness about 0.5 cm (¼ ") and cut into squares of about 8 cm (3 "). Place a little Filling in center of each square and fold into triangle form. Press ends together with the aid of a beaten egg yolk mixed with a little water.

Cook Filled Pastries in boiling salted water about 15 minutes.

Remove from pot carefully with slotted spoon. Serve with soup. OR . . .

In large frying pan heat some oil and brown Pastries on both sides; drain on paper toweling.

Serve with **Mushroom-Wine Sauce**.

P.S. Great as either an appetizer or a side dish.

MEAT-STUFFED MUSHROOMS
Hors d'oeuvres with class

6–8 portions
Cooking time: about 20 minutes

½ kilo (1 lb.) chopped meat or turkey meat (white and dark)	1 tbsp. prepared mustard
3 tbsp. scallions, chopped	2 tbsp. flour
3 tbsp. soy sauce	20 large mushroom caps
¼ tsp. pepper	¾ cup broth
	¼ cup dry red wine

In large bowl mix together meat, scallions, one tablespoon soy sauce, salt, pepper, mustard and one tablespoon flour.

Form balls suitable for mushroom caps and fill. In large frying pan mix together rest of soy sauce, flour, broth and wine.

Place stuffed mushrooms in pan carefully (stuffing facing up). Be careful that the broth does not reach the top of the mushroom caps. If there is extra filling, form small meat balls and place in pan. Cover and cook over low flame about 20 minutes.

P.S. If you love meatballs and mushrooms, you can make more batches in the same sauce. Just keep taking out and putting in. They are delicious as hors d'oeuvres or as a side dish.

DRESSED COCKTAIL FRANKS
Everybody goes crazy over these!

Portions depend on how fast they're gobbled up.
Baking time: about 20 minutes

1 recipe **Plain Pastry Dough**	1 egg, slightly beaten
40–50 cocktail franks	sesame seeds

Preheat oven 400° F, 210° C.

Roll out dough thin, about 0.3 cm (⅛ ") and cut into squares. With rolling pin roll over each square to make a thin rectangle. Width should be large enough to wrap each cocktail frank, leaving ends open.

Wrap frankfurters; place on greased lipped cookie sheet, seam side down.

Brush jackets with beaten egg and sprinkle with sesame seeds. Bake in hot oven about 20 minutes.

P.S. Great with mustard as hors d'oeuvres.

MEAT LOAF SANDWICH

Revital's favorite

About 8 portions
Baking time: 1 ¼ hours
Food processor comes in handy

1 kilo (2 lbs.) chicken breast,
  skinned and boned
1½ kilo (3 lbs.) chopped meat
  or turkey meat (white and dark)
5 cloves garlic, crushed
2 onions, chopped
¼ cup parsley, chopped
2 eggs
¼ cup wheat germ
¼ cup fresh bread crumbs OR
  3 slices white bread, soaked
  and squeezed out
about ⅓ cup raw oatmeal
2 tbsp. prepared mustard
3 tbsp. ketchup
1 tsp. pepper
2 scallions, chopped
2 onions, diced

TOPPING
3 tbsp. oil
3 cloves garlic, crushed
¼ kilo (½ lb.) mushrooms, sliced
½ tsp. salt
¼ tsp. pepper
½ tsp. paprika

SAUCE
½ cup orange juice
½ cup dry red wine
¼ cup apricot jam
2 tbsp. prepared mustard
2 tbsp. soy sauce
¼ tsp. pepper
2 tsp. paprika
1 tsp. marjoram

Preheat oven 350° F, 180° C.

Slit and pound chicken breasts to make them thin; set aside.

In large bowl place chopped meat; add garlic, onions, parsley, scallions, eggs, wheat germ, breadcrumbs or sliced bread, oatmeal, pepper, mustard and ketchup and mix together until well blended.

TOPPING: In large frying pan heat oil and sauté garlic and onion a few minutes, stirring occasionally. Add mushrooms and seasoning and continue sautéing about 10 minutes, stirring occasionally. Set aside.

Use large baking pan (big enough so that there's room on the top even after the Sauce is poured). If necessary, use two pans.

Cover bottom of pan with half amount of chicken breast; spread chopped meat on top; arrange rest of chicken breast on top and cover with Topping.

SAUCE: Process all ingredients in food processor. Place in pitcher with spout.

COOKING: Bake sandwich in moderate oven all together 1 ¼ hours. Bake uncovered 15 minutes; pour Sauce over sandwich; cover and continue baking 45 minutes; uncover, baste and bake 15 more minutes. Baste again. Allow time for settling.

OPTIONAL: Garnish with cooked broccoli pieces.

SUGGESTED SIDE DISHES: Cut up potatoes tossed with seasoned, sautéed onion or **Cabbage Roll**.

Exciting QUICHES, PIES & CASSEROLES

Are quiches an impossible dream? I thought so before I began making them. Now when I'm rushed I prepare a quiche — that's how easy it is. I used to make them just for company, but it has become a favorite family affair (if you're watching your cholesterol and calories use milk instead of cream). When you get the feel of making quiches, try experimenting with variations of the Filling.

The basic quiche is made up of five layers: crust, grated cheese, filling, grated cheese and topping (sweet cream, eggs and wine). My secret in making it easier is having the pastry dough (crust) and grated cheese in the freezer for ready use (pastry dough has to be thawed out before using). Cheeses can be grated in the fine grater attachment of the mixer or food processor. Be sure to allow time for quiches to settle after baking.

Casseroles, also, are a meal in themselves. If you want just a light meal, prepare a casserole and serve with a tossed salad.

Have FUN!

PIZZA QUICHE

Be sure to have enough for seconds

6–8 portions
Allow time for settling

⅓–½ recipe **Plain Pastry** or **Cream Cheese Pastry**

250 grams (8 oz., 2½ cups) hard
   cheese, grated
2 tbsp. flour
50–60 grams (¼ cup) butter
2–3 onions, sliced
½ tsp. salt
¼ tsp. pepper
1 tsp. paprika
2 cloves garlic, crushed
1 tomato, peeled and sliced

¼ tsp. basil
1 tbsp. dill, chopped
4 olives, pitted and halved

TOPPING
3 eggs
1 cup sweet cream
pinch of ground nutmeg, optional
⅛ tsp. salt and pepper
¼ cup dry or semi-dry white wine

On floured board roll out dough thin to 0.3 cm (⅛″) thickness. Place dough in pie pan 25 cm (10″) round, overlapping over sides; fold in circumference and flute edges as desired.

Preheat oven 425° F, 220° C.

In large bowl mix together grated cheese and flour.

In large frying pan, over low flame, melt butter; increase heat and sauté onions, salt, pepper, paprika and garlic about 15 minutes, stirring occasionally. Sprinkle ⅓ of the cheese mixture over bottom of crust in pie pan. Spread sautéed onion over cheese. In same frying pan heat tomatoes about one minute.

Arrange tomatoes over onions; sprinkle with basil, dill, olives and remaining grated cheese.

In blender, blend Topping ingredients and pour carefully over cheese.

Bake in hot oven 10 minutes; lower heat to 350° F (180° C) and continue baking another 30 minutes, until browned.

Allow to settle at least 15–20 minutes.

Serve warm. May be reheated without losing flavor.

P.S. For hard cheeses I use a combination of Swiss and cheddar.

LAYERED ZUCCHINI QUICHE

With a difference!

8–10 portions
Baking time: 50 minutes
Allow time to settle

¼ cup Parmesan cheese
¼ cup cheddar cheese
about ½ recipe **Plain Pastry**

FILLING
½ cup breadcrumbs
750 grams (1½ lbs.) zucchini,
   thinly sliced

2 eggs, separated
1 cup sour cream
1 scallion, chopped
2 tbsp. dill, chopped
2 tbsp. flour
1 tsp. salt
¼ tsp. pepper
1 tbsp. butter
¼ tsp. marjoram

Grate cheeses and place in medium bowl and mix. Work in half of cheese into Plain Pastry dough.

On floured board roll out dough thin to 0.3 cm (⅛″) and wide enough to fit over pie pan 27 cm (11″) or two pans 23 cm (9″) round, overlapping sides. Fold up circumference and flute edges as desired.

Add breadcrumbs to rest of grated cheeses, mix and set aside.

Cook zucchini in a little salted water about 5 minutes and drain.

Preheat oven 450° F, 230° C.

In medium bowl beat together egg yolks and sour cream. Add scallions, dill, flour, salt and pepper and mix until smooth.

In mixer, at high speed, beat egg whites until stiff, but not dry.

Fold egg yolk-sour cream mixture into egg whites.

Prepare layers of sliced zucchini and egg mixture. Finish off with egg mixture. Sprinkle with breadcrumb-cheese mixture and dot with butter.

Bake in hot oven 10 minutes; lower heat to 325° F (165° C) and continue baking 40 minutes.

Allow to set about 15 minutes. Can be left in oven ½ hour or more.

P.S. Quiche does not lose its flavor when rewarmed.

ONION-MUSHROOM QUICHE   *Delicate elegance*

About 6 portions
Baking time: 35–40 minutes
Food processor comes in handy
Allow time for settling

⅓–½ recipe **Shortcrust Pastry** or **Plain Pastry**

FILLING
50–60 grams (¼ cup) butter
2 cloves garlic, crushed
1 large onion, diced
1 cup mushrooms, sliced
½ tsp. basil
1 tsp. salt
¼ tsp. pepper
1 cup hard cheese, grated

TOPPING
4 eggs
½ cup sweet cream
⅛ tsp. salt and pepper
¼ cup dry or semi-dry white wine
pinch of nutmeg, if desired

On floured board roll out dough thin about 0.3 cm (⅛″). Spread on pie pan 25 cm (10″) with overlapping sides. Fold in circumference and flute.

In large frying pan, over low flame, melt butter. Increase heat slightly and sauté garlic and onion about 5 minutes, stirring occasionally. Add mushrooms, basil, salt and pepper and continue sautéing another 10 minutes, stirring occasionally.

Preheat oven 350° F, 180° C.

Arrange layers: cheese-mushrooms-cheese-mushrooms. Sprinkle with scallion and parsley.

In blender blend Topping ingredients and pour over Filling carefully.

Bake in moderate oven 35–40 minutes.

Allow to settle about 20 minutes. Can be left in oven ½ hour or more.

Delicious even when rewarmed.

P.S. For hard cheeses I use a combination of Swiss and cheddar.

VARIATION: Add ⅓ cup chopped tuna fish to Filling.

SCALLION QUICHE

An improved Quiche Lorraine

About 6 portions
Baking time: about 30 minutes
Allow time for settling

½ recipe ***Plain Pastry*** *or* ***Cream Cheese Pastry***

FILLING
30 grams (2 tbsp.) butter
⅔ cup scallions, chopped
1½ cups hard cheese, cubed
½ cup Parmesan cheese, cubed
½ tsp. salt
¼ tsp. pepper

TOPPING
3 eggs
1 cup sweet cream
¼ cup dry or semi-dry white wine
¼ tsp. salt
⅛ tsp. pepper
pinch of nutmeg, optional

Preheat oven 450° F, 230° C.

On floured board roll out pastry dough thin to about 0.3 cm (⅛″) thickness and wide enough to fit into a 25 cm (10″) pie pan overlapping on sides. Fold in circumference and flute as desired.

Pierce crust with fork in a few places and bake in pre-heated oven about 5 minutes.

In small frying pan over low flame melt butter; increase heat slightly and gently sauté scallions. Sprinkle over bottom crust.

Mix together cheese cubes; spread over scallions and sprinkle with seasoning.

In blender blend all Topping ingredients and pour over cheeses carefully.

Bake in hot oven 15 minutes. Lower heat to 350° F (180° C) and continue baking another 15 minutes.

Allow to settle about 15 minutes. Can be left in oven ½ hour or more. Quiche can be rewarmed without losing flavor.

P.S. For hard cheeses I use a combination of Swiss and cheddar.

ZUCCHINI QUICHE WITH TOPPING

Another delicious variation

6–8 portions
Baking time: 30 minutes
Allow time for settling
Food processor comes in handy

⅓–½ recipe ***Plain Pastry***

FILLING
50–60 grams (¼ cup) butter
1 onion, chopped
3 cloves garlic, crushed
3 medium zucchini, diced
1 scallion, sliced
½ gamba, diced
1 tsp. salt
¼ tsp. pepper
¼ tsp. marjoram
1 tsp. dill
¼ cup Parmesan cheese, grated
¼ cup Cheddar cheese, grated
1 tbsp. flour

TOPPING
3 eggs
1 cup sweet cream
¼ cup dry or semi-dry white wine
¼ tsp. salt
⅛ tsp. pepper
pinch of nutmeg, optional

Preheat oven 450° F, 230° C.

On floured board roll out dough thin to about 0.3 cm (⅛″) for a 27 cm (11″) round pie pan overlapping on sides. Fold in circumference and flute edges as desired. Pierce with fork in a few places and bake in preheated oven 5 minutes. Set aside.

In large frying pan heat butter and sauté onion and garlic 3–4 minutes.

Add zucchini, scallion, gamba, salt, pepper and marjoram and continue sautéing about 8 minutes more, stirring occasionally. Set aside.

In medium bowl mix together grated cheeses and flour.

Sprinkle ½ of cheese mixture over pie crust. Spread vegetables over cheese mixture, then sprinkle vegetables with remaining cheese.

In blender blend Topping ingredients and pour over quiche slowly and carefully.

Bake in hot oven 15 minutes. Lower heat to 350° F (180° C) and continue baking another 15 minutes.

Allow to set about 20 minutes. Can be left in oven ½ hour or more.

P.S. Can be rewarmed without losing flavor.

ZUCCHINI SQUARES

An everyday affair

About 6 portions
Cooking and baking time: about 1 hour
Food processor comes in handy

2–3 tbsp. butter	½ cup cottage cheese
2 onions, diced	½ tsp. paprika
250 grams (½ lb.) mushrooms, sliced	⅛ tsp. marjoram
6 medium (600 grams,	1 tsp. salt
1¼ lbs.) zucchini, sliced	¼ tsp. pepper
3 scallions, sliced	¼ cup flour
2 tbsp. dill, chopped	2 tbsp. plus 1 tbsp. wheat germ
2 tbsp. parsley, cut up	or breadcrumbs
3 eggs	2 tbsp. sesame seeds
1 cup plus 2 tbsp.	5 stuffed olives, halved
hard cheese, grated	

Preheat oven 350° F, 180° C.

In frying pan heat butter over low flame. Increase heat and sauté onion, mushrooms and paprika about 10 minutes. Set aside. Cook zucchini about 10 minutes and drain. Place in large wooden bowl and chop (can be done in food processor). Pour off excess water.

Add sautéed onion, mushrooms, scallions, dill, parsley, eggs, grated cheese, cottage cheese and seasoning. Mix together. Add flour and 2 tablespoons wheat germ or breadcrumbs and mix.

Spread into suitable flat greased baking pan and dot with olives.

In small bowl mix together one tablespoon wheat germ, two tablespoons hard cheese and one tablespoon sesame seeds. Sprinkle mixture over casserole. Sprinkle with paprika.

Bake into moderate oven about 45 minutes.

Allow to set about 15 minutes. Cut into squares and serve.

P.S. For hard cheeses I use a combination of Swiss and cheddar.

CABBAGE-MUSHROOM PIE

All covered up!

6–8 portions
Baking time: 40 minutes
Allow time for settling
Food processor come in handy

About ¾ recipe **Plain Pastry**

FILLING
4 tbsp. butter
1 large onion, diced
1 small cabbage, grated
½ tsp. basil
½ tsp. marjoram
1 tsp. salt
¼ tsp. pepper
1–2 tsp. caraway seeds

250 grams (½ lb.) mushrooms, sliced
100–125 grams (½ cup) cream cheese
3 hard boiled eggs, sliced
1 tbsp. dill, chopped

GLAZE
1 egg yolk
1 tsp. water
1 tbsp. dill, chopped
1 tbsp. sesame seeds

Divide pastry dough into two balls: one ⅔ and one ⅓. On floured board roll out ⅔ dough thin to about 0.3 cm (⅛") for a 23 cm (9") round pie pan, overlapping on sides.

Preheat oven 400° F, 200° C.

In large frying pan, over low flame, melt two tablespoons butter. Increase heat and sauté onions about 5 minutes, stirring occasionally. Add cabbage and seasoning and continue sautéing until soft, stirring occasionally. Add caraway seeds. In separate pan sauté mushrooms with remaining butter.

Spread cream cheese over bottom crust and then form layers: sliced egg sprinkled with dill-cabbage mixture sprinkled with mushrooms.

Roll out remaining dough to cover pie and place on top of Filling.

Press together circumference and flute edges as desired. Pierce top with fork in a few places.

GLAZE: Mix together egg yolk and water. Brush on crust and sprinkle with sesame seeds.

Bake in hot oven 15 minutes. Lower heat to 350° F (180° C) and continue baking about 25 more minutes. Allow 15–20 minutes to settle.

BROCCOLI-CHEESE PIE

Adds color and great taste

About 6 portions
Baking time: 55 minutes; allow time for settling
Food processor comes in handy

About ⅓ recipe **Plain Pastry** or ½ recipe **Cream Cheese Pastry**

FILLING
800 grams (1½ lb.) frozen broccoli
2 cups cottage cheese
50–60 grams (¼ cup) butter, melted
3 eggs, beaten
2 tbsp. sesame seeds

1 cup cheddar cheese, grated
2 tbsp. flour
1 small onion, chopped
¼ tsp. marjoram
¾–1 tsp. salt
½ tsp. pepper
2 tbsp. pine nuts or chopped walnuts

On floured board roll out pastry dough thin to about 0.3 cm (⅛") for a 23 cm (9") round pie pan overlapping on sides. Fold up circumference and flute edges as desired.

Preheat oven 350° F, 180° C.

Thaw out broccoli; drain and dry out in frying pan over medium-low flame, stirring continuously. Process can be done in microwave oven. Squeeze out excess water.

Place broccoli in large bowl and chop. (Process can be done in food processor.) Add remaining ingredients and mix well.

Spread over pie crust and bake in moderate oven about 55 minutes. Allow to settle about 20 minutes.
TO SERVE: Sprinkle with additional walnuts.
P.S. Nice side dish to fish or **Vegetable Omelette**.

SPINACH PIE
Even the kids love spinach

About 6 portions
Baking time: 40 minutes
Allow time for settling

⅓ recipe **Plain Pastry**	2 cups cottage cheese
800 grams (2 lbs.)	1–1½ tsp. salt
cooked and chopped spinach	¼–½ tsp. pepper
1 tbsp. butter	½ cup Parmesan cheese, grated
1 scallion, sliced	2 eggs, slightly beaten
2 tbsp. pine nuts	2 tbsp. almonds, chopped

On floured board roll out dough thin to 0.3 cm (⅛″) for a 27 cm (11″) or 25 cm (10″) deep dish pie pan, overlapping on sides. Fold in circumference and flute edges as desired.

If using frozen spinach, dry it out over medium-low flame (pouring off excess liquid). Process can be done in microwave oven.

Preheat oven 450° F, 230° C.

In frying pan, over low flame, melt butter; increase heat and sauté spinach with scallions and pine nuts about 5 minutes. Transfer to bowl; add rest of ingredients (except 1 tbsp. Parmesan cheese and almonds); mix together and pour over pie crust.

Bake in hot oven 10 minutes. Lower heat to 325° F (165° C) and bake another 40 minutes. Sprinkle with Parmesan cheese and almonds. Allow to settle about 15 minutes.

BROCCOLI KUGEL
An interesting treat

About 6 portions
Baking time: 40 minutes

800 grams (1½ lbs.) frozen broccoli

SAUCE	3 eggs, beaten
2 tbsp. margarine	½ tsp. salt
2 tbsp. flour	¼ tsp. pepper
½ cup milk or broth	⅛ tsp. marjoram
½ cup mayonnaise	2 tbsp. pine nuts
1 tbsp. onion soup powder	breadcrumbs

Cook broccoli and drain. Place in large wooden bowl and chop coarsely.
Preheat oven 325° F, 165° C.
SAUCE: In small pot, over low flame, melt margarine and remove from flame. Add flour and stir until smooth. Return to flame; add milk slowly and cook, stirring constantly, until thickened.

Mix into broccoli together with mayonnaise, onion, soup powder, eggs, seasoning and pine nuts.
Grease a 20 cm (8") square baking pan, sprinkle with breadcrumbs and spread broccoli mixture on top. Sprinkle with more breadcrumbs and bake in moderate-low oven 40 minutes.

BROCCOLI ROLL

An entertainment extravaganza

About 8 portions
Baking time: 50 minutes
Food processor comes in handy

Mushroom-Wine Sauce
1 recipe **Plain Pastry**

FILLING
800 grams (1½ lbs.) fresh or
    frozen broccoli
1 tbsp. margarine
2 tbsp. pine nuts OR
    chopped almonds
1 onion, chopped
½ cup breadcrumbs

3 cloves garlic, crushed
1 tbsp. sesame seeds
1 tsp. salt
¼ tsp. pepper
2 eggs, beaten

GLAZE
1 egg yolk
1 tbsp. water
1–2 tbsp. sesame seeds

Prepare Mushroom-Wine Sauce and set aside.

Divide pastry dough into three pieces and roll out each one thin, to about 0.3 cm (⅛").

Cook broccoli until soft and drain.

Chop broccoli and place in large wooden bowl. (Chopping process may be done in food processor.)
Preheat oven to 375° F, 190° C.

In small saucepan melt ½ tablespoon margarine and sauté pine nuts or almonds about 2 minutes, being careful mixture doesn't burn. Add to broccoli along with the remaining Filling ingredients and 2 tablespoons Mushroom-Wine Sauce. Mix together until well blended.

Place ⅓ of Filling on each pastry sheet; fold in sides; roll up carefully and place on greased aluminum-foil-covered cookie sheet.

For glaze, mix together egg yolk and water and brush on broccoli rolls. Sprinkle with sesame seeds.

Slit rolls with knife in a few places and bake in moderate-high oven about 50 minutes.

TO SERVE: Place rolls on long serving platter, cut into thick slices, and serve with Mushroom-Wine Sauce.

P.S. Try adding chicken livers to the Mushroom-Wine sauce for added flavor.

VARIATION: Use ½ of Filling ingredients; prepare ½ kilo (1 lb.) ground beef or ground turkey meat (mixed with 1 egg, ¼ cup breadcrumbs, 2 teaspoons prepared mustard, 2 cloves garlic, crushed, and 1 onion, chopped) and spread over each pastry dough before spreading with broccoli mixture. Bake in moderate oven (350° F, 180° C) about 1¼ hours.

CABBAGE ROLL

Out of this world

About 6 portions
Baking time: about 1 hour
Food processor comes in handy

⅔ recipe **Plain Pastry**

FILLING
50–60 grams (¼ cup) butter
2 cups cabbage, grated
1 carrot, grated
1 small green pepper, diced
1 large onion, chopped
½ red pepper, diced
1 tsp. caraway seeds

1 tsp. paprika
1 tsp. salt
¼ tsp. pepper
¼ tsp. marjoram

GLAZE
1 egg yolk beaten with 1 tbsp. water
2 tbsp. sesame seeds

Preheat oven 350° F, 180° C.

Prepare pastry as directed. Cut dough in half and, on floured board, roll out each piece thin (about 0.3 cm, ⅛").

In large frying pan heat butter over low flame; increase heat and sauté vegetables about 10 minutes, stirring occasionally. Add seasoning and cool slightly.

Spread ½ of mixture on each sheet of dough; fold in sides and roll up as you would a jelly roll.

Place carefully on greased aluminum-foil-covered cookie sheet. Brush with egg yolk mixture; sprinkle with sesame seeds and bake in moderate oven about 1 hour.

Cut into thick slices and serve.

P.S. This roll does not need any sauce, since the sautéed vegetables keep it moist and delicious.

TUNA-PASTA CASSEROLE

250 grams (8 oz.) pasta, cooked and drained	1½ tsp. salt
	½ tsp. pepper
1 can (190 grams; 7 oz.) tuna, flaked and drained	½ tsp. basil
	4 eggs
3 cups grated cheese	2 cups milk
1 onion, diced	¼ tsp. oregano

Preheat oven 325° F, 175° C.

In large bowl mix together pasta, tuna, cheese, onion, salt, pepper, and basil. Spread into desired baking pan. In blender, blend eggs, milk and oregano. Gently pour over pasta.

Bake in moderate oven about 45 minutes.

VARIATION: For a richer version, substitute **Mushroom Cream Sauce** for the milk.

CARROT KUGEL
Better than cake

6–8 portions
Baking time: 1 hour
Food processor comes in handy

1¼ cup flour	½ cup brown sugar
½ tsp. baking soda	3 eggs
½ tsp. baking powder	2 tsp. vanilla extract
½ tsp. salt	¼ cup lemon juice
50–60 grams (¼ cup) margarine	3½ cups carrots, grated

Preheat oven 350° F, 180° C.

In bowl sift flour, baking soda, baking powder and salt and set aside.

In mixer, at medium speed, beat margarine and sugar about one minute; add eggs, and vanilla extract. Continue beating a couple of minutes. Lower speed; add flour mixture and lemon juice and mix just until blended.

With wooden spoon fold in carrots.

Spread in greased ring mold or rectangular baking pan and bake in moderate oven one hour.

VANILLA-CARROT PUDDING
Vanilla flavor all the way

About 6 portions
Baking time: about 40 minutes

2 kilo (4 lbs.) carrots, cooked
⅓ cup margarine, melted
⅓ cup brown sugar
5 eggs

1 tbsp. vanilla extract
2 tsp. flour
½ tsp. baking powder
2 tbsp. bread or cornflakes crumbs

Preheat oven 350° F, 180° C.

In bowl mash carrots; add rest of ingredients except crumbs and mix.

Grease deep baking pan; sprinkle with one tablespoon crumbs and spread carrot mixture evenly. Sprinkle with last tablespoon crumbs and bake in moderate oven about 40 minutes.

YAM-APPLE CASSEROLE
Just the right sweetness

1 kilo (2 lbs.) yams
  (about 4 medium)
4 cooking apples

SAUCE
⅔ cup brown sugar
⅓ cup butter
½ cup apple or orange juice
1½ tbsp. lemon juice
¼ cup maple syrup
1 tsp. cinnamon
½ tsp. ginger

Cook yams in skins (in enough water to cover) until tender. Drain, peel and slice.

Peel and slice applies. Pat dry.

Preheat oven 350° F, 180° C.

In saucepan bring the remaining ingredients to a boil and cook 10 minutes, stirring occasionally.

Layer sliced yams and apples in greased deep casserole, starting and ending with yams. Pour Sauce over casserole contents.

Bake in moderate oven about 30 minutes.

Remove from oven and baste.

P.S. Delicious with **Roast Turkey** and everything else.

There's nothing like homemade **BREADS**

It's really fun to work with yeast doughs. A dough hook attachment to the mixer makes bread-making a real delight, but whatever you have for kitchen gadgets, making bread will give you a great feeling, especially when you taste your freshly baked bread.

There's nothing like homemade bread and rolls — try it. If using fresh yeast, be sure it's fresh. Learn how to judge when dissolving yeast that the water is not too hot or too cold. Follow the directions.

It took me a bit of time to start baking with yeast doughs. Experience is everything. Don't be afraid — show who's boss and attack that dough.

WHITE BREAD (CHALLAH)

It's worth the effort

Yield: 4 medium loaves
Baking time: about 40 minutes

8 cups flour	*1 ½ cups water*
¾ – 1 cup sugar	*¾ cup oil*
4 tsp. salt	*3 eggs*
50–60 grams (2 oz.) fresh yeast	*1 egg, beaten (for brushing)*

In large bowl mix together flour, sugar and salt; make well in center.

In small bowl place one-cup very warm water; break up yeast; add one-teaspoon suger; mix slightly; cover with light cotton towel and leave 10-15 minutes.

Add yeast to flour together with oil, eggs, and ½ cup water and form dough. On floured board knead dough 8-10 minutes until smooth and satiny. Process can be done in mixer with dough hook (follow directions).

To let rise, place dough in large lightly oiled bowl; cover with slightly damp cotton towel and leave for 1 ½ hours. Punch down a few times and leave dough to rise another hour. (In winter, if room is cool, allow for dough to rise 1 ½ hours each time.)

On floured board divide dough into desired sizes and shape into desired forms.* Place on well-floured cookie sheets (allowing room for spreading); cover with slightly damp cotton towel and leave in warm spot about 50 minutes. Brush gently with beaten egg and sprinkle with poppy or sesame seeds and bake in moderate-high oven (375° F, 190° C) 30–40 minutes. (For fluffier bread do not preheat oven.)

To test for doneness, tap bottom of challah with fingers. It should have a hollow sound.

P.S. Cool before storing. Heat and serve.

Note: I use part whole wheat flour (about 2 cups). It gives a little heavier texture.

A RICHER VARIATION:

about 8 cups flour,	*only 1 cup water*
50–60 grams yeast,	*1 cup oil*
4 tsp. salt	*4 eggs*
1 cup sugar	

Follow directions as above but allow to rise overnight in a warm spot; punch down and let rise another 1 ½ hours. After shaping, brush with egg, sprinkle with poppy or sesame seeds and let rise one hour.

*To form a 6-BRAIDED CHALLAH
(The key is in the back-and-forth rhythm of braiding: find it and the bread practically braids itself!)

Step 1: Take desired amount of dough; divide it into 6 equal pieces and, on floured board, roll each piece with palm of hand to form medium thick strips.

Step 2: Divide strips into 2 groups of 3. Designate a top (starting point) and align the strips at the top. Place one group on top of the other and press the top end together with knife handle. Keeping the top end pressed together, separate the two groups on the board.

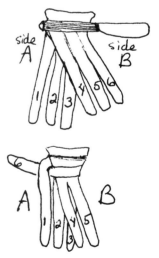

Step 3: (Forming the braid) Number the strips in your mind. Lift strips 6 and 1 with opposite hands. Cross strip 6 under strip 1; place 6 above all the strips (over A) and bring 1 next to side A.

  Lift strips 2 and 6 (above); bring 6 under 2; place 6 next to side B and place strip 2 above strips (over B). Lift 5 and 2; bring 5 under 2; place 5 over strip and 2 on right side. Continue the procedure until the end, pulling the strips slightly in the process so that the braid is somewhat firm.

Place carefully onto floured cookie sheets and continue with directions.

SEMI-WHOLE WHEAT BREAD
Melts in your mouth!

Baking time: about 45 minutes

3½ cups whole wheat flour
about 2½ cups regular flour
1¼ tsp. salt
1 tbsp. caraway seeds

30 grams (1 oz.) fresh yeast
1½ tsp. brown sugar
2 cups lukewarm water
50–60 grams (¼ cup or 2 oz.) butter

In large bowl sift together flour and salt; mix in caraway seeds and make hole in center. Set aside.

Dissolve yeast and sugar in one cup lukewarm water 5–10 minutes (until frothy). Add to flour mixture together with rest of water and butter and form dough.

On floured board knead dough about 8 minutes until smooth and satiny. Process can be done in mixer with dough hook (follow directions).

Place dough in large oiled bowl, turning over so that both sides are oiled. Cover with slightly damp cotton towel or place in closed polyethylene bag, and leave in warm spot one hour.

On floured board knead again and form two round loaves. Place on greased cookie sheet and leave in warm spot 45 minutes, until double in size.

Heat oven 400° F, 200° C.

Bake in hot oven about 45 minutes.

P.S. Great with cheeses, soups or just smeared with butter.

ONION ROLLS
The top of the topped rolls

24 rolls
Baking time: about 30 minutes

20 grams (⅔ oz.) yeast
½ cup warm water
about 5½ cups flour
⅓ cup sugar
2 tsp. salt
⅓ cup oil
2 eggs
½ cup water

TOPPING
1 medium onion, chopped
¼ tsp. salt
1 tbsp. oil
¼ cup poppy seeds
1 egg, slightly beaten

Dissolve yeast in warm water about 5 minutes.

In large bowl sift flour and salt and make well. Add sugar, yeast mixture, oil, eggs and water and form dough.

On floured board knead dough about 8 minutes. Process can be done in mixer with dough hook (follow directions).

Place dough in large greased bowl, turning over (so that both sides are oiled). Cover with cotton towel or place in a closed polyethylene bag, and leave in warm spot 1½ hours.

Knead a few seconds; divide into 24 pieces; roll out each piece into a bar, hold one end and form a spiral.

Place on greased cookie sheet (allowing room for spreading). Cover and leave about ½ hour.

To prepare Topping, squeeze out water from onions. In bowl mix together onion, salt, oil and poppy seeds. Brush each roll with beaten egg and top with onion mixture.

Heat oven 350° F, 180° C.

Bake in moderate oven about 30 minutes.

PLAIN ROLLS

Extra special!

Yield: 10 rolls
Baking time: 25–30 minutes

about 3½ cups flour
½ cup milk
50–60 grams (¼ cup) butter,
 room temperature
2 tbsp. sugar
2 tsp. salt

½ cup water
30 grams (1 oz.) yeast
1 egg, slightly beaten
30 grams (2 tbsp.) butter

OPTIONAL TOPPING
 poppy or caraway seeds,

In bowl sift flour and set aside.

In small saucepan bring milk to a boil; remove from flame; add butter, sugar and salt and mix until dissolved. Add water (to bring to lukewarm); add yeast; mix and allow to soften 5–10 minutes. Mix in egg.

Gradually add yeast mixture to flour and form dough. Knead about eight minutes until dough is smooth and satiny. Process can be done in mixer with dough hook (follow directions).

Place dough in oiled bowl, turning over so that both sides are oiled. Cover with slightly damp cotton towel or place in closed polyethylene bag, and leave in warm spot one hour.

Punch down a few times and leave another hour.

On floured board knead dough a few seconds, divide into 10 pieces and form rolls of desired shapes. Place on greased, floured cookie sheet (allowing space for spreading); cover and leave in warm spot 40 minutes.

Heat oven 425° F, 220° C.

Melt 2 tablespoons butter; brush on rolls. Sprinkle with sesame seeds and bake in hot oven 25–30 minutes.

PIZZAZZY ITALIAN PIZZA

Number of portions depends on who's eating
Baking time: 25 minutes (prepare dough beforehand)

CRUST
20 grams (¾ oz.) yeast
1 cup warm water
about 3¼ cups flour
¼ tsp. salt
2 tbsp. butter, melted

FILLING
about 1 tbsp. oil
1–1½ cups **Tomato Sauce**
250 grams (½ lb.) hard cheese
 (Swiss-cheddar-Parmesan mixture)
salt, pepper, oregano and garlic

Choice of Toppings: onion, anchovy, mushrooms, olives, etc.

Soften yeast in warm water 5–10 minutes.

In bowl sift flour and salt and make well in center. Add yeast mixture and butter and gradually form dough.

On floured board knead until smooth and satiny. Process can be done in mixer with dough hook (follow directions).

Place dough in oiled bowl, turning over so that both sides are oiled. Cover with slightly damp cotton towel or place in closed polyethylene bag, and leave to rise in warm spot two hours.

Divide dough according to size of pans; knead a few seconds; stretch and roll out as thin as possible (about 0.3 cm, ⅛″).

Preheat oven 450° F, 230° C.

Place dough on flat pans; sprinkle with oil; arrange Filling in layers (Tomato Sauce, cheeses, spices). If desired, sprinkle with choice of Topping.

Bake in hot oven about 25 minutes.

P.S. I always sprinkle my pizza with granulated garlic and oregano. (Fresh garlic is even better.)

DATE BREAD
Warm and delicious

Baking time: about 50 minutes

2 cups (about 350 grams, ¾ lb.) pitted dates	1 cup sugar
1½ cups boiling water	2 eggs
1 tsp. baking soda	1 cup regular flour, sifted
50–60 grams (¼ cup) butter OR margarine, room temperature	1 cup whole wheat flour, sifted
	1 cup walnuts, coarsely ground
	¼ cup raisins

Place dates in large bowl. Mix baking soda in boiling water and pour over dates. Allow to cool. Preheat oven 350° F, 180° C.

In mixer, at medium speed, beat butter and sugar about one minute. Add eggs and continue beating a few minutes.

Lower speed to lowest; add dates and both kinds of flour and beat just until last of flour is added.

With wooden spoon fold in walnuts and raisins.

Pour into greased loaf pan and bake in moderate oven about 50 minutes.

P.S. A cakey type of bread.

GARLIC BREAD IN BUTTER
Makes a meal into a happening

Baking time: 15 minutes

1 long French bread	¼ tsp. salt
50–60 grams (¼ cup) butter OR margarine	⅛ tsp. pepper
4 cloves garlic, crushed	½ tsp. paprika
	2 tbsp. parsley, chopped

Preheat oven 375° F, 190° C.

In small saucepan, over low flame, melt butter or margarine; remove from flame; add all remaining ingredients and mix. Let cool to room temperature.

Place bread on piece of aluminum foil (long enough and wide enough to cover entire bread). Cut bread into thick pieces – almost through to the bottom of bread, leaving an uncut edge.

Spread garlic butter on each side of every piece; wrap in aluminum foil and bake in moderate-high oven about 15 minutes.

P.S. Goes great with hot soups and pretty much with all hot meals.

GARLIC BREAD IN OIL: (30 minutes baking time) For ingredients use: 1 long French bread, olive or sunflower oil, garlic – fresh, crushed or granulated, and oregano or basil (fresh, chopped is the best). Preheat oven 350° F, 180° C. Slice bread into 2.5 cm (1″) slices (12–16 slices) and place on cookie sheet (keeping each slice separate) and bake 15 minutes. Spread ½ teaspoon oil on each slice and continue baking another 15 minutes. Remove from oven and sprinkle with garlic and oregano or basil.

VARIATION: After baking, sprinkle each slice with grated cheese and a drop of olive oil and broil 2 min.

Make your own PASTRY DOUGHS

Why buy prepared pastry doughs? With or without the food processor they're really very easy to prepare.

The two types that I use the most and that are always in the freezer for ready use are the Plain Pastry and the Sweet Cookie Doughs. Besides the Sweet Yeast Dough (which is in a class of its own) the others are nice variations that should definitely not be overlooked.

For Pre-Baked Pie Crust, preheat oven 425° F, 220° C. Roll out Plain Pastry Dough; place in pie plate; flute edges and prick all over with fork. Cut a round piece of aluminum foil and place on top. Pour one cup dried beans over the foil to weigh it down and bake crust in hot oven 12–15 minutes; remove beans and aluminum foil and bake a few minutes more. (Store beans for reuse.)

PLAIN PASTRY DOUGH
The most versatile dough I know

Food processor makes it easy

2⅓ cups flour
pinch of salt
about ⅓ cup ice cold water

150–190 grams (¾ cup) butter OR
margarine, room temperature

In large bowl sift flour and salt. Cut in butter or margarine until crumbly; slowly pour in water and knead with hand until dough is formed. Knead as little as possible. Process may be done in food processor with metal cutting blade — place flour and salt in processor; add butter or margarine and beat for a few seconds. While still beating, add water. Turn processor off as soon as ball of dough is formed.

On floured board knead a few seconds with hand to form soft, not sticky, dough.

P.S. Great for all quiches, food pies, food rolls, dessert pies (except fruit pies — which I find are better with the **Sweet Cookie Dough**).

Note: If recipe calls for only partial amount of dough, it's worth making the entire amount and freezing it for ready use (thaw out before using). If desired, cut dough into thirds before freezing: ⅓ dough is perfect for a 9″ (23 cm) or 10″ (25 cm) round pie plate.

SWEET COOKIE DOUGH
I always have pieces in the freezer, ready for use

about 4½ cups flour
3 tsp. baking powder
200–250 grams (1 cup) margarine
  OR ½ cup oil plus
  100–125 grams (½ cup)
  margarine, room temperature

¾ cup sugar
3 eggs, slightly beaten
½ cup orange juice

In large bowl sift flour, baking powder and salt. Make well in center; add rest of ingredients; mix and knead until dough is formed. Add enough flour to form soft, slightly sticky dough.

Process can be done in mixer with dough hook.

Refrigerate at least one hour or overnight.

Divide dough into workable sizes. On floured board knead each piece, adding enough flour to make soft, not sticky, dough.

VARIATION for pie crust:

3½ cups flour	3 eggs
pinch of salt	¾ cup oil
¾ cup sugar	⅓ cup chilled orange juice
3 tsp. baking powder	

P.S. Excellent as pie crust for fruit pies, cheese cakes or **Crumbly Cookies** and **Filled Rolled Cake**. Use as much as needed. The rest can be frozen for future use.

SHORTCRUST PASTRY DOUGH
Great for all quiches and food pies

Food processor makes it easy

2 cups flour	150–190 grams (¾ cup) butter, softened
pinch of salt	1 tsp. lemon juice
1 tsp. sugar	3 tbsp. ice cold water

In large bowl sift flour and salt; cut in butter until crumbly; sprinkle with lemon juice; add water and knead with hand until soft, not sticky, dough is formed. Knead as little as possible.

Process can be done in food processor (see **Plain Pastry Dough** for directions).

Use amount of dough according to size of pan.

P.S. Advisable to cut into two or three pieces before freezing.

VARIATION: Mix ¼ cup grated cheddar-Swiss cheeses into dough.

CHEDDAR CHEESE PASTRY DOUGH
For quiches, food pies etc.

2 cups flour	1 tsp. lemon juice
¼ tsp. salt	1–2 tbsp. ice water
½ tsp. sugar	¼ cup cheddar cheese, grated
150–190 grams (¾ cup) butter, room temperature	

In large bowl sift flour, salt and sugar. Cut in butter until crumbly; sprinkle over lemon juice and ice water. Add cheeses and knead until soft, not sticky, dough is formed. Process can be done in food processor with metal blade. Adjust amount of flour and water (if sticky, add flour, if flaky add a little water).

This amount of dough is good for 2 one-crust pies (23 cm or 9″) or 1 two-crust pie.

CREAM CHEESE PASTRY DOUGH

Try this one for a change!

1¼ cup flour
1 tsp. sugar
½ tsp. salt

75–80 grams (⅓ cup) butter,
room temperature
100–125 grams (½ cup) cream cheese

In large bowl sift flour, sugar and salt; cut in butter until crumbly.

Add cheese and form dough (knead as little as possible).

Divide dough in half and on floured board roll out to fit a 23 cm (9″) round pie plate.

P.S. Amount of dough is good for 2 one-crust pies or 1 two-crust pie.

Great for quiches, pizza and food pies.

SWEET YEAST DOUGH

Can't be beat!

40 grams (1½ oz.) yeast
¼ cup warm water
1 cup milk
100–125 grams (½ cup) butter
¾ cup sugar

½ tsp. salt
about 6 cups flour
2 eggs
1 tsp. lemon rind, finely grated

Dissolve yeast in warm water 5–10 minutes.

In small saucepan heat milk (carefully, do not boil); add butter, sugar and salt. Mix until butter is melted; remove from heat and let sit until mixture has cooled to luke-warm.

In large bowl sift flour; make well in center; add yeast mixture, milk mixture, eggs and grated lemon rind and form dough. Add enough flour to form soft, not sticky, dough. On floured board knead 8–10 minutes until smooth and satiny. Process can be done in mixer with dough hook (follow directions).

Place in large oiled bowl, turning once so that both sides are greased. Cover with slightly damp cotton towel or place in polyethylene bag, and leave in warm spot about 1½ hours. Punch down a few times and leave another 1½ hours.

Use for **Cinnamon Buns** and **Swedish Tea Ring**.

CHEESE CAKE CRUST

Give your cake the best

Food processor comes in handy

1½–1¾ cups flour
2 tsp. baking powder
pinch of salt
1½ tbsp. sugar

100–125 grams (½ cup) butter,
room temperature
1 egg, slightly beaten
2 tbsp. water
2 tsp. lemon rind, finely grated

In large bowl sift flour, baking powder, salt and sugar. Cut in butter until crumbly; add egg, water and lemon rind and form dough. Process can be done in food processor with metal blade. Knead a little by hand to form soft, not sticky, dough.

On floured board roll out dough and place in spring form or desired pan, going a little up sides. Dough can also be pressed into pan with fingers. If you prefer a thinner crust, use some of the dough and make cookies. Fill with desired **Cheese Cake Filling**.

QUICK SWEET PIE CRUST
Fast and still delicious

about 1 cup flour
3 tbsp. powdered sugar
1 egg yolk

75–80 grams (⅓ cup) butter OR margarine,
   room temperature

Knead all ingredients together to form soft, not sticky, dough.

Roll out or press down with fingers into 23 cm (9″) round pie plate or spring form pan, pressing a little up sides also. Topping for fruit pies: use one of the **Crumb Toppings**.

Muffins

PLAIN MUFFINS
Breakfast bonanza

12 muffins
Baking time: about 25 minutes

2 cups flour
1 tbsp. baking powder
½ cup sugar
1 cup milk

100–125 grams (½ cup) butter, melted
½ tsp. salt
3 eggs

Preheat oven 425° F, 220° C.

Sift flour, baking powder and salt.

In large bowl beat eggs; add butter, sugar and milk and mix together. Add to flour mixture slowly and blend together with a wooden spoon until batter is smooth.

Grease muffin tins (or use paper liners) and fill.

Bake in hot oven about 25 minutes.

OPTIONAL TOPPING: Spread with melted butter and sprinkle with cinnamon

P.S. Delicious with butter, cottage cheese or whatever.

VARIATION: Use 2 eggs, ⅓ cup (75–80 grams) butter and 2 cups milk. OR Add one mashed banana or peeled, diced peach (use less milk)

HONEY-RAISIN BRAN MUFFINS   *A breakfast treat*

12 muffins
Baking time: about 20 minutes

1⅓ cup whole wheat flour
4 tsp. baking powder
¼ tsp. salt
2 tbsp. flaked coconut
3 cups raisin bran cereal
                OR
2½ cups bran cereal plus
¾ cup raisins

1 cup milk
⅓ cup honey
1 tsp. grated orange rind
2 eggs, slightly beaten
⅓ cup oil
2 pears, peeled and grated

Preheat oven 425° F, 220° C.

In bowl sift flour, baking powder and salt; add coconut and set aside.

In separate large bowl mix together raisin bran cereal, milk and honey; add grated orange rind, eggs and oil; and mix.

Squeeze out water from pears; add to bran mixture together with flour mixture and stir together with wooden spoon just until blended (be careful not to overmix).

Fill greased muffin tins and bake in hot oven about 20 minutes.

P.S. Great with cottage cheese. If using Whole wheat flour reduce amount by 1 tablespoon.

BRAN MUFFINS   *Fruity goodness*

12 muffins
Baking time: 20–25 minutes

1½ cup bran cereal
1 cup milk
1 egg, slightly beaten
¼ cup oil
1 cup whole wheat flour
1 tbsp. baking powder
½ tsp. baking soda
¼ tsp. salt

¼ cup sugar
1½ tsp. cinnamon
2 tbsp. flaked coconut
2 fresh fruits, apples or pears,
   peeled and grated or mashed bananas
1 tsp. grated lemon rind
⅓ cup raisins
1 tsp. vanilla

Preheat oven 400° F, 200° C.

In medium bowl mix together bran cereal and milk and set aside a few minutes until milk is absorbed. Add egg and oil; mix and set aside.

In large bowl sift together flour, baking powder, baking soda, salt, sugar and cinnamon. (If using apples, mix sugar and cinnamon mixture into apples).

Add coconut, bran mixture, raisins, and vanilla to flour mixture and stir until blended. Don't overbeat (batter will be thick).

Squeeze water out of grated apples or pears and fold into batter with grated lemon rind.

Fill greased muffin tins and bake in hot oven 20–25 minutes.

Topping suggestion: Dip warm muffins in melted butter combined with a little cinnamon.

VARIATION: Corn Muffins (12 muffins) – In large bowl sift 1 cup flour, 1 tablespoon baking powder, ½ teaspoon salt. Add 1 cup cornmeal, ⅓ cup sugar, ⅓ cup melted butter, 1 cup milk or sour cream, 2 eggs and 1 teaspoon vanilla. Mix until smooth.

Fill greased or paper-lined muffin tins and bake at 400° F, (200° C) for 15–20 minutes.

CREPES & PANCAKES

Creative, fun-filled

It's easier than you think! In the beginning, the idea of crêpes (and blintzes) seemed beyond me, but after making the initial effort I found that it's easy, fun and delicious. The batter takes no time to prepare — but of course the process of making the crêpes makes up for it.

They may take a bit of time and patience, but it's well worth it. The only way to be good at it is by doing it again and again — until it becomes natural. Many times the first crêpe does not come out perfect (the frying pan needs that time to get used to the idea). Don't despair and don't give up.

Tips for crêpes

• Don't overbeat the batter; mix until just blended. If a few small lumps are left, leave them; they will come out in the process of cooking .
• Make the crêpes as thin as possible — pour the batter into the frying pan and spread by tipping the frying pan or use the back of a spoon.
• Crêpes are ready (fry on one or both sides according to instructions) when edges begin coming up — don't wait until they become brown.
• Crêpes can be stored in refrigerator or freezer. Flat unfilled crêpes can be stacked, separated with waxed paper and then placed in a plastic bag. If frozen, allow to thaw out from freezer before using.

Potential problems with crêpes

• Crêpe sticks to pan = batter too thin; improper greasing of pan; pan not clean
• Crêpes crack = batter too thin; overfrying; pan too hot
• Tough texture = overbeating of batter
• Crêpes don't brown = pan too cool

Pancakes

Batter takes no time at all to prepare. Making them is fun and eating them is heavenly.

AMERICAN BREAKFAST PANCAKES
A great way to say "Good morning"

12–15 pancakes

1¼ cup flour
1 tbsp. sugar
½ tsp. salt
2½ tsp. baking powder

3 eggs, separated
1 cup milk
50–60 grams (¼ cup) butter, melted
maple syrup and/or pats of butter

In large bowl sift together flour, sugar, salt and baking powder.

In a separate bowl beat egg yolks, milk and melted butter; add to flour mixture and with wooden spoon mix until just blended (don't overbeat). Batter does not have to be very smooth.

In mixer at high speed beat egg whites until stiff, but not dry, and fold into batter. Grease griddle or frying pan lightly with pieces of butter. Drop batter by full tablespoons onto *heated* pan or griddle, over medium-low flame, and brown on both sides. Continue until all batter is used up.

Serve immediately with maple syrup with/without pat of butter.

HEARTY PANCAKES
Morning ecstasy

8–10 pancakes

¾ cup flour
¾ tsp. baking powder
¼ tsp. salt
⅛ tsp. pepper
1 egg, slightly beaten

½ cup milk
2 tbsp. sour cream or cottage cheese
1 tsp. oil
about 1 tbsp. butter, for frying
maple syrup and/or pats of butter

In large bowl sift flour, baking powder, salt and pepper.

In separate bowl mix together egg, milk, sour cream or cottage cheese and oil; add to flour and mix just until blended.

In large frying pan heat butter. Drop blobs of batter (about 2–3 tablespoons) and brown lightly on both sides. Drain on paper toweling.

Serve with maple syrup and/or pats of butter.

ZUCCHINI CREPES
With a difference

8 crêpes

CREPES
1 cup flour
1 tsp. baking powder

FILLING
1 cup sour cream
1 cup Parmesan cheese, grated
1 cup Swiss cheese, grated
2 tbsp. sesame seeds

1 tsp. salt
1 tsp. garlic powder
¼ tsp. pepper
5 eggs
⅔ cup milk
2 cups zucchini, grated
1 tsp. olive oil

Preheat oven 350° F (180° C) 10 minutes before baking.

CREPES: In big bowl sift flour, baking powder and seasoning. Make well in center.

In separate medium bowl beat eggs and milk.

Separately, mix zucchini with one teaspoon oil. Add to flour along with egg mixture; mix to form batter.

Spread frying pan with a little oil and heat. Pour ¼ cup batter into frying pan and spread thin with the back of a spoon. Over medium flame fry on both sides. Continue until all the batter is used up.

FILLING: Spread one tablespoon sour cream on each crêpe. Combine the hard cheeses and sprinkle a little over each crêpe. (Leave some for topping).

Grease flat baking pan. Roll up crêpes and place in pan side by side, close together. Sprinkle with rest of grated cheeses and sesame seeds and bake in moderate oven 15–20 minutes.

P.S. For that Saturday-night snack or Sunday night's meal.

SPINACH-FILLED CREPES
One of a kind

About 20 crepes

CREPES
2 cups flour
½ tsp. salt
4 eggs
1 cup milk
1 cup cold water
50–60 grams (¼ cup) butter,
melted

FILLING
2 cups cheddar cheese
*2 cups medium **White Sauce***
800 grams (1½ lbs.) spinach, cooked,
drained and chopped
1 onion, chopped
salt and pepper to taste
2 tbsp. pine nuts

Preheat oven 350° F, 180° C. Prepare crepes according to directions in **Fish-Filled Crêpes** (see index).
FILLING: Stir cheddar cheese into White Sauce over low flame until cheese melts.

In bowl mix together spinach, half the Sauce, onion, salt, pepper and pine nuts.

Place about 1 tablespoon of Filling down center of each crêpe and roll up. Arrange crêpes side by side in greased shallow baking pan. Pour rest of Sauce over crêpes and bake in medium heat 15–20 minutes (until top browns).

P.S. It's a meal in itself or a side dish.

EGG ROLLS (Chinese Crêpes)
Going Chinese

About 18 egg rolls
Food processor comes in handy

CREPES
2 cups flour
½ tsp. salt
2 eggs, beaten
2¼ cups water
1 tsp. oil

FILLING
1 cup cooked chicken breast, shredded
½ tsp. salt
¼ tsp. pepper

1 tsp. sugar
1 tsp. cornflour
2 tbsp. soy sauce
2 tbsp. oil
2 cups cabbage, finely grated
2 cups bean sprouts
2 scallions, chopped
1 onion, thinly sliced
¼ cup canned bamboo shoots
1 carrot, grated
2 tbsp. almonds, blanched and slivered
1 egg, for brushing
*1 cup **Duck Sauce***

CREPES: In large bowl sift flour and salt.

In separate bowl mix together eggs, water and oil. Add egg mixture to flour and mix just until blended.

In frying pan heat a little oil; pour enough batter to make thin crêpe. (Tip pan to spread batter over entire surface). Fry on both sides. (Don't despair if the first crêpe is not too successful).

FILLING: In medium bowl mix together chicken pieces, salt, pepper, sugar, cornflour and soy sauce and set aside. *Note* – If not using chicken then mix cornflour, soy sauce & seasoning just before adding to vegetables.

In large frying pan heat oil, fry all the vegetables about 10 minutes. Add chicken mixture and almonds; fry a few minutes more; let cool.

Place a heaping tablespoon of Filling onto each crêpe and roll up. Brush seam with beaten egg.

In pan, fry crêpes on both sides (open side down first) and drain on paper toweling. Serve with Duck Sauce.

FISH-FILLED CREPES

A special treat!

About 20 crêpes
A bit of doing but well worth it

CREPES
2 cups flour
½ tsp. salt
4 eggs
1 cup cold milk
1 cup cold water
50–60 grams (¼ cup) butter,
   melted

FILLING
2 tbsp. butter
2 scallions, chopped
2½ cups fish filet,
   cooked, drained and flaked

1 tsp. salt
¼ tsp. pepper
½ cup dry vermouth

CHEESE – WINE SAUCE
2 tbsp. cornflour
2 tbsp. milk
⅓ cup dry vermouth
1½ cups sweet cream
½ tsp. salt
⅛ tsp. pepper
1 cup hard cheese, grated
2–3 tbsp. sesame seeds

CREPES: In large bowl sift flour and salt. In separate bowl beat eggs with milk and water; Add to flour mixture and mix together until just blended (mixture does not have to be very smooth). Add melted butter and mix slightly.

Grease frying pan with a little butter and heat. Pour enough batter to form thin crêpe about 18 cm (7″), tipping pan to spread batter over bottom and/or use back of spoon to spread batter.

Fry on both sides over medium heat until batter is used up.

FILLING: Melt butter in frying pan; add scallions and fry a few minutes, stirring continuously. Add fish and continue frying another minute. Add seasoning and vermouth and continue frying over low flame until most of the liquid evaporates (about 10 minutes) stirring occasionally.

Preheat oven 450° F, 220° C.

CHEESE – WINE SAUCE: Dissolve cornflour in milk. Pour vermouth into small saucepan, bring to boil and cook, uncovered over medium-low flame until liquid halves (about 5 minutes). Remove from flame. Add sweet cream, cornflour mixture and spices, stir and continue cooking, stirring continuously. Add ½ cup grated cheese and cook an additional 2 minutes. Leave about 10 minutes to settle.

Add half of Sauce to fish mixture and mix together. Place one level tablespoon of Filling down length of each crêpe and roll up. Place crêpes on lightly greased baking pan close together (if necessary use two baking pans). Spread rest of sauce over crêpes.

Sprinkle with additional ½ cup grated cheese and sesame seeds. Bake in hot oven about 20 minutes. Leave for about 10 minutes to settle.

FRENCH-STYLE CREPES SUZETTE   *Deliciously elegant*

About 15 crêpes

CREPES
2½ tbsp. sugar
¼ cup flour
½ tsp. salt
3 eggs
½ cup milk
1 tbsp. vanilla extract
1 tsp. butter, melted

SAUCE
100–125 grams (½ cup) butter
½ cup sugar
grated rind and juice of one lemon
grated rind and juice of one orange
¼ cup orange liqueur

CREPE: In bowl sift together sugar, flour and salt.

In separate bowl beat eggs together with milk and vanilla extract; add to flour mixture together with butter and mix until just blended (don't overbeat). Batter does not have to be smooth.

Grease 16 cm (6.5″) frying pan with butter and heat. Pour enough batter to make thin crêpes (about 2 tablespoons). Tip pan or use back of spoon so that batter spreads over bottom of pan. Over medium flame fry lightly on both sides (don't brown, crêpes should not be dry). Don't despair if the first crêpe is not successful.

SAUCE: In large saucepan melt butter; add sugar and heat, stirring constantly, until butter is melted. Add rinds, juices and liqueur and heat. Place each crêpe into sauce, fold in half and then in quarters. Serve warm with additional sauce.

PINEAPPLE CREPE SUZETTES Listed below are the ingredients for about 15 French-style Crêpes Suzettes.

¾ cup sugar
2½ tbsp. cornflour
2½ cups milk
3 egg yolks, slightly beaten

1 tsp. vanilla extract
1 small can cubed pineapple
  (drain and reserve 2 tbsp. syrup)
1 tbsp. cherry liqueur

In bowl, combine sugar and cornflour.

In pot bring milk to boiling point; pour over sugar mixture, mix and return to pot. Cook over low flame, stirring occasionally until it thickens.

In small bowl mix egg yolks with two tablespoons of the mixture, and add to pot. Stir mixture about two minutes until it thickens. Remove from flame and cool.

Add vanilla extract, syrup and liqueur. Fill crêpes and roll up.

Decorate with pineapple cubes.

CREPES DELUXE   *A fantastic full dessert!*

About 8 portions

12 cheese (or fruit) crêpes
2 cups cottage cheese
8 eggs
1 tbsp. brandy

2 cups sour cream
1 tsp. vanilla extract
½ cup sugar
¼ cup orange juice

Preheat oven 350° F, 180° C.
In baking pan arrange crêpes close together and cover with cottage cheese.
In blender blend the rest of the ingredients and pour over crêpes.
Bake in moderate oven about one hour. Serve warm.

CHEESE CREPES (BLINTZES) *Grandma's old-fashioned-recipe*

About 16 crêpes

FILLING
3 cups dry white cheese
2 eggs
½ cup sugar
½ cup matzo meal
½ tsp. vanilla extract
oil or butter for frying

CREPES
⅔ cup flour
pinch of salt
2 eggs, beaten
1 cup milk
1½ tbsp. oil or melted butter

sour cream

In mixer, mix together Filling ingredients and refrigerate until ready to use.

In large bowl sift flour and salt and make well in center.

In separate bowl beat the eggs with the milk; add to flour and mix with wooden spoon. Add oil or melted butter and mix just until blended. (The batter does not have to be very smooth. Small lumps will come out in frying).

Grease frying pan with oil or butter; heat over medium flame; pour enough batter to make a thin crêpe. Tilt pan or use back of spoon to spread batter. Brown one side only. (Don't despair if the first crêpe is not too successful). When crêpe starts coming away from sides remove from pan.

With brown side up, place 1 tablespoon Filling in each crêpe, and fold up like an envelope.

In large frying pan heat oil and fry crêpes on both sides (open side first). Drain on paper toweling.

Serve with sour cream.

Freezeable: best to freeze before frying filled blintzes.

PIES

and other dreamy desserts

Pies are my favorite company dessert. Serving a fruit pie à la mode (topped with ice cream) or a pie that has all the richness inside is always a special treat.

There's no end to the variety of desserts. Pies, cakes, ice creams, fruits – there are so many variations and so many different ingredients. Only your imagination can limit your creativity!

LEMON MERINGUE PIE

*Sharon loves the light,
delicate texture*

*Cooking time: about 15 minutes
Baking time: 12–15 minutes*

about ⅓ recipe **Plain Pastry Dough**

FILLING
2 cups boiling water
1¼ –1½ cups sugar
pinch of salt
½ cup sifted cornflour
2 tsp. lemon rind, grated

3 eggs, separated
⅓ –½ cup lemon juice
2 tsp. butter or margarine

Meringue *(see index)*

Prepare Plain Pastry dough according to directions.

On floured board roll out thin (about 0.3 cm, ⅛″); place in round pyrex pie pan (23 cm, 9″) and bake as directed for prebaked pie crust.

*Prepare all Filling ingredients before starting.

*Preparation of Filling requires complete attention.

In medium pot mix together sugar, salt, cornflour and lemon rind.

Add boiling water and with wooden spoon stir quickly until completely smooth. (It may be necessary to press cornflour against sides of pot).

Over medium-low flame cook 8–10 minutes, stirring constantly, until mixture is thick.

Mix 2 tablespoons of mixture into egg yolks and add to mixture in pot.

Add lemon juice and butter; mix and continue cooking another 5 minutes, stirring constantly.

Remove from flame and cool slightly.

Pour over baked pie crust.

Preheat oven 325° F, 165° C.

Prepare Meringue with egg whites and cover Filling – making sure Meringue touches circumference all around to prevent shrinkage. With spatula form peaks.

Bake in moderate-low oven 12–15 minutes until peaks are golden.

Let cool to room temperature – refrigerating too soon will cause tear drops to form on Meringue.

To cut at serving time – dip knife in hot water to keep Meringue from sticking.

P.S. Whenever there's a party, this is my specialty. Everyone has a piece or two of my Lemon Meringue Pie, before they survey what else is available.

APPLE PIE PERFECTION

Have enough for second helpings

About 8 portions
Food processor comes in handy
Baking time: 1 ¼ – 1 ½ hours

about ⅓ recipe **Sweet Cookie Dough** *(see index)*
or **Quick Sweet Pie Crust** *using desired* **Crumb Topping**

FILLING
6 cooking apples
2 tbsp. brandy
1 tbsp. cinnamon

¼ cup sugar
⅓ cup cornflakes crumbs
¼ cup walnuts, ground

Preheat oven 350° F, 180° C.
Prepare pastry dough according to directions.
Divide amount needed to ⅔ and ⅓.
On floured board roll ⅔ out to medium thickness (about 0.5 cm, ¼″) to cover bottom of 25 cm (10″) or 27 cm (11″) round pie plate with overlapping sides.
Peel core and chop apples (chopping is easy in food processor).
Transfer to large bowl; add rest of ingredients and mix until well blended.
Spread onto pie crust (apples may pile up, but will settle down during baking).
Roll out remaining ⅓ pastry dough and cover apples. Pierce with fork in several places.
Fold in circumference and flute edges as desired.
Bake in moderate over 1¼–1½ hours.

LATTICE TOP: For a change, try covering your pie with a lattice top. Roll out dough to medium thickness (about 0.5 cm, ¼″). With knife cut strips of about 1 cm (¾″) wide. Carefully place over apples in an under-over pattern.

BLUEBERRY FILLING: 4 cups blueberries, ⅓ cup sugar, 3 tablespoons flour, ½ teaspoon cinnamon and 1 teaspoon lemon juice. (Bake until crust is golden.)

FLUFFY CHOCOLATE PIE

Fantastic fluffity filling topped
with whipped cream

⅓–½ recipe **Plain Pastry Dough**

FILLING
1 cup sugar
⅓ cup cocoa powder
½ cup boiling water
1 tbsp. plain gelatin
¼ cup cold water
4 eggs, separated

2 tbsp. flaked coconut
2 tsp. vanilla extract
pinch of salt
1–1½ cup whipping cream
2 tbsp. powdered sugar
1 tsp. grated chocolate (garnish)

Prepare Pastry Dough according to directions for pre-baked pie crust using a 25 cm (10″) round pie plate.
In small saucepan dissolve cocoa powder in boiling water and leave for 10 minutes.
Dissolve gelatin in cold water about 5 minutes.

In mixer, at medium speed, beat egg yolks with ½ cup sugar about 3 minutes, until thickened.

Meanwhile add dissolved gelatin to cocoa mixture and over low flame cook a few minutes, stirring continuously.

Remove from heat; mix 2 tablespoons egg yolk mixture into cocoa and add cocoa mixture to egg yolks together with flaked coconut and one teaspoon vanilla extract. At low speed beat just until blended. Finish mixing with wooden spoon.

Cool quickly by placing bowl into a larger bowl of ice water for about 10 minutes (until mixture starts to thicken). During cooling time mix with wooden spoon a couple of times (to prevent top from hardening).

In separate mixer bowl, at high speed, beat egg whites with salt until stiff, but not dry. Slowly add ½ cup sugar and continue beating until meringue becomes firm.

With wooden spoon fold meringue into chocolate mixture and spread onto baked pie crust.

Refrigerate a few hours.

In mixer, at medium-high speed, beat whipping cream. When somewhat stiff, add powdered sugar and one teaspoon vanilla extract.

Continue beating until desired stiffness. (Caution: overbeating creates butter).

Spread over pie and decorate with grated chocolate.

P.S. For best whipping results: place bowl and beater in freezer for a short while before using and remove cream from refrigerator just before beating.

STRAWBERRY PIE   *Light and smooth*

About ½ recipe **Plain Pastry**

FILLING

1 tbsp. lemon juice	*2 tbsp. flaked coconut*
1½ cups strawberries, sliced	*4 eggs, separated*
1 cup sugar	*pinch of salt*
1 tsp. plain gelatin	*1 cup whipping cream*
½ cup boiling water	*2 tbsp. powdered sugar*
1 tbsp. brandy	*1 tsp. vanilla extract*

Prepare Pastry Dough according to directions for pre-baked pie crust using a 25 cm (10″) round pie plate.

In bowl mix together strawberries with ¾ cup sugar. Leave about 20 minutes.

Dissolve gelatin in cold water about 5 minutes.

In large bowl melt gelatin mixture in boiling water; add brandy, lemon juice, coconut and strawberries; mix and let cool.

In mixer, at medium speed, beat egg yolks until thick.

Lower speed; add strawberry mixture and beat just until blended.

In separate bowl, at high speed, beat egg whites with salt until stiff, but not dry. Add remaining ¼ cup sugar slowly and beat until Meringue is firm.

Fold strawberry mixture into Meringue.

In separate bowl, at medium-high speed, beat whipping cream. Add powdered sugar and vanilla extract when cream begins to stiffen and continue beating until firm. (Caution: overbeating will create butter.)

With wooden spoon fold whipped cream into strawberry mixture.

Pour Filling onto baked pie crust. Decorate as desired with strawberries and/or additional whipped cream. Refrigerate.

P.S. For best whipped cream results place bowl and beater in freezer for a short time before using and remove whipping cream from refrigerator just before whipping.

PEACHY PEACH PIE

My favorite
cool summer dessert à la mode

Baking time: 40–50 minutes

about ¼ recipe **Sweet Cookie Dough**

FILLING
7–8 peaches (about 1 kilo, 2 lbs.)	¼ tsp. cinnamon
1 tsp. lemon juice	2 tbsp. brandy
⅓ cup sugar	1 tbsp. butter or margarine
1–2 tbsp. flaked coconut	3 tbsp. flour

Prepare Sweet Pastry Dough according to directions.

On floured board roll out ¾ of the amount needed to medium thickness (about 0.5 cm, ¼″) and to 25 cm (10″) round. Place on round pie pan (23 cm, 9″) so that pastry dough overlaps on sides of pan.

Preheat oven 450° F, 230° C.

*Skin and slice peaches. Drain, if necessary. Add rest of Filling ingredients (except butter or margarine); mix and spread over crust.

Roll out rest of remaining pastry dough to medium thickness and cut into strips of 1½–2 cm (about ¾″).

Arrange strips into lattice top by an under-over procedure. Dot with butter or margarine. Press ends of strips gently onto circumference on bottom crust. Fold under bottom crust and flute edges.

Bake in hot oven 10 minutes; lower heat to 350° F (180° C) and continue baking 25–30 minutes more.

P.S. No matter how full everyone is they always have room for my Peach Pie, especially when I serve it à la mode (topped with ice cream)

SUGGESTION: Try it sometime with a **Crumb Topping** instead of lattice top crust.

* TO SKIN PEACHES: In large pot boil enough water to immerse all of the peaches. Place peaches in boiling water. Remove from flame and leave one to two minutes and drain. Rinse under cold water. Pierce skin gently with knife and peel off skin.

122   _Easy and Elegant_

FRUITY CHEESE PIE

Baking time: 35 minutes

*About ¼ recipe **Sweet Cookie Dough** OR*

COOKIE CRUST
100 grams (3 oz.) cookies crumbs
20 grams (1½ tbsp.) butter
1 tsp. cinnamon
2 tbsp. flaked coconut

FILLING
5 strawberries, sliced OR
  2 peaches, skinned and sliced

2 eggs
1 cup sugar
2 tbsp. flour
400–500 grams (2 cups) cottage cheese
1 cup sour cream
1 tbsp. vanilla extract
½ tsp. lemon rind,
  thinly grated
1 tbsp. flaked coconut

Preheat over 450°, 230°C.

DOUGH CRUST: Roll out pastry dough to medium thickness about 0.5 cm (¼") to fit 25 cm (10") deep dish pie plate, allowing dough to overlap on sides. Fold in circumference and flute edges as desired.

COOKIE CRUST: In bowl mix together Cookie Crust ingredients and pat down on bottom and sides of pie plate.

FILLING: Arrange fruit on top of crust.

In blender blend rest of Filling ingredients and pour gently over fruit.

Bake in hot oven 10 minutes. Lower heat to 350° F (180°C) and bake another 25 minutes. Open oven door and leave cake to cool in oven about one hour.

Other Desserts

HONEYED PEARS

1½ kilos (3 lbs.) small soft pears
¼ tsp. salt
¼ tsp. cinnamon (optional)

¼ – ⅓ cup honey
1 tbsp. lemon juice
¼ cup brandy

Wash pears and place in large pot. (If desired pare, core and halve pears.) Add 3 cups water. Bring to boil; add rest of ingredients and cook over low flame 2½ hours.

Serve as a dessert or as a side dish, or modify recipe to create a sauce as below.

HONEYED APPLE-PEAR SAUCE: Cut 1½ kilos (3 lbs.) cooking apples (Cortland, Granny Smith) into thick wedges. Place in pot. Fill with enough water to cover ¾ of apples. Add ¼ teaspoon salt and cook about 10 minutes. Add to pot ½ kilo (1 lb.) pears cut into wedges. Cook another 10 minutes. Add about ¼ cup honey. Allow to cool. Strain in food mill. Add ½ teaspoon cinnamon if desired.

P.S. For variety, add strawberries instead of pears.

CHOCOLATE MOUSSE
Chocolate chocolaty goodness

About 8 portions

200 grams (7 oz.)
   bittersweet chocolate chips
½ cup strong coffee liquid
1 tbsp. brandy

1 tbsp. vanilla extract
6 eggs, separated
2 tbsp. flaked coconut
almonds, blanched and chopped

In double boiler melt chocolate and coffee. Remove from flame; add brandy and vanilla extract and beat in mixer at medium speed.

Add egg yolks, one at a time, and coconut and beat until thick.

In separate bowl, at high speed, beat egg whites until stiff but not dry.

With wooden spoon fold chocolate mixture into egg whites.

Pour into individual serving bowls or one large serving bowl.

Sprinkle with chopped almonds.

Refrigerate.

PINEAPPLE MOLD
All whipped up!

About 6 portions
Prepare a few hours or a day in advance

1 cup canned crushed pineapple
2 packages lime gelatin

2 cups boiling water
1 cup whipping cream whipped
2 tbsp. flaked coconut

Drain pineapple (if crushed pineapple is not available, sliced pineapple may be crushed in blender).

Dissolve gelatin in boiling water and refrigerate until partially cooled. Fold in drained pineapple, coconut, whipped cream and coconut.

Pour into ring form pan or desired deep serving bowl. Refrigerate until firm.

TO REMOVE FROM PAN:

Method I: Go around mold with knife about 2 cm (¾″) deep. Prepare a larger bowl with very hot water and immerse mold for about 2 seconds (be careful water does not overflow into jello mold). Immediately place serving platter over mold and invert mold with platter. If mold does not fall onto platter, tap top of mold a few times. Refrigerate immediately.

Method II: Go around circumference of mold with knife. Turn mold over onto serving platter; wet a cotton towel with very hot water and cover mold a few seconds. Process may have to be done a second time before mold falls onto platter. Refrigerate immediately.

FROZEN MOCHA MOUSSE

For very special occasions

16–18 portions
Prepare a few hours or a day in advance

⅔ cup coffee liqueur
About 200 grams (½ lb.)
    lady finger cookies
3 tbsp. instant coffee powder
½ cup boiling water
400 grams (1 lb.)
    bittersweet chocolate, cut up

3 eggs, separated
½ cup sugar
2 tsp. vanilla extract
1 tbsp. coffee liqueur
2 cups whipping cream, whipped
2 tbsp. flaked coconut

Use 25 cm (10″) tube pan or a large spring form pan.

Place ⅔ cup coffee liqueur in small flat bowl; dip each lady finger gently and quickly in liqueur and line sides of pan. Dip and place a few broken lady fingers on bottom.

In bowl dissolve coffee powder in boiling water. Add chocolate and in double boiler melt over low flame.

In mixer, at medium speed, beat egg yolks, sugar, vanilla extract and one tablespoon coffee liqueur until thick.

Add melted chocolate and continue beating another few minutes. If desired, crush a few lady finger cookies and add to mixture.

In separate bowl, at high speed, beat egg whites until stiff but not dry.

Fold chocolate mixture into egg whites.

Fold in whipped cream and flaked coconut; place carefully in lady finger lined pan.

Freeze at least a few hour before serving.

P.S. Remove from deep freeze 10-15 minutes before serving. Remove from pan carefully as follows: Prepare serving platter. With long thin metal spatula go around lady fingers. Carefully remove center part of pan. Loosen mousse from center tube and bottom of pan. Place two wide metal spatulas under mousse and raise carefully.

CHOCOLATE CHIP ICE CREAM

Make yourself a sundae

8–10 portions

1 cup whipping cream
4 eggs, separated
½ cup sugar
1 tbsp. vanilla extract

½ tsp. instant coffee powder
    dissolved in 1 tbsp. water
100–125 grams (½ cup) chocolate chips
5–6 plain cookies, crushed

In mixer, at medium-high speed, beat whipping cream until firm. Refrigerate until ready to use.

In separate mixer bowl, at high speed, beat egg whites until almost stiff. Add sugar gradually; add vanilla extract, egg yolks and coffee and beat until stiff meringue is formed.

With wooden spoon fold whipped cream into egg white mixture.

Fold in chocolate chips and crushed cookies.

Place in individual serving bowls or one large serving bowl and freeze.

P.S. For that sundae — pour over chocolate syrup, sprinkle with chopped walnuts and top it with a maraschino cherry.

Note: For best whipped cream results place bowl and beater in freezer about 15 minutes before using. Refrigerate cream until ready to use.

SPUNKY FRUIT SALAD

My favorite winter fruit salad

About 12 portions
Preferable to prepare one day in advance

2 grapefruit
2 oranges
1 apple
2 pears
2 bananas
2 persimmons, if available
2 kiwi fruit, if available

5 dates
1 cup sliced strawberries
2 tbsp. raisins
2 tbsp. frozen orange and apple juice
  concentrate
⅓ cup Curacao or fruit liqueur
¼ cup sweet red wine
chopped almonds or walnuts

In large bowl cut up grapefruit and oranges by peeling and cutting segments in between membranes. Squeeze out juice or orange only and discard membranes.

Cut up rest of fruit and add together with raisins, coconut, juices, liqueur and wine and toss. Refrigerate overnight.

TO SERVE: place in individual fruit bowls, or sherbet glasses, and sprinkle with almonds or walnuts. Or serve in large bowl as part of buffet.

P.S. If you fancy to be fancy, top each serving with whipped cream or ice cream, or dress with a combination of 1 cup sour cream, 3 tablespoons maple syrup and a pinch of salt.

COCONUT CREAM FRUIT SALAD

Delicious summer refreshment

About 10 portions

1 melon, cut up
400 grams (¾ lb.) seedless grapes
3 peaches, cut up
2 bananas, sliced
4 apricots, cut up

TOPPING
1½ cups sour cream
¼ cup apricot jam
½ cup chopped walnuts
⅓ cup coconut, flaked

SPRINKLE: ¼ cup chopped almonds

In large bowl mix fruit and place in individual serving bowls.

In separate bowl mix together Topping ingredients and place about 2 tablespoons on each fruit salad. Sprinkle with almonds.

Serve chilled. Place additional Topping in center of table for extra helpings.

CREAM PUFFS

Deliciously light

32 cream puffs
Baking time: about 35 minutes

1 cup flour
½ tsp. salt
100–125 grams (½ cup) margarine,
  room temperature
1 cup boiling water

4 eggs
Lemon Cream Puff Filling (below)
  or whipped cream

Chocolate Glaze

Preheat oven 425° F, 220° C.

In bowl sift flour and salt and set aside.

In medium saucepan melt margarine in boiling water over low flame; add flour mixture and stir until batter leaves sides of pan. Remove from flame and cool slightly.

Transfer batter to mixer bowl and beat, at medium speed, about one minute. Add eggs, one at a time, and beat a few minutes more until batter is smooth.

Drop full teaspoons of batter onto greased cookie sheet, allowing space for spreading. Each cream puff should come to a point on top.

Bake in hot oven about 35 minutes.

Remove from pan and let cool.

Cut off about ⅓ from the top; fill each bottom part with a little Lemon Cream Puff Filling or whipped cream and cover with upper part.

Dip bottom part of cream puff in Chocolate Glaze and leave on waxed paper to harden.

LEMON CREAM PUFF FILLING   *Zesty and Delicious*

¾ cup flour	3 eggs, slightly beaten
¾ cup sugar	2 tbsp. flaked coconut
pinch of salt	2 tsp. lemon extract

In medium saucepan sift flour, sugar and salt; add eggs and cook over low flame, stirring continuously, until smooth.

Cook a few minutes more. Remove from flame; add coconut and lemon extract; stir and let cool.

SWEET RICE PUDDING   *A delicious no-cake dessert*

About 6 portions
Cooking & baking time: about 1 hour

¾ cup white rice	½ cup sugar
2 cups water	1 tsp. vanilla extract
1 tbsp. butter	2 tbsp. apricot jam
2¼ cups milk	¼ cup raisins
3 eggs, slightly beaten	½ tsp. cinnamon

Preheat oven 350°F, 180°C.

Rinse rice in cold water and drain. Cook in two cups water and one tablespoon butter about 20 minutes. Add milk and bring to boil.

Lower flame and cook over medium-low flame about 5 minutes, stirring continuously.

In blender blend rest of ingredients except raisins and cinnamon.

Add blended mixture slowly to rice, stirring continuously. Add raisins and mix together.

Spread mixture in large flat baking pan and sprinkle with cinnamon.

Place pan in large baking pan filled with water about 1–2 cm (½–¾") depth and bake in moderate oven 40 minutes.

Serve warm or cold.

CAKES *with Character*

Love for cakes, pies and cookies is international. Wherever you go, someone has a sweet tooth. The Viennese are known for the richness of their whipped cream; the Greeks love their sweet, sticky pastries.

I prefer cakes with a distinctive taste. A good cake can stand on its own without frosting. It seems that no matter how much is eaten beforehand, everyone has room for a piece of my cakes (or two pieces). When I don't serve a pie as a company dessert, I usually serve a cheese cake, yeast cake or just a good-tasting batter cake with fruit — sliced or in individual fruit salads — and cookies on the side.

Glazes and frostings are added for extra taste and to fancy it up. Frostings can give the artist in you a chance to emerge — so plan to be creative.

Another big plus for cakes is that, in general, they are freezeable. But there's nothing like a fresh piece of cake.

TIPS

- Before starting, prepare all the ingredients
- Don't play around with the recipe too much and don't cut corners
- If using a different size pan than indicated, adjust timing
- Always preheat oven unless otherwise indicated
- Butter, margarine and eggs should be at room temperature
- For basic batter cakes don't overbeat batter after adding flour
- Grease pans with butter or margarine
- Sprinkle a little flour on greased cake pan, shake around bottom and sides and discard excess (use cocoa powder for chocolate cakes)
- Bake immediately upon preparing batter unless otherwise indicated
- Place baking pan in center of oven without touching sides
- Don't depend on exact indicated time only, for batter cakes; test doneness by inserting a toothpick; it should come out clean
- Try not to open oven door during first third of baking time
- Cool cake completely before storing

(See Hints Section for other tips)

CINNAMON-NUT COFFEE CAKE

One of my basics

Baking time: about 1 hour

FILLING
¼ cup sugar
1 tbsp. cinnamon
½ cup walnuts, ground
2 tbsp. flaked coconut
2 tbsp. raisins

BATTER
3 cups flour

4 tsp. baking powder
pinch of salt
2 tbsp. flaked coconut
1¾ cup sugar
1 cup oil
4 eggs
1½ tsp. vanilla extract
¾ cup orange juice
1 tbsp. lemon juice

Preheat oven 350° F, 180° C.

In small bowl mix together Filling ingredients (except raisins) and set aside.

In separate bowl sift together flour, baking powder and salt; add coconut and set aside.

In mixer at medium speed beat sugar and oil. Add eggs, one at a time, and vanilla extract. Continue beating a few minutes until thickened.

Lower speed to lowest; add flour mixture alternately with juice, starting and ending with flour. Beat just until last of flour is added. With wooden spoon, continue mixing just until blended.

Pour ⅔ of the batter into a 10″ tube pan; sprinkle with ⅔ Filling and all of the raisins. Add rest of batter and sprinkle with remaining Filling mixture.

Bake in moderate oven about 1 hour.

CRUMBLY COFFEE CAKE

Crumbly goodness

Baking time: about 50 minutes

FILLING
1 tbsp. flaked coconut
2 tsp. cinnamon
¼ cup sugar
¼ cup walnuts, ground
2 tbsp. raisins

BATTER
2 cups flour
2 tsp. baking powder
pinch of salt
2 tbsp. flaked coconut
100–125 grams (½ cup) butter or margarine,
    room temperature
1 cup sugar
3 eggs
1 tsp. vanilla extract
½ cup orange juice

Preheat oven 350° F, 180° C.

In small bowl, mix together Filling ingredients (except raisins) and set aside.

In bowl sift together flour, baking powder and salt. Add coconut and set aside.

In mixer, at medium speed, beat butter or margarine and sugar. Add eggs, one at a time, and vanilla extract and continue beating a few minutes until thickened.

Lower speed to lowest; add flour alternately with juice and continue beating just until last of flour is added. With wooden spoon continue mixing just until blended.

Pour ⅔ of batter into greased square pan, 23 cm (9″), sprinkle with ⅔ Filling and raisins; add rest of batter and sprinkle with remaining Filling.

Bake in moderate oven about 50 minutes.

MOCHA OATMEAL CAKE

Healthful and still delicious

Baking time: about 50 minutes

1 cup oatmeal
2 tbsp. instant coffee powder
1⅓ cups boiling water
2 cups flour
1¼ tsp. baking soda
pinch of salt
3 tbsp. cocoa powder

¼ cup flaked coconut
150−190 grams (¾ cup) butter OR
   margarine, room temp.
1 cup regular sugar
1 cup brown sugar
2 eggs
2 tsp. vanilla extract

Preheat oven 350° F, 180° C.

In medium bowl mix oatmeal with coffee powder, which has been dissolved into boiling water. Cover with cotton towel and leave about 20 minutes.

Meanwhile, in separate bowl, sift flour, baking soda, salt and cocoa powder. Add coconut and set aside.

In mixer, at medium speed, beat butter or margarine and sugars about 1 minute. Add eggs, one at a time, and vanilla extract and continue beating about 5 minutes until thickened.

Lower speed to lowest; add oatmeal mixture and beat about one minute; add flour mixture and beat just until last of flour is added. With wooden spoon continue mixing just until blended.

Pour into greased 25 cm (10″) tube pan or bundt pan and bake in moderate oven about 50 minutes.

P.S. The cake is firm and chewy.

CINNAMON BUNS

*There are few things as good
as a fresh yeast cake*

Baking Time: about 25 minutes

½ recipe **Sweet Yeast Dough**

FILLING
½ cup sugar
2 tsp. cinnamon
¼ cup walnuts, ground

2 tbsp. flaked coconut
2 tbsp. raisins
50−60 grams (¼ cup) butter, melted
¼ cup milk

Prepare Sweet Yeast Dough according to recipe.

Preheat oven 375° F, 190° C.

In small bowl mix together sugar, cinnamon, walnuts, coconut and raisins; reserving ¼ cup for topping.

Roll out yeast dough into medium thick rectangle (about 0.5 cm, ¼″); brush with melted butter; spread over with walnut mixture and roll up.

Slice roll into 2.5 cm (1″) slices and place, cut side up, in greased center-ringed spring form pan or any flat baking pan, leaving room for spreading.

Cover with slightly damp cotton towel and leave to rise about ½ hour.

Brush top with milk and sprinkle with remaining walnut mixture.

Bake in moderate-high oven about 25 minutes.

SOUR CREAM COFFEE CAKE

I double the recipe since it's eaten before it has time to cool

Baking time: about 50 minutes

TOPPING
3 tbsp. sugar
1 tsp. cinnamon
¼ cup walnuts, finely ground
2 tbsp. flaked coconut
2 tbsp. raisins

1 tart apple, grated, optional

BATTER
1½ cups flour
2 tsp. baking powder
2 tbsp. flaked coconut
1 cup sour cream
1 tsp. baking soda
1 tsp. vanilla extract
100–125 grams (½ cup) butter, room temperature
¾ cup sugar
1 egg

Preheat oven 350° F, 180° C.

In small bowl mix together Topping ingredients (except raisins); set aside.

In separate bowl sift flour, baking powder and salt; add coconut and set aside.

In small bowl mix together sour cream, baking soda and vanilla extract and set aside.

In mixer at medium speed beat butter and sugar; add egg and continue beating a few minutes until thickened.

Lower speed to lowest; add flour alternately with sour cream mixture (starting and ending with flour). Beat just until last of flour is added. With wooden spoon continue mixing just until blended.

Pour ½ of batter into small greased spring form pan (23 cm, 9″). Squeeze water out of apple and sprinkle over batter; sprinkle with ⅔ of Topping and all of the raisins. Spread rest of batter on top and sprinkle with remaining Topping.

Bake in moderate oven about 50 minutes.

CRUMBLY SOUR CREAM COFFEE CAKE

Its the greatest!

Baking time: 40–50 minutes

TOPPING
¾ cup brown sugar
2 tbsp. butter, room temperature
3 tbsp. flour
1 tsp. cinnamon
1 tbsp. flaked coconut

BATTER
2¼ cups flour
1 tsp. baking powder
1 tsp. baking soda
200–250 grams (1 cup) butter, room temperature
1 cup sugar
3 eggs
1 tsp. vanilla extract
1 cup sour cream

Preheat oven 350° F, 180° C.

In bowl or food processor, mix together Topping ingredients and set aside.

In separate bowl sift flour, baking powder and baking soda; add coconut and set aside.

In mixer, at medium speed, beat butter and sugar; add eggs and vanilla extract and beat a few minutes until thickened.

Lower speed to lowest; add flour mixture alternately with sour cream (starting and ending with flour). Beat just until last of flour is added. With wooden spoon continue mixing just until blended.

Pour batter into small greased spring form pan (23 cm, 9″).

Sprinkle with Topping and bake in moderate oven 40–50 minutes.

CHOCOLATE NUT YEAST BUNS

The topping keeps it deliciously moist

24 buns
Baking time: 50 minutes
With dough hook it's no more work than any other cake

FILLING
200–250 grams (1 cup) butter,
  room temperature
2 tbsp. cocoa powder
1 tsp. coffee powder
¼ cup brown sugar
¼ cup regular sugar
1 cup walnuts, ground
¼ cup flaked coconut
⅓ cup raisins
4 tsp. cinnamon

DOUGH
30 grams (1 oz.) fresh yeast
1 cup lukewarm milk
About 5 cups flour
200–250 grams (1 cup) butter,
  room temperature
1 egg
1 tsp. vanilla extract
pinch of salt
½ cup sugar

TOPPING
1 cup milk
1 cup sugar
1 tsp. vanilla extract

In bowl or food processor mix together Filling ingredients; set aside.

Dissolve yeast in milk 5–10 minutes to soften.

In large bowl sift flour; make well in center and add yeast mixture, butter, egg, vanilla extract, salt and sugar. Knead together to form dough; transfer to floured board and knead about 8 minutes, until smooth and satiny. (Process may be done in mixer with dough hook; read instructions How To).

Place dough in oiled bowl (large enough to allow for rising); turn over once so that both sides are oiled; cover with cotton towel and leave in warm spot for 2 hours. Punch down and leave another 2 hours. On wooden board knead a few seconds; divide dough in half and roll out each piece thick to 0.75 cm (½″) thickness. Spread half of Filling on each piece of dough and roll up.

Grease a large baking pan or two smaller ones (not a spring form or tube), large enough to allow for spreading. Cut each roll into 3 cm (1¼″) slices (making 24 buns all together) and place, open side up in baking pan, leaving a little space between each one for spreading.

Cover and leave in warm spot for about 20 minutes.

Preheat oven 350° F, 180° C (10 minutes before using).

Bake in moderate oven about 50 minutes.

Prepare Topping just as cake is ready to come out of the oven by bringing the milk and sugar to a boil over medium-low heat; remove from flame and add vanilla extract.

Pour Topping gently over cake immediately upon removal from oven.

SWEDISH TEA RING

A beautiful form—and delicious cake

Baking time: about 30 minutes

½ recipe **Sweet Yeast Dough**

FILLING
2 tbsp. sugar
1 tbsp. cinnamon
¼ cup walnuts, ground
2 tbsp. flaked coconut

2 tbsp. raisins
3 tbsp. butter, melted

Vanilla Glaze
½ tsp. almond extract
¼ cup almonds, cut up

Prepare Sweet Yeast Dough according to directions.

Preheat oven 375° F, 190° C.

In small bowl mix together sugar, cinnamon, walnuts, coconut and raisins and set aside.

On floured board roll out pastry dough to medium thickness about 0.5 cm (¼″). Brush with melted butter; sprinkle with sugar-walnut mixture; roll up; place on greased cookie sheet and form round ring.

With scissors make deep cuts in ring about 2.5 cm (1″) apart. Turn ring slightly on its side outwardly; cover with cotton towel and let rise about ½ hour.

Bake in moderate-high oven about 30 minutes.

Prepare Vanilla Glaze with the addition of almond extract. Spread Glaze over cake while cake is still warm and sprinkle with almonds.

FILLED ROLLED CAKE

Besides cookies, this is great to keep in the freezer for those unexpected times

Baking time: 30–40 minutes

1 recipe **Sweet Cookie Dough**

FILLING
1 cup walnuts, ground
¼ cup sugar

1 tbsp. cinnamon
2 tbsp. flaked coconut
½ cup raisins

4 tbsp. dark fruit jam

Prepare dough according to directions.

Preheat oven 350° F, 180° C.

In small bowl mix together Filling ingredients.

Divide dough into four pieces.

On floured board roll out each piece to medium, about 0.5 cm (¼″), thickness; spread 1 tablespoon jam on each piece and sprinkle ¼ of the Filling.

Carefully roll up and place on 2 greased cookie sheets. With sharp knife slit top of rolls 2 cm (¾″) apart.

Bake in moderate oven 30–40 minutes, until golden brown.

RICH MARBLE CAKE

Black and white—and eaten all over

Baking time: about 1 hour

MARBLE
¼ cup sugar
¼ cup cocoa powder
¼ cup boiling water
1 tsp. vanilla extract

BATTER
3½ cups flour
3½ tsp. baking powder
pinch of salt

¼ cup flaked coconut
1¾ cup sugar
100–125 grams (½ cup) margarine,
   room temperature
½ cup oil
4 eggs
1 tsp. vanilla extract
½–1 tsp. almond extract
1 cup orange juice
1 tbsp. lemon juice

Preheat oven 350° F, 180° C.

In small bowl mix together Marble ingredients and refrigerate.

In bowl sift flour, baking powder and salt; add coconut and set aside.

In mixer, at medium speed, beat sugar, margarine and oil; add eggs, one at a time, vanilla and almond extract. Continue beating a few minutes until mixture thickens.

Lower speed to lowest; add flour mixture alternately with juices (starting and ending with flour) and beat just until last of flour is added. With wooden spoon continue mixing just until blended.

Mix ½ cup batter into Marble mixture.

Pour batter into greased 25 cm (10″) tube pan or bundt pan; pour over marble mixture and with knife swerve Marble through batter by forming figure eights.

Bake in moderate oven about 1 hour.

P.S.   If desired, frost with **Glaze** or **Frosting** (see Icings).

MARBLE CAKE

*I usually double the recipe—
It's a handy cake to have in the freezer*

2 cups flour
pinch of salt
3 tsp. baking powder
2 tbsp. flaked coconut
⅔ cup oil
1⅓ cup sugar

3 eggs
1½ tsp. vanilla extract
¼ tsp. almond extract
⅔ cup orange juice
1 tbsp. lemon juice
3 tbsp. cocoa powder

Preheat oven 350° F, 180° C.

In bowl sift flour, baking powder and salt; add coconut and set aside.

In mixer, at medium speed, beat oil and sugar about ½ minute; add eggs, one at a time; vanilla and almond extracts. Continue beating a few minutes until mixture thickens.

Lower speed to lowest; add flour mixture alternately with juices (starting and ending with flour). Beat just until last of flour is added. With wooden spoon continue mixing until just blended.

Pour ¾ batter into greased loaf pan.

Form Marble by adding cocoa powder to remaining batter and mix.

Pour Marble over white batter and with knife swerve through batter by forming figure eights.

Bake in moderate oven about 1 hour.

Cake is done when toothpick, inserted, comes out dry.

P.S. Sometimes I double the recipe, leave out the cocoa and put in a little less sugar. Of course, then it's not a Marble Cake but. . . it's delicious.

MARBLE CHIFFON CAKE

Light and airy,
melts in your mouth

Baking time: 65–70 minutes

MARBLE
¼ cup cocoa powder
¼ cup sugar
2 tbsp. flaked coconut
2 tsp. vanilla extract
¼ cup boiling water

BATTER
2¼ cups flour
4 tsp. baking powder
1¾ cup sugar
pinch of salt
½ cup oil
5 eggs yolks
¾ cup cold water
7 eggs whites
½ tsp. cream of tartar (optional)

Preheat oven 325° F, 165° C.

In small bowl mix together Marble ingredients and refrigerate.

In large bowl sift flour, baking powder, sugar and salt.

Make well in center; pour in oil, egg yolks and water and with mix wooden spoon.

In mixer, at high speed, beat egg whites with cream of tartar until stiff but not dry. Fold batter into egg whites. Mix about ¼ of batter into Marble mixture.

Pour ⅔ of remaining batter into ungreased 25 cm (10″) tube pan; pour Marble mixture over and with knife gently swerve through batter by forming figure eights. Add remaining batter.

Bake in moderate-low oven 55 minutes; increase heat to 350° F, 180° C, and bake 10–15 minutes longer.

Remove from oven; turn over onto bottle and leave until cooled (this will prevent sagging). Remove from bottle and turn upright. With long thin metal spatula go around sides of tube pan; remove center of pan; with spatula go around center tube and bottom. Prepare cake plate; with two wide metal spatulas gently raise cake and place on cake plate.

P.S. Sometimes I use 6 eggs, separated, and it comes out fine.

LEMON CHIFFON CAKE

Fluffily light

Baking time: 65–70 minutes

2¼ cups flour
1½ cups sugar
4 tsp. baking powder
pinch of salt
2 tbsp. flaked coconut
½ cup oil
6 eggs, separated

½ cup cold water
¼ cup lemon juice
2 tsp. vanilla extract
2 tsp. grated lemon rind
½ tsp. cream of tartar, optional
Coconut Lemon Filling, optional
flaked coconut

Preheat oven 325° F, 165° C.

In large bowl sift flour, sugar, baking powder and salt. Add coconut; make well in center; add oil, egg yolks, water, lemon juice, vanilla extract and lemon rind and with wooden spoon stir together.

In mixer, at high speed, start beating egg whites; add cream of tartar and continue beating until stiff, but not dry. Fold batter into egg whites.

Pour into *ungreased* tube pan (25 cm, 10″) and bake in moderate-low oven 55 minutes. Increase heat to moderate (350 F°, 180° C) and bake 10–15 minutes more.

Turn cake over onto bottle neck and allow to cool completely. Remove from bottle; turn right side up; remove cake from pan by loosening sides with long thin metal spatula; remove center of pan and go around tube and bottom.

Prepare cake plate and with two wide spatulas lift cake and place on cake plate.

Filling and Topping: Cut cake in half widthwise and fill with ¼–⅓ Coconut Lemon Filling. Place top half of cake over Filling and ice top and sides with remaining Icing. Sprinkle with extra flaked coconut.

ORANGE-DATE CAKE

What a great combination!

Baking time: 25–30 minutes

BROWNY TOPPING
1 tbsp. margarine, melted
2 tsp. cinnamon
½ cup walnuts, ground
1 tbsp. flaked coconut
½ cup brown sugar

BATTER
2 cups flour
2 tsp. baking powder

pinch of salt
2 tbsp. flaked coconut
½ cup sugar
½ cup oil
2 eggs
2 tsp. grated orange rind
1 tsp. vanilla extract
¼ tsp. almond extract
½ cup orange juice
1 cup dates, cut up
1–2 mashed bananas

Preheat oven 375° F, 180° C.

In bowl, mix together Browny Topping ingredients and set aside.

In bowl sift flour, baking powder and salt; add coconut and set aside.

In mixer, at medium speed, beat sugar and oil; add eggs, one at a time, orange rind and vanilla extract. Continue beating a few minutes, until thickened.

Lower speed to lowest and add bananas. Add flour alternately with orange juice (starting and ending with flour). Beat just until last of flour is added. With wooden spoon, fold in dates.

Pour batter into greased baking pan 24x14x3 cm (9½x5½x1″).

Sprinkle with Topping and bake in moderate oven 25–30 minutes.

Serve warm or cooled.

P.S. Doubling the recipe is twice as good. Use 33x22x5 cm (13x9x1½″) baking pan. Bake 40–45 minutes.

ORANGE-GLAZED CAKE

Glazes give extra deliciousness

Baking time: about 1 hour

3 cups flour
4 tsp. baking powder
200–250 grams (1 cup) butter or
    margarine, room temperature
1¾ cups sugar
4 eggs, separated
2 tsp. lemon rind, thinly grated
2 tsp. vanilla extract

¼ cup lemon juice
2 tbsp. flaked coconut

ORANGE GLAZE
1 cup powdered sugar
2 tbsp. orange juice
1 tsp. lemon juice
1 tbsp. flaked coconut

Preheat oven 350° F, 180° C.

In bowl sift flour, baking powder and salt and set aside.

In mixer, at medium speed, beat butter or margarine and sugar ½ minute. Add egg yolks, lemon rind and vanilla extract and continue beating about 5 minutes until thickened. Lower speed to lowest; add flour alternately with juice (starting and ending with flour) and beat just until last of flour is added.

Add coconut and continue mixing with wooden spoon just until blended.

In mixer, at high speed, beat egg whites until stiff but not dry. Fold batter into egg whites.

Pour into 23 cm (9″) greased spring form pan and bake in moderate oven about 1 hour.

Leave cake in pan 20–30 minutes. Remove outer ring of pan. If possible remove cake from bottom with two wide metal spatulas.

In small bowl mix together Glaze ingredients and spread over cake while still warm. (Sometimes Glazes can be poured gently over cake straight from bowl).

APPLE CAKE

Everyone asks for the recipe

Baking time: about 1 hour
Food processor makes it easier

FILLING
5–6 tart apples
2 tsp. cinnamon
2 tbsp. flaked coconut
¼ cup sugar

BATTER
3 cups flour

4 tsp. baking powder
pinch of salt
¼ cup flaked coconut
2 cups sugar
1 cup oil
4 eggs
2 tsp. vanilla extract
¼ cup orange juice
1 tbsp. lemon juice

FILLING: Peel, core and slice apples (slicing can be done in food processor). Place in large bowl and mix together with sugar, cinnamon and coconut and set aside.

Preheat oven 350° F, 180° C.

In bowl sift flour, baking powder and salt; add coconut and set side.

In mixer, at medium speed, beat sugar and oil about ½ minute; add eggs, one at a time and vanilla extract and continue beating about 5 minutes, until thickened.

Lower speed to lowest; add flour alternately with juices and beat just until last of flour is added. With wooden spoon continue mixing just until blended.

Spread half of batter in large, greased, rectangular baking pan 35x25x5 cm (13½x10x2″); spread apple mixture over batter and cover with remaining batter.

If desired, sprinkle top with **Rich Crumb Topping**.

Bake in moderate oven about 1 hour.

APPLE NUT CAKE

Moist and full of everything good

Baking time: about 1 hour
Food processor comes in handy

2 cups flour
1 tsp. baking soda
¼ cup flaked coconut
5 tart apples
1 tsp. cinnamon
1 cup oil

1½ cups sugar
3 eggs
1 tsp. vanilla extract
100 grams (3½ oz.)
   chocolate chips
½ cup walnuts, coarsely ground

Preheat oven 350° F, 180° C.

In bowl sift flour and baking soda; add coconut and set aside.

Peel, core and chop apples (chopping may be done in food processor). Place in large bowl; mix together with cinnamon and set aside.

In mixer, at medium speed, beat oil and sugar about 1 minute; add eggs, one at a time and vanilla extract and continue beating about 5 minutes until thickened. Lower speed to lowest; add flour and beat just until last of flour is added. With wooden spoon fold in apples, chocolate chips and walnuts. (Batter might be thick).

Pour batter into greased loaf pan 32x23x5 cm (12½x9x2″) or 25 cm (10″) tube pan and bake in moderate oven about 1 hour.

P.S. Chocolate chips can be made by cutting up bittersweet chocolate (freeze before cutting).

FLUFFY CHEESE CAKE

Who can resist?

Baking time: 1 hour

About 1 recipe **Cheese Cake Crust**

1 kilo (4 cups) cream cheese	*2 tbsp. lemon juice*
1¼ cups sugar	*2 cups milk*
3 eggs, separated	*3 tbsp. cornflour*
1 tsp. vanilla extract	

Preheat oven 350° F, 180° C.

Roll out dough thin (about 0.3 cm, ⅛″ thickness) and place on bottom and about ¼ up sides of 23–25 cm (9–10″) spring form pan. (Dough can be pushed into baking pan with fingers.)

Prebake crust about 10 minutes.

In mixer beat cheese, sugar, egg yolks, lemon juice, milk (which has been combined with cornflour) and vanilla extract until smooth.

In separate mixer bowl, at high speed, beat egg whites until stiff, but not dry. Fold cheese mixture into egg whites and pour over pie crust.

Bake in moderate oven one hour. Open oven door and leave cake to cool one to two hours.

Refrigerate. When cake is cool, remove from sides of pan.

P.S. You can make cookies out of leftover Pastry Dough.

CHEESY CHEESE CAKE

I love that cheesy flavor

Baking time: 1¼ hours

about 1 recipe **Cheese Cake Crust**

4 eggs	*2 tsp. vanilla extract*
1½ cups sugar	*1 tbsp. lemon rind, thinly grated*
500 grams (2 cups) cream cheese	*2 tbsp. lemon juice*
1½ cups cottage cheese	*1½ tbsp. flour*
	*see **Whipped Cream Topping for Cheese Cake***

Preheat oven 350° F, 180° C.

Prepare Crust dough and roll out thin (about 0.3 cm, ⅛″) to fit bottom and ¼ up sides of 23–25 cm (9–10″) spring form pan.

Prebake crust about 10 minutes and set aside.

In mixer, at medium speed, beat eggs; add sugar and beat until thickened. Lower speed; add rest of ingredients (except Whipped Cream Topping) and beat until smooth. Pour mixture over crust and bake in moderate oven 1¼ hours.

Open oven door and allow cake to cool about 1 hour.

Prepare Topping according to directions and pour gently over cooled cake. Refrigerate a few hours or overnight and then remove sides of pan.

P.S. You can make cookies out of left over pastry dough.

VARIATION: Sliced strawberries, apricots or skinned sliced peaches can be spread over crust before adding Filling. I love that fruity–cheesy flavor even more.

STRAWBERRY CHEESE CAKE
Light, fluffy and delicious

Baking time: 1 hour

About 1 recipe **Cheese Cake Crust** or ¼ recipe **Sweet Pastry Dough**

5 large strawberries, cut up	¼ cup flaked coconut
400–500 grams (2 cups) cream cheese	¼ cup cornflour
400–500 grams (2 cups) cottage cheese	4 eggs, separated
1 cup sour cream	1 tsp. vanilla extract
1⅓ cups sugar	½ tsp. lemon rind, thinly grated

Preheat oven 350° F, 180° C.

Prepare Pastry Dough according to directions. Use enough for bottom and ¼ up sides of 25 cm (10″) spring form pan. Cheese Cake Crust: can be spread into pan with fingers (prebake about 10 minutes) or Sweet Pastry Dough: roll out thin (about 0.3 cm, ⅛″) Spread strawberries over crust.

In mixer, at medium-low speed, beat cheeses, sour cream, sugar, coconut, cornflour, egg yolks, vanilla extract and lemon rind until smooth.

In separate mixer bowl, at high speed, beat egg whites until stiff but not dry. Fold cheese mixture into egg whites and carefully pour over strawberries.

Bake in moderate oven one hour. Open door and leave about 2 hours. Let cool (top may crack somewhat) and then refrigerate.

Remove spring form after cake is cold.

P.S. You can make cookies out of leftover pastry dough.

VARIATION: Instead of strawberries use apricots or skinned peaches.

P.S. You can make cookies out of leftover pastry dough.

SOUR CREAM-TOPPED CHEESE CAKE
A special treat

Baking time: 1 hour and 10 minutes

1 recipe **Cheese Cake Crust**

FILLING	1½ tbsp. flour
500 grams (2 cups) cream cheese	1 tsp. baking powder
1 cup sour cream	
1 cup sugar	TOPPING
3 eggs	2 cups sour cream
1 tsp. vanilla extract	⅓ cup sugar
2 tbsp. flaked coconut, optional	1 tsp. vanilla extract

Preheat oven 350° F, 180° C.

Prepare pie crust according to directions. Roll out thin (about 0.3 cm, ⅛″) and place on bottom and ¼ up sides of 25 cm (10″) spring form pan. Prebake crust about 10 minutes.

FILLING: In mixer at medium-low speed, beat all Filling ingredients until smooth. Pour over pie crust and bake in moderate oven 1 hour.

TOPPING: (Prepare just before pie is done.) In small bowl mix the ingredients together; carefully spoon over pie and continue baking another 10 minutes. Open oven door and leave about 2 hours.

Let cool and refrigerate. Remove spring form after pie is cold.

P.S. You can make cookies out of leftover pastry dough.

CHOCOLATE CHIP CAKE
A very special birthday cake

Baking time: 40–45 minutes

2 cups flour
4 tsp. baking powder
½ tsp. baking soda
pinch of salt
2 tbsp. flaked coconut
¼ cup regular sugar
1 cup brown sugar

100–125 grams (½ cup) butter or
margarine, room temperature
3 eggs
1½ tsp. vanilla extract
1½ cups milk or milk substitute
175 grams (6 oz.) chocolate chips
see Walnut Filling
and Chocolate Frosting

Preheat oven 350° F, 180° C.

In bowl sift flour, baking powder, baking soda and salt. Add coconut and set aside.

In mixer, at medium speed, beat sugars and butter or margarine. Add eggs, one at a time, and vanilla extract and continue beating about 5 minutes.

Lower speed to lowest; add flour mixture alternately with milk (starting and finishing with flour) and beat just until blended (don't overbeat).

With wooden spoon fold in chocolate chips.

Pour batter into 2 greased and floured round layer cake pans (23cm, 9″) and bake in moderate oven 40–45 minutes.

Let cakes cool in pan about 20 minutes. Remove from pans and let cool completely.

Place one layer on cake plate upside down.

Spread with Walnut Filling.

Place second layer on top (right side up).

Frost with Chocolate Frosting.

CHOCO-CHOCOLATE CAKE
A special frosty layer cake

Baking time: About 45 minutes

2¼ cups flour
1½ tsp. baking soda
pinch of salt
2 tbsp. flaked coconut
1½ cups sugar

100–125 grams (½ cup) and 1 tbsp.
margarine, room temperature
2 eggs
1 tsp. vanilla extract
½ cup cocoa powder
1¼ cups ice water

Preheat oven 350° F, 180° C.

In bowl sift flour, baking soda and salt; add coconut and set aside.

In mixer, at medium speed, beat sugar and margarine about 1 minute. Add eggs, one at a time, and vanilla extract and continue beating about 5 minutes until thickened.

Lower speed to lowest and add cocoa powder. Add flour alternately with water (starting and ending with flour); beat just until last of flour is added. With wooden spoon continue mixing until blended.

1: Spread batter into greased rectangular baking pan (32x23x5 cm, 13x9x3″) and bake in moderate oven about 45 minutes.

OR

2: Layer Cake – Spread batter into two round layer cake pans (23cm, 9″) and bake at 375° F, 190° C about 25 minutes.

Fill and frost with **White Frosting**. Decorating with sliced strawberries gives that extra special taste.

CHOCOLATE CHIP BANANA CAKE
I never mind having overripe bananas

Baking time: about 1 hour

4 cups flour
1 tsp. baking powder
1 tbsp. baking soda
pinch of salt
¼ cup flaked coconut
1 cup oil

2½ cups sugar
5 eggs
2 tsp. vanilla extract
6 ripe bananas, mashed
½ cup orange juice
1 tbsp. lemon juice
2 cups (400–500 grams) chocolate chips

In bowl sift flour, baking powder, baking soda and salt; add coconut and set aside.

In mixer, at medium speed, beat oil and sugar; add eggs, one at a time and vanilla extract and continue beating about 5 minutes until thickened.

Lower speed to lowest and add mashed bananas. Add flour alternately with juices (starting and ending with flour) and beat just until last of flour is added. With wooden spoon fold in chocolate chips.

Pour batter into 2 greased loaf pans 24x14x7 cm (9½x5½x2½″) and bake in moderate oven about one hour.

Cake can also be baked in 25 cm (10″) tube pan. Timing is about 2 hours.

P.S. Either buy ready-made chocolate chips or cut up bars of chocolate with sharp knife (freeze beforehand for easier cutting).

CHOCOLATE CHIP CUPCAKES
Not the usual

About 16 cupcakes
Baking time: about 25 minutes

TOPPING
½ cup brown sugar
1 egg
pinch of salt
1 cup chocolate chips
2 tbsp. flaked coconut
½ cup walnuts, ground
1 tsp. vanilla extract

BATTER
1 cup and 2 tbsp. flour
½ tsp. baking soda
2 tbsp. flaked coconut
100–125 grams (½ cup) butter or
  margarine, room temperature
⅓ cup regular sugar
⅓ cup brown sugar
1 tsp. vanilla extract
1 egg

Preheat oven 375° F, 190° C.

Line cupcake tins with paper liners.

TOPPING: In bowl mix together brown sugar, egg and salt; add chocolate chips, coconut, walnuts and vanilla extract; mix and set aside.

In separate bowl sift flour with baking soda and salt; add coconut and set aside.

In mixer, at medium speed, beat butter or margarine, sugars and vanilla extract. Add egg and continue beating until smooth and thickened.

Lower speed to lowest; add flour and mix just until last of flour is added. With wooden spoon continue mixing just until blended.

Pour batter into paper liners, ½ full.

Bake in moderate-high oven 10–12 minutes.

Remove from oven; pour 1 tablespoon Topping on each cupcake and continue baking another 15 minutes.

CHOCOLATE MOCHA CAKE

A moist chocolaty cake

Baking time: about 1 hour

3 cups flour
½ tsp. baking powder
pinch of salt
¼ cup flaked coconut
2 tbsp. coffee powder
1½ cups hot water
2½ cups sugar

¾ cup oil
3 eggs
2 tsp. vanilla extract
½ tsp. almond extract
¾ cup cocoa powder
1½ tsp. baking soda
¾ cup boiling water

Preheat oven 350° F, 180° C.

In bowl sift flour, baking powder and salt; add coconut and set aside.

Dissolve coffee powder in hot water and set aside.

In mixer, at medium speed, beat sugar and oil. Add eggs, one at a time and extracts and continue beating about 5 minutes until thickened.

Lower speed to lowest and add cocoa powder. Add coffee alternately with flour. Add baking soda dissolved in boiling water and beat just until blended. (Batter will be very "liquidy".)

Pour batter into large greased rectangular baking pan 35x25x5 cm (13½x10x2″) and bake in moderate oven about 1 hour. Test doneness with toothpick.

Cakes may be baked in two loaf pans; adjust timing.

P.S. For extra goodness frost with desired frosting.

CHOCOLATE DATE CAKE

Chocolate dates are delicious

Baking time: about 40 minutes

1½ tsp. instant coffee powder
1 cup boiling water
1 cup dates, cut up
1¾ cups flour
¾ tsp. baking soda
2 tbsp. cocoa powder
pinch of salt
2 tbsp. flaked coconut

50–60 grams (¼ cup) margarine,
   room temperature
1¼ cups sugar
2 eggs
1 tbsp. vanilla extract
100 grams (3½ oz.) chocolate chips
¼ cup walnuts, coarsely chopped

Preheat oven 350° F, 180° C.

In medium bowl dissolve coffee powder in boiling water; add dates; mix and let cool.

In bowl sift flour, baking soda, cocoa powder and salt; add coconut and set aside.

In mixer, at medium speed, beat margarine and sugar; add eggs, one at a time, and vanilla extract and continue beating a few minutes until thickened.

Lower speed to lowest and add date mixture. Add flour, spoon by spoon and mix just until last of flour is added. With wooden spoon fold in chocolate chips and walnuts.

Pour batter into greased square baking pan 28x28x4 cm (11x11x½″) and bake in moderate oven about 40 minutes.

P.S. If using other size pan adjust timing.

CHOCOLATE CREAM ROLL

For that special occasion

Baking time: 15–18 minutes

FILLING and FROSTING (for one cake)
or FILLING: (for two cakes)
2 eggs, separated
1 cup powdered sugar
¼ cup cocoa powder
1 tbsp. instant coffee powder
2 tbsp. flaked coconut
1 tsp. vanilla extract
200–250 grams (1 cup) margarine,
  room temperature

BATTER (one cake)
½ cup flour
1¼ tsp. baking powder
¼ cup cocoa powder
pinch of salt
2 tbsp. flaked coconut
4 eggs, separated
¾ cup sugar
1 tsp. vanilla extract
¼ cup cold water

FILLING: In mixer beat egg yolks with ¾ cup sugar. Add rest of ingredients, except egg whites, and beat until smooth.

In separate bowl at high speed beat egg whites until almost firm. While its beating, add ¼ cup sugar and beat a little more.

Preheat ovwn 350° F, 180° C.

Grease lipped cookie sheet; cover with waxed paper and grease. Set aside.

BATTER: In bowl sift flour, baking powder, cocoa powder and salt; add coconut and set aside.

In mixer, at medium speed, beat egg yolks, sugar and vanilla extract a few minutes until creamy.

Lower speed; add flour mixture alternately with water (starting and ending with flour) and beat until blended.

In separate mixer bowl, at high speed, beat egg whites until firm (but not dry). With wooden spoon, fold batter into egg whites.

Spread batter on waxed paper-lined cookie sheet and bake in moderate oven 15–18 minutes.

Meanwhile prepare two pieces of waxed paper sprinkled heavily with remaining powdered sugar. Remove cake from oven; leave about 2 minutes; go around sides with knife so that cake is not sticking to pan; turn pan over onto powdered waxed paper; remove pan and leave for about 2 minutes. Remove top waxed paper carefully; roll up with powdered waxed paper and leave ½ hour.

Unroll and fill with ½ of Filling; roll up without waxed paper and carefully transfer onto long serving plate.

Frost with remaining Filling (if desired) or prepare a second cake and fill with remaining Filling. Freeze at least a few hours. Remove from freezer about 10 minutes before serving.

VARIATION: Instead of Filling, spread cakes with ice cream (allowing ice cream to soften before spreading). Freeze immediately.

CRUMBLY WHIPPED CREAM CAKE

What can be better?

Baking time: about 55 minutes

3 cups flour
4 tsp. baking powder
pinch of salt
1½ cup sugar
2 tbsp. flaked coconut

100–125 grams (½ cup) butter or margarine,
  room temperature
½ cup oil
2 tsp. vanilla extract
1 cup whipping cream
3 eggs

Preheat over 350° F, 180° C.

In mixer bowl, sift flour, baking powder and salt; add sugar, coconut, butter or margarine, oil and vanilla extract. Beat ingredients until crumbly. Set aside ½ cup for Topping.

In separate bowl at medium-high speed, beat whipping cream until almost stiff; add eggs, one at a time; continue beating until firm. With wooden spoon fold crumbly mixture into whipped cream. (Batter will be thick).

Pour batter into greased 25 cm (10″) tube pan; sprinkle reserved ½ cup of crumbs on top and bake in moderate oven about 55 minutes.

When cooled remove from pan by going around sides with thin metal spatula; remove center and go around center tube and bottom; prepare cake plate; place two wide metal spatulas underneath; raise cake and place on plate.

STRAWBERRY SHORTCAKE

Better than strawberries and cream

Baking time: about 15 minutes

500 grams (1 lb.) strawberries
2 tbsp. sugar
¾ cup flour
pinch of salt
2 tbsp. flaked coconut

5 eggs, separated
¾ cup sugar
1 tsp. vanilla extract
4 tsp. powdered sugar
1–1½ cups whipping cream

Preheat oven 375° F, 190° C.

Grease lipped cookie sheet; cover with waxed paper and grease waxed paper. Set aside.

Set aside ¼ of the whole strawberries.

Slice remaining strawberries; place in bowl; add 2 tablespoons sugar; mix and set aside.

In bowl sift flour and salt; add coconut and set aside.

In mixer, at medium speed, beat egg yolks, sugar and ½ teaspoon vanilla extract until thickened. Lower speed to lowest; add flour and beat until last of flour is added. Continue mixing with wooden spoon.

In separate bowl, at high speed, beat egg whites until stiff, but not dry. Fold batter mixture into egg whites.

Pour batter onto cookie sheet.

Bake in moderate-high oven 15–20 minutes.

While cake is baking, sprinkle 2 tablespoons powdered sugar on cotton towel. Remove cake from oven and turn over onto powdered sugar. Remove waxed paper and let cool. Cut cake in half and place half on cake plate.

In mixer, at medium-high speed, beat whipping cream with ½ teaspoon vanilla extract and 2 tablespoons powdered sugar.

Spread half of the whipped cream over bottom cake. Sprinkle with sugared sliced strawberries. Place second half of cake on top; spread with remaining whipped cream and place whole strawberries on top.

To cover cake sides with whipped cream, use 1½ cups cream. For final touch, add extra sliced strawberries over cream.

P.S. For best whipped cream results make sure bowl, beater and cream are very cold.

SOUR CREAM-TOPPED CAKE
Ruven's favorite

Baking time: about 15 minutes

CAKE
200–250 grams (1 cup) butter
⅔ cup sugar
2 eggs
1 tsp. lemon rind,
    thinly grated
¼ cup flaked coconut
2¼ cups self-rising flour

SOUR CREAM TOPPING
150–190 grams (¾ cup) butter
¾–1 cup sugar
1 tsp. vanilla extract
3 cups sour cream
2 eggs
2 tbsp. flaked coconut

Preheat oven 350° F, 180° C.

In mixer, at medium speed, beat butter and sugar about 1 minute. Add eggs and lemon rind and continue beating about 3 minutes.

Lower speed to lowest; add coconut and flour slowly and beat just until last of flour is added. Continue mixing with wooden spoon just until blended.

Place one cup of batter into small greased baking dish (to be used for Crumb Topping). Pour rest of batter in large, flat greased rectangular baking pan.

Bake both batters in moderate oven – large one for 15 minutes (it should remain very light in color so as not to be dry) and small one for about 20 minutes until golden. Let cool.

Meanwhile in blender blend Topping ingredients until smooth.

Refrigerate until cake has cooled somewhat and then pour Topping over cake.

In small bowl crumble up small piece of cake and sprinkle over Sour Cream Topping.

Refrigerate overnight to allow for settling.

COCONUT-PINEAPPLE-TOPPED CAKE
Top of the line

Baking time: about 25 minutes

1½ cups flour
½ cup sugar
3 tsp. baking powder
pinch of salt
2 tbsp. flaked coconut
1 egg, slightly beaten
1¼ cups canned pineapple, drained
    and chopped, (reserving liquid)
½ cup canned pineapple syrup
¼ cup orange juice

¼ cup oil
1 tsp. vanilla extract

TOPPING
⅓ cup honey
50–60 grams (¼ cup) butter,
    room temperature
½ cup cornflakes crumbs
¼ cup flaked coconut

Preheat oven 400° F, 200° C.

In bowl sift flour, sugar, baking powder and salt. Add coconut and set aside.

In separate large bowl mix egg with pineapple syrup, orange juice, oil and vanilla extract. Add flour mixture and mix until blended.

Pour batter into greased square baking pan 28 cm (11″), or 23 cm (9″) spring form pan.

TOPPING: In mixer, at medium speed, beat honey and butter until thickened. Lower speed; add cornflakes crumbs, coconut and pineapple. Pour over batter and bake in moderate-high oven about 25 minutes.

VARIETY CAKE

3 cups flour	1¾ cups sugar
4 tsp. baking powder	4 eggs
pinch of salt	1½–2 tsp. vanilla extract
2 tbsp. flaked coconut	1 cup orange juice
200–250 grams (1 cup) butter or margarine, room temperature	1 tbsp. lemon juice

In bowl sift flour, baking powder and salt; add coconut and set aside.

In mixer, at medium speed, beat butter or margarine and sugar about ½ minute; add eggs, one at a time, and vanilla extract. Continue beating 4–5 minutes, until mixture thickens.

Lower speed to lowest; add flour mixture and orange juice alternately (starting and ending with flour), beating just until last of flour is added (overbeating will cause tough-textured cake). With wooden spoon continue mixing just until blended.

LOAF CAKE: Preheat oven 350° F, 180° C. Pour batter into greased and floured loaf pan. If desired, sprinkle with **Crumb Topping** (see index). Bake in moderate oven about 1 hour.

LAYER CAKE: Preheat oven 375° F, 190° C. Pour batter into two layer cake pans (23 cm, 9″) and bake in moderate-high oven about 30 minutes. Let cool. Place one layer upside down on cake plate; prepare desired **Chocolate Filling** or **Frosting**, spread about ¼ Chocolate Frosting on top. Place second layer right side up on top of bottom layer. Frost top and sides.

CUPCAKES: (Yield: about 28) Preheat oven 375° F, 180° C. Place paper liners in cupcake tins and fill ⅔ full with batter. Bake in moderate-high oven 20–25 minutes. Frost with desired glaze or frosting (see index); or for **Fast Chocolate Glaze** – place one square of bittersweet chocolate on each cupcake as soon as they come out of the oven. Leave for about 1 minute (allowing chocolate to melt), then spread over cupcake with thin metal spatula.

HONEY NUT CAKE

A honey of a cake

Baking time: about 45 minutes

3 cups flour	1 cup sugar
2 tsp. baking powder	½ cup oil
1 tsp. baking soda	4 eggs
pinch of salt	1 cup honey
½ tsp. cinnamon	2 tbsp. brandy
½ tsp. ginger	1 cup strong coffee, cooled
2 tbsp. flaked coconut	¼ cup walnuts, coarsely chopped

Preheat oven 350° F, 180° C.

In bowl sift flour, baking powder, baking soda, salt, cinnamon and ginger; add coconut and set aside.

In mixer, at medium speed, beat sugar and oil ½ minute; add eggs, one at a time, honey and brandy and continue beating about 5 minutes, until thickened. Lower speed to lowest; add flour alternately with coffee (starting and finishing with flour). Beat just until last of flour is added. With wooden spoon fold in walnuts.

Pour batter into 2 greased loaf pans 24x14x7 cm (9½x5½x2½″) and bake in moderate oven about 45 minutes.

CHOCOLATE CHIP SQUARES

All goodness

35 squares
Baking time: about 30 minutes

2¾ cups flour
3 tsp. baking powder
2 tbsp. flaked coconut
½ cup walnuts, coarsely chopped
2 cups chocolate chips

⅔ cup oil
2 cups brown sugar
3 eggs
1 tsp. vanilla extract
¼ cup orange juice

Preheat oven 350° F, 180° C.

In bowl sift flour and baking powder; add coconut and set aside.

In separate bowl prepare chocolate chips and walnuts and set aside.

In mixer, at medium speed, beat oil and sugar about 1 minute. Add eggs, one at a time, and vanilla extract and continue beating a few minutes until thickened.

Lower speed to lowest; add flour alternately with juice (starting and ending with flour) and beat just until blended. With wooden spoon fold in chocolate chips and walnuts.

Spread batter onto greased lipped cookie sheet and bake in moderate oven about 30 minutes. Cool and cut into squares.

P.S. Either buy ready-made chocolate chips or make your own by cutting up bittersweet chocolate bars. Freeze before cutting.

Note: These are always in the freezer for ready use – but when unexpected company comes I sometimes find one square left; so I suggest reviewing the situation periodically.

CHOCOLATY BROWNIES

Creamy goodness

About 30 brownies
Baking time: about 30 minutes

1 cup flour
¾ cup cocoa powder
pinch of salt
2 tbsp. flaked coconut
2 cups sugar

4 eggs
200–250 grams (1 cup) margarine, melted
1 tsp. vanilla extract
¼ cup walnuts, coarsely chopped

Preheat oven 350° F, 180° C.

In bowl sift flour, cocoa and salt; add coconut and set aside.

In mixer, at medium speed, beat sugar and eggs a few minutes until thick.

Lower speed to lowest; add margarine. Add flour mixture, vanilla extract and walnuts and beat until smooth.

Pour batter into greased square baking pan (about 23 cm, 9″) and bake in moderate oven about 30 minutes (be sure not to dry out).

Or bake in an 8″ square pan for about 40 minutes.

Cut into squares while still warm and allow to cool in pan.

P.S. If brownies come out a little too soft, then just call it fudge and enjoy it. Sometimes I purposely under-bake it. My family prefers it fudgy.

The added touch of GLAZES, FROSTINGS & FILLINGS

Glazes, frostings and fillings give added taste to cake. The cake should be able to stand on its own two feet when it comes to tastiness, but a good frosting will take it to the next level. And we all know that a cake with a glaze or frosting always looks fancier and more exciting than a plain cake – so why not give it that little something extra. Take a look at the glazes and you will find that they are easier to prepare than you thought.

Have fun and everyone will join in. Just make sure no one samples the frosting before cutting the cake.

MERINGUE

Especially good for Lemon Meringue Pie

3 egg whites, room temperature
pinch of salt
¼ tsp. baking powder

⅓ cup sugar
1 tsp. lemon juice OR
½ tsp. vanilla extract

Preheat oven 325° F, 160° C.

In mixer at high speed beat egg whites and salt until almost stiff.

Add baking powder and then gradually add sugar and lemon juice or vanilla extract. Continue beating until stiff and thick.

Spread meringue over pie, touching the circumference all around (to prevent shrinking). Form peaks on top.

Bake in moderate-low oven 12–15 minutes until peaks turn golden.

BROWN SUGAR MERINGUE

Very tasty

2 egg whites
1 cup brown sugar

1 tbsp. lemon juice
½ cup walnuts, ground

Preheat oven 400° F, 200° C.

In mixer, at high speed, beat egg whites until almost stiff. Gradually add sugar. Add lemon juice and walnuts and beat until stiff and thick.

Spread over cake or pie about 5 minutes before it's done – forming peaks on top.

Return to oven and bake in hot oven 8–10 minutes.

CREAMY CHOCOLATE FROSTING

Full richness

200 grams (6 ½ oz.)
    chocolate chips
¼ cup sugar
¼ cup water
4 egg yolks, room temperature
2 tbsp. flaked coconut

100–125 grams (½ cup) margarine,
    room temperature
1 tsp. vanilla extract
½ tsp. instant coffee powder
2 tsp. coffee liqueur

In double boiler over hot, not boiling, water, melt chocolate, sugar and water, stirring occasionally. Let cool.

In mixer, at medium speed, beat chocolate mixture. Add egg yolks, one at a time and continue beating about two minutes.

Lower speed; add margarine (a little at a time), vanilla extract, coffee liqueur and coconut. Increase to medium speed and beat about 7 minutes until thick and smooth.

If frosting is not thick enough, refrigerate about one hour before spreading.

P.S. Great for layer cakes or one large cake.

CHOCOLATE FROSTING
A standard

200 grams (6½ oz.) chocolate chips
1 tbsp. margarine, room temperature
1 tsp. vanilla extract
pinch of salt

1¼ cup powdered sugar, sifted
¼ cup milk or cooled strong coffee
2 tbsp. flaked coconut

In double boiler over hot, not boiling, water melt chocolate and margarine.

Transfer to mixer bowl; add vanilla extract, salt, sugar, milk or coffee and coconut and beat at medium-high speed until creamy and spreading consistency.

P.S. Good for top and sides of layer cake. Fill middle layer with desired Filling.

Note: Chocolate chips can be made by cutting up bittersweet chocolate (freeze chocolate before cutting).

CHOCOLATE FILLING & FROSTING
Extra goodness

3 egg yolks
¾ cup cocoa powder
1 cup powdered sugar, sifted

1 tsp. vanilla extract
100–125 grams (½ cup) margarine,
   room temperature
2 tbsp. flaked coconut

In mixer, at medium-high speed, beat all ingredients about 5 minutes.

P.S. Good for middle and top layers of layer cake or for top and sides and change the filling.

WHITE FROSTING
Especially on Chocolate Cake

200–250 grams (1 cup) margarine,
   room temperature
1 cup sugar OR
   1¼ cup powdered sugar
pinch of salt

2 eggs, room temperature
¼ tsp. instant coffee powder
2 tsp. water
1 tsp. vanilla extract
2 tbsp. flaked coconut

In mixer, at medium speed, beat margarine, sugar and salt.

Add eggs, one at a time and beat about ½ minute. Add coffee powder, water, vanilla extract and coconut; increase speed and beat at high speed 8–10 minutes until thick and smooth.

P.S. Enough for filling, top and sides of layer cake.

Note: For decorative designing on a chocolate frosting prepare a more liquidy frosting by adding a little more water.

WHIPPED CREAM TOPPING

*An added
touch of deliciousness*

For cheese cake

1 cup whipping cream
3 tbsp. sugar
1 tsp. vanilla extract

2 cups sour cream
2 tbsp. flaked coconut

In mixer, at medium-high speed, beat whipping cream, sugar and vanilla extract until firm (Caution: overbeating results in butter).

With wooden spoon fold in sour cream and coconut.

Spread on cooled cheese cake.

P.S. For best results when whipping cream, place bowl and beater in freezer for a while before using. Remove cream from refrigerator just when ready to use.

RICH CRUMB TOPPING

Crunchily good

Food processor makes it easy

¾ cup sifted regular or
    whole wheat flour
¼ cup regular sugar
¼ cup brown sugar
1 tsp. cinnamon

1 tsp. lemon rind, finely grated
pinch of salt
¼ cup walnuts, chopped
2 tbsp. flaked coconut
50–60 grams (¼ cup) butter or
    margarine, room temperature

In bowl mix together flour, sugars, cinnamon, lemon rind, salt, walnuts and coconut.

Cut in butter or margarine until crumbly. (Adjust amount of butter or margarine for proper consistency). Process can be done in food processor.

Sprinkle over cake or pie before baking.

P.S. If pie calls for top and bottom crusts, prepare only bottom crust and use Rich Crumb Topping as top crust.

SIMPLE CRUMB TOPPING

Crumbly good

Food processor makes it easy

about 3 tbsp. regular or
    whole wheat flour
1 tsp. cinnamon

⅓ cup brown sugar
1½ tbsp. butter or margarine,
    room temperature
2 tbsp. flaked coconut

In bowl sift flour and cinnamon. Add coconut, brown sugar and butter or margarine and mix until crumbly. (Adjust amount of flour for proper consistency). Process can be done in food processor.

Sprinkle over cake or pie before baking.

OATMEAL TOPPING
Gives fruit pies an exciting flavor

Food processor makes it easy

2 cups oatmeal
2 tbsp. flaked coconut
¼ cup regular or
   whole wheat flour
¼ tsp. salt

½ tsp. cinnamon
½ cup. almonds, ground
50–60 grams (¼ cup) butter or
   margarine, room temperature
3 tbsp. honey

In bowl mix all ingredients and sprinkle over cake or pie before baking. Process may be done in food processor.

P.S. Enough for two 23 cm (9″) pies.

SUGGESTION: For a two crust pie, prepare only bottom crust and use Oatmeal Topping as top crust. It's nutritionally delicious.

COCOA GLAZE
Add flavor and elegance

75–80 grams (⅓ cup) butter or
   margarine, room temperature
½ tsp. vanilla extract
about 3 tbsp. boiling water

about 1½ cup powdered sugar, sifted
½ cup cocoa powder
2 tbsp. flaked coconut

In saucepan, over low flame, melt butter or margarine and remove from flame.

Add rest of ingredients and stir quickly until smooth. (Adjust for correct consistency – if too thin add a little more powdered sugar – if too thick add a little more boiling water.)

Spread on cake immediately (Glaze hardens all by itself). It's possible to simply pour the Glaze, or else use spatula.

MOCHA GLAZE
Makes a cake something special

1 tsp. butter or margarine
2 tbsp. cocoa powder
2 tbsp. flaked coconut

2 tbsp. strong, hot coffee
1 cup powdered sugar, sifted
1 tsp. vanilla extract

In small saucepan, over low heat, melt butter or margarine and remove from flame.

Add rest of ingredients and quickly stir together until smooth.

(Adjust for proper consistency − if too thin add a little more powdered sugar − if too thick add a little boiling water).

Spread on cake immediately.

P.S. Great on **Marble Cake.**

VANILLA GLAZE
A cinch to prepare

½ cup powdered sugar, sifted
about 4 tsp. boiling water

1 tsp. vanilla extract
2 tbsp. flaked coconut

In bowl, stir together all ingredients and spread on cake immediately.

CHOCOLATE GLAZE
A standard

200 grams (6½ oz.)
chocolate chips

¼ cup milk or strong coffee
1 tbsp. vanilla extract

In small greased saucepan, over low heat, melt chocolate. Add milk or coffee and vanilla extract and stir until smooth.

Spread on cake immediately or use for dipping cookies or cream puffs.

ORANGE GLAZE
Just stir and spread

1 cup powdered sugar
2 tbsp. flaked coconut

2 tbsp. orange juice
½–1 tsp. lemon juice

In bowl stir all ingredients (adjust consistency – if too thin add powdered sugar – if too thick add a little more lemon juice).

Spread on cake immediately.

P.S. Great on **Orange-Glazed Coffee Cake**.

NUT FILLING
That rich flavor

¼ cup brown sugar
2 tbsp. flour
½ cup milk or strong coffee
2 tbsp. flaked coconut

30 grams (2 tbsp.) butter or margarine,
room temperature
½ cup walnuts, ground
2 tsp. vanilla extract

In small saucepan mix together sugar and flour. Add milk or coffee and over low heat cook 3 minutes, stirring continuously.

Remove from flame. Add coconut, butter or margarine, walnuts and vanilla extract and stir together. Let cool.

P.S. Especially good for Filling of bottom layer of **Chocolate Chip Cake**.

LEMON COCONUT FILLING & TOPPING

A light delicate texture

¼ cup cornflour
¼ cup cold water
1 cup boiling water
1 cup sugar

½ cup lemon juice
lemon rind from 1½ lemons,
  finely grated
1 egg, slightly beaten
1 cup flaked coconut

In small saucepan mix together cornflour with cold water until smooth.

Add boiling water, sugar, lemon juice, lemon rind and egg and cook over low heat, stirring continuously, until thick.

Remove from flame and let cool. Mix in half the amount of coconut.

P.S. For **Lemon Chiffon Cake** (see Cake section) carefully cut cake in half crosswise (forming two layers). Spread some of the Filling on bottom layer; place top layer on top and frost sides and top of cake.

Sprinkle rest of flaked coconut over top and sides.

CRUNCHY, MUNCHY COOKIES

If you think cookies are kid stuff, just put a bowl in front of adults and see what happens

I usually serve cookies as an accompaniment to a dessert. It happens often that the pie is finished so quickly that there is a need for something munchy and crunchy to go with the coffee and tea. Cookies are great to nibble on after the meal, or any time.

All cookies are freezeable and they're just as delicious straight from the freezer. My family actually prefers them frozen (so much for freshly baked cookies). I suggest making a double batch if you want to have some for unexpected guests, and periodically review the situation in the freezer. I find sometimes there's one cookie left in the cookie jar (no one wants to be the one to wash the jar).

TIPS

- Cool cookie sheets before re-using, otherwise you may get burnt cookie bottoms.
- Most cookie doughs are easier to roll out if refrigerated for a short period of time.
- Remove cookies from sheets immediately, otherwise they may harden and crack when removing (unless otherwise indicated).
- Cool completely before storing.

POTENTIAL PROBLEMS

- Cookies too hard — too little fat; too much sugar
- Cookies too soft — too much fat; not enough kneading before forming
- Burnt bottom — reusing cookie sheet while it's still hot

ACORN COOKIES

50–60 cookies
Baking time: about 15 minutes

2½ cups flour
pinch of salt
2 tbsp. flaked coconut
200–250 grams (1 cup) butter
    or margarine, room temperature

¾ cup sugar
1 tbsp. vanilla extract
1 cup walnuts, ground

Chocolate Glaze

Preheat oven 350° F, 180° C.

In bowl sift flour and salt; add coconut and set aside.

In mixer, at medium speed, beat butter or margarine and sugar until smooth.

Lower speed; add vanilla extract and walnuts. Add flour slowly and beat until well blended. Cover and refrigerate about one hour. Take one full teaspoon at a time; roll into ball with palm of hand and form acorn-like cookie, pointed at one end (see picture). Place on ungreased cookie sheet, leaving space for spreading.

Bake in moderate oven about 15 minutes until golden.

Remove immediately from cookie sheet with metal spatula and let cool.

Prepare Chocolate Glaze: place in narrow bowl or glass; dip wide base of cookie into Glaze and place carefully on waxed paper.

Leave at least 10 minutes until Glaze hardens.

P.S. To freeze, place waxed paper between layers.

CHOCOLATE CHIP COOKIES

70–80 cookies
Baking time: about 15 minutes

200 grams (7 oz.) chocolate chips
2½ cups flour
3 tsp. baking powder
pinch of salt
2 tbsp. flaked coconut
1 cup walnuts, chopped

200–250 grams (1 cup) butter
    or margarine, room temperature
¾ cup regular sugar
¾ cup brown sugar
2 eggs, slightly beaten
1 tsp. vanilla extract

Preheat oven 325° F, 165° C.

In bowl sift flour, baking powder and salt; add coconut and set aside.

In mixer, at medium speed, beat butter or margarine and both kinds of sugar; add eggs and beat well.

Lower speed; add walnuts, chocolate chips and vanilla extract. Add flour mixture and beat until well blended.

Drop by spoonfuls on greased cookie sheet, leaving space for spreading.

Bake in moderate-low oven about 20 minutes.

Remove from pan immediately with metal spatula.

P.S. Buy ready-made chocolate chips or cut bittersweet chocolate into pieces (freeze before cutting).

CRESCENTS

About 70 cookies
Baking time: about 20 minutes

200–250 grams (1 cup) butter
  or margarine, room temperature
½ cup sugar
2 tbsp. whiskey or brandy

1 tsp. vanilla extract
about 2½ cups sifted flour
½ cup walnuts or almonds, ground
about ½ cup powdered sugar, sifted

Preheat oven 375° F, 190° C, 10 minutes before using.

In mixer, at medium speed, beat butter (or margarine) and sugar; add whiskey or brandy and vanilla extract and beat well.

Lower speed; add flour and walnuts or almonds and beat well. Knead a little with hands (adjust flour — dough should be soft but not sticky).

Take one teaspoon of dough at a time. With palm of hands form ball and then form thick short crescent.

Place on ungreased cookie sheet.

Bake in moderate-high oven about 20 minutes until golden.

Remove from cookie sheet immediately and let cool.

Dip in powdered sugar until well coated.

P.S. No matter how fantastic the dessert, I usually have these in a bowl, on the table as sweet, crunchy nibblers.

OATMEAL COOKIES

60–70 cookies
Baking time: about 15 minutes

100 grams (3½ oz.)
  chocolate chips
2 cups flour
pinch of salt
1 tsp. baking powder
1 tsp. baking soda
200–250 grams (1 cup) margarine,
  room temperature

2 cups brown sugar
3 eggs
1 tsp. vanilla extract
grated rind of ½ lemon
1½ cups flaked coconut
3 cups raw oatmeal
½ cup walnuts, coarsely
  chopped

Preheat oven 350° F, 180° C.

In bowl sift flour, salt, baking powder and baking soda and set aside.

In mixer, at medium speed, beat margarine and brown sugar; add eggs, vanilla extract and grated lemon rind and continue beating about 5 minutes.

Lower speed to lowest; add flour, coconut and oatmeal and beat until smooth. Add walnuts and chocolate chips and beat just until blended.

Drop by teaspoonfuls onto greased cookie sheets, leaving room for spreading.

Bake in moderate oven about 15 minutes.

Remove carefully with metal spatula.

P.S. Either buy ready-made chocolate chips or cut up bittersweet chocolate (freeze before cutting).

SUGAR COOKIES

Crunchily delicious

About 80 cookies
Baking time: about 20 minutes

about 5 cups flour
4 tsp. baking powder
¼ tsp. salt
2 tbsp. flaked coconut
200–250 grams (1 cup) butter or
   margarine, room temperature

1 ¾ cups sugar
3 eggs
1 tbsp. vanilla extract
⅓ cup liquid (milk, strong coffee
   or orange juice)

In bowl sift flour, baking powder and salt; add coconut and set aside.

In mixer, at medium speed, beat butter or margarine and sugar about 1 minute; add eggs, one at a time, and vanilla extract and beat a few minutes. Lower speed to lowest; add flour mixture alternately with liquid and beat until well blended.

Refrigerate a few hours.

Preheat oven 350° F, 180° C.

Divide dough into 4 pieces.

On floured board take each piece and adjust amount of flour to make soft, not sticky, dough. Roll out to medium thickness (about 0.5 cm, ¼″) and cut with glass or round cookie cutter.

Place on greased cookie sheet and bake about 20 minutes.

Remove from cookie sheet with metal spatula.

THUMBPRINT COOKIES

With your own personal touch!
and tasty too

About 30 cookies
Baking time: about 25 minutes.

2¼ cups flour
pinch of salt
2 tbsp. flaked coconut
200–250 grams (1 cup) butter or
   margarine, room temp.

½ cup sugar
2 eggs, separated
1 tsp. almond extract
¼ cup almonds, ground

Preheat oven 350° F, 180° C.

In bowl sift flour and salt; add coconut and set aside.

In mixer, at medium speed, beat butter or margarine and sugar; add egg yolks and almond extract and beat a few minutes.

Lower speed to lowest; add flour and beat until smooth. Continue kneading a little with hands.

In small bowl beat egg whites lightly.

Take a full teaspoon of dough and form small balls. Dip each ball in the egg whites and roll in ground almonds.

Place on greased cookie sheets; press each roll down with thumbprint and bake in moderate oven about 25 minutes.

Remove from cookie sheet with metal spatula.

ALMOND COOKIES

Almond delight

About 70 cookies
Baking time: about 15 minutes

about 3 cups flour
1½ tsp. baking powder
pinch of salt
¼ cup flaked coconut
2 eggs, room temperature
¾ cup sugar

⅔ cup oil
1 tbsp. orange juice
2 tsp. almond extract
1 tsp. vanilla extract
1 tbsp. water
½ cup almonds, blanched

Preheat oven 350° F, 180° C.

In bowl sift flour, baking powder and salt; add coconut and set aside.

In mixer, at medium speed, beat one egg and sugar; add oil, orange juice and extracts and beat a few minutes more. Lower speed, add flour mixture and beat until smooth. Continue kneading a little by hand until dough is soft and not sticky (adjust flour).

Form balls of about 2.5 cm (1″) diameter and place on greased cookie sheets, leaving space between each one for spreading. Press each cookie down with fork to about 1 cm (⅓″) thickness.

Mix remaining egg with water; brush each cookie with egg mixture and place one almond on each cookie.

Bake in moderate oven about 15 minutes.

Remove from cookie sheet with metal spatula.

ALMOND CAKES (MANDELBROIT)

Something a little different

About 45 slices
Baking time: 55 minutes

about 5 cups flour
1 tbsp. baking powder
pinch of salt
¼ cup flaked coconut
3 eggs

1 cup sugar
½ cup oil
½ tsp. vanilla extract
grated rind of 1 lemon
½ cup almonds, ground

Preheat oven 350° F, 180° C.

In bowl sift flour, baking powder and salt; add coconut and set aside.

In mixer, at medium speed, beat eggs, sugar, oil, vanilla extract and lemon rind a few minutes. Lower speed; add flour mixture and almonds and beat another minute.

Knead dough a little by hand (dough should be soft, not sticky; adjust flour).

Refrigerate about 15 minutes.

On floured board form three long logs about 8 cm (3¼") wide; place on greased cookie sheet and bake in moderate oven about 40 minutes.

Remove from oven and with sharp knife cut logs into 2 cm (¾") wide slices. Replace on cookie sheet, cut side up, and bake 15 minutes more.

Remove from cookie sheet with metal spatula.

P.S. It's not the ordinary cookie and you may think it's the best thing you ever tasted.

CRUMBLY NUT COOKIES

Crunchily good

About 80 cookies
Baking time: about 15 minutes.

1 recipe **Sweet Cookie Dough**

FILLING
1 tbsp. cinnamon
2 tbsp. flaked coconut

¼ cup sugar
100–125 grams (½ cup)
  walnuts, ground

Prepare dough according to directions.
Preheat oven 350° F, 180° C.
In medium bowl mix Filling ingredients and set aside.
On floured board roll out dough to medium thickness (about 0.5 cm, ¼″); cut into rounds of about 7 cm (2½″) and place on greased cookie sheets. Sprinkle each round with a little Filling and press down gently with fingers.
Bake in moderate oven about 15 minutes.
P.S. You don't have to use all the dough; make the whole recipe and freeze portions of dough as crust for fruit pies.

COOKIE DOUGH RUGELACH

Fantastic no-yeast rugelach

48 rugelach
Baking time: about 35 minutes

FILLING
⅓ cup sugar
1 cup walnuts
2 tbsp. cinnamon
¼ cup flaked coconut
½ cup raisins

DOUGH
5½ cups flour
1 tsp. baking powder
¼ cup flaked coconut
1 cup sugar
1 cup oil
3 eggs
½ cup orange juice

In bowl mix together Filling ingredients and set aside.
Sift together flour and baking powder; add coconut and set aside.
In mixer, at medium speed, beat sugar and oil; add eggs one at a time and beat a couple of minutes.
Lower speed and add flour mixture alternately with orange juice.
Knead a little by hand and adjust amount of flour to form soft, not sticky dough.
Preheat oven 350° F, 180° C.
Divide dough into three pieces. On floured board roll out each piece to medium thickness (about 0.5 cm, ¼″); brush with a little oil and sprinkle each piece with ⅓ of the Filling.
With sharp knife cut widthwise and lengthwise (resulting in 4 quarters; cut each quarter in two and again in two, resulting in 16 triangles from each piece of dough).
Roll from outside to in and place (point side down) on greased cookie sheets, leaving a little space between each one.
Bake in moderate oven about 35 minutes.
Remove from cookie sheet with metal spatula.

CREAM CHEESE RUGELACH

Can't be beat

32 rugelach
Baking time: about 30 minutes

DOUGH
About 2 cups flour
pinch of salt
200–250 grams (1 cup)
  cream cheese
200–250 grams (1 cup) butter,
  room temperature
1 tbsp. sugar

FILLING
2 egg whites
½ cup sugar
½ cup walnuts
2 tsp. cinnamon
2 tbsp. flaked coconut
About ½ cup raisins

DOUGH: In large bowl sift flour and salt; add cheese, butter and sugar and knead until soft, not sticky. On floured board roll out into a large rectangle; fold over into 3 layers and refrigerate about 2 hours.

FILLING: In mixer, at high speed, beat egg whites until moderately stiff. Add sugar and beat until stiff. Fold in walnuts, cinnamon and coconut.

Preheat oven 375° F, 190° C.

Divide dough in half; on floured board roll out each half into a large circle of medium thickness about 0.5 cm (¼″) and spread ½ of Filling on each circle.

With sharp knife cut circle lengthwise and widthwise (forming 4 quarters); cut each quarter in four and then again, resulting in 16 triangles. Place 3 raisins on each triangle.

Roll up each triangle, rolling the base of the triangle toward the top – wide to narrow point. Place on ungreased cookie sheet – point side down. (Allow a little space for spreading.)

Bake in moderate-high oven about 30 minutes, until golden brown.

Remove from cookie sheet with metal spatula.

P.S. Meringue will ooze out a bit onto the outside; let it be.

YEAST RUGELACH

From my mother's kitchen; they have to be good

48 rugelach
Baking time: about 30 minutes

DOUGH
About 7 cups flour
pinch of salt
40 grams (1½ oz.) yeast
½ cup warm orange juice
200–250 grams (1 cup) butter or
  margarine, room temperature
3 eggs, room temperature
¾ cup sugar
2 tbsp. oil

FILLING
2 tbsp. cinnamon
⅓ cup sugar
1 cup walnuts, chopped
½ cup raisins
¼ cup flaked coconut

Easy and Elegant

In large bowl sift flour and salt. Make well in center; add crumbled yeast and orange juice. Mix together with a little flour. Cover with slightly damp cloth towel or place in closed polyethylene bag, and leave about 20 minutes.

Add butter, eggs, sugar and 2 tablespoons oil; mix together by slowly adding more and more flour and form soft dough.

Knead about 8 minutes until smooth and satiny.

Process can be done in mixer with dough hook, in which case soften yeast only in warm orange juice about 10 minutes.

Place dough in large oiled bowl, turning once so that both sides of dough are oiled. Cover with towel and leave in warm spot to let rise one hour; punch down and leave another hour.

In medium bowl mix together Filling ingredients.

Divide dough into three pieces. On floured board roll out each piece to medium thickness (about 0.5 cm, ¼"); smear with a little oil and sprinkle each piece with ⅓ of Filling.

Cut each piece in half in width and length (making four quarters); cut each quarter in half and then again (forming 16 triangles). Roll each triangle from wide to narrow point; place on greased cookie sheets point side down (leaving space for spreading); cover with towel and leave in warm spot about 20 minutes to rise.

Preheat oven 350° F, 180° C, ten minutes before using.

Bake in moderate oven about 30 minutes, until golden brown.

Remove from cookie sheet with metal spatula.

GRANOLA

It's habit-forming

Baking time: about 1 hour

2 cups flaked coconut	1 tbsp. cinnamon
1 cup wheat germ	½ cup oil
1 cup shelled sunflower seeds	¾ cup honey
½ cup sesame seeds	1 tbsp. vanilla extract
½ cup unsalted peanuts	½ tsp. salt
½ cup almonds, halved	⅓ cup raisins
7 cups raw oatmeal	

Preheat oven 250° F, 120° C.

In large bowl mix together coconut, wheat germ, sunflower seeds, sesame seeds, peanuts, almonds, oatmeal and cinnamon.

In large frying pan, over low flame, heat oil, honey, vanilla extract and salt and stir until smooth.

Pour over granola; add raisins and mix.

Spread mixture into lipped cookie sheet and bake in slow oven about one hour, stirring occasionally. Let cool and store in closed glass jars.

P.S. I could eat a whole jar all by myself.

SALTY CHEESE TWISTS

Better than bought

About 35 crackers
Baking time: about 15 minutes

about 2 cups flour
1 tsp. salt
150–190 grams (¾ cup) butter,
    room temperature

2 eggs
3 tbsp. milk
1 cup hard yellow cheese, grated
Caraway seeds

Preheat oven 425° F, 220° C.

In bowl sift flour and salt; cut in butter and mix until crumbly. Add one egg and the white of the other egg and mix. Add milk and knead dough until soft, but not sticky (adjust flour).

Refrigerate about one hour.

On floured board roll out dough to medium thickness (about 0.5 cm, ¼″); cut into 6 cm (2¼″) long strips; twist each two strips together and place on greased cookie sheet with a little space between each one.

Brush each twist with egg yolk; sprinkle with grated cheese and caraway seeds and bake in hot oven about 15 minutes.

P.S. Delicious by itself or with cheeses, soups, etc.

SESAME RINGS

Non-sweet crunchy crackers

About 50 rings
Baking time: about 1 hour

about 6½ cups flour
4 tsp. baking powder
¼ tsp. salt
200–250 grams (1 cup) margarine,
    room temperature

1 cup oil
1 cup water
1 egg, slightly beaten
about 150–190 grams
    (¾ cup) sesame seeds

Preheat oven 350° F, 180° C.

In mixer bowl sift flour, baking powder and salt. Cut in margarine and beat at low speed. Add oil, water and 2 tablespoons sesame seeds. Increase to medium speed and beat until smooth. Continue kneading a little with hands until soft dough is formed.

Taking about 2 teaspoons of dough at a time, roll into short logs with palm of hands and form rings. Dip each ring in beaten egg and then in sesame seeds.

Place on ungreased cookie sheets and bake in moderate oven about one hour until golden brown.

Remove immediately with metal spatula.

Preparing for **PASSOVER**

Passover is a holiday different from all others. On all other holidays, any and every recipe can be used. On Passover, ingredients must be changed.

Cooking for Passover is easier than you think. Besides the basic recipes, there are quite a few dishes which are very adaptable (e.g., borscht, certain salads, chicken and meat recipes). There are others which can be adjusted by using matzo meal instead of breadcrumbs, wheat germ, etc. (e.g., Sweet and Sour Meat Balls, Fish Cakes).

One of my standard side dishes is cooked potato (not necessarily mashed but rather cut up) mixed with sautéed onions, garlic, paprika and mushrooms (if desired), seasoned well with salt and pepper.

—FOLLOWING ARE MY BASIC RECIPES—

HORSERADISH

½ cup horseradish root
2 cups beets
½ cup vinegar

1 tsp. salt
2 tbsp. sugar
⅛ tsp. pepper

Finely chop horseradish root and beets in blender. Place in bowl; add rest of ingredients and mix together.

CHOROSES

6 apples
½ cup walnuts
¼ cup dates

wine
1 tsp. cinnamon
½ tsp. ginger

Chop apples, dates and walnuts. Mix together.
Add other ingredients. Amount of wine is according to consistency desired.
If you want, you can make it in advance and let the mixture marinate. It's up to you.
The consistency should be like chutney.

MATZO BALLS (Knaidlach)

4 eggs
½ cup soda water
⅓ cup oil
½ tsp. ground ginger

1 tsp. salt
¼ tsp. pepper
1–1¼ cups matzo meal

In medium bowl beat eggs. Add soda water, oil, ginger, salt, and pepper and mix.
Add matzo meal slowly and mix until blended (batter should be soft and a little loose). Adjust amount of matzo meal.
Refrigerate about 20 minutes
In large pot bring to boil a lot of water with 2 teaspoons salt added. With wet hands form balls from batter and drop into boiling water. Shake pot; cover and cook over medium low flame about 30 minutes.
Remove with slotted spoon.
To warm up place in soup and cook about 10 minutes.

POTATO PUDDING (KUGEL)

1½ kilos (3 lbs.), potatoes
1 small onion, optional
5–6 eggs
½ cup and 2 tbsp. oil

⅓ cup and 2 tbsp. oil
about 1 Tablespoon salt
½–¾ tsp. pepper

Preheat oven 350° F, 180° C.
Peel and blend potatoes in blender with onion and eggs.
Place contents of blender in large bowl; add ½ cup oil, salt, pepper, potato starch and baking powder and mix.
Pour 2 tablespoons oil in a six-quart-deep casserole dish; grease sides and heat in oven about eight minutes.
Remove from oven and pour in potato mixture.
Bake in moderate oven about 2 hours.

MATZO KUGEL

9 matzos
5 eggs, beaten
2 cups cottage cheese

½ cup milk
2 tsp. salt
¼ tsp. pepper

Preheat oven 350° F, 180° C.
Break up matzos and soak in warm water about 10 minutes; drain and squeeze out water.
In large bowl combine and mix together all ingredients.
Pour and spread into suitable flat greased baking pan and bake in moderate oven about 50 minutes.

POTATO PANCAKES (LATKES)

1 kilo (2 lbs.) potatoes
4 eggs
2 tbsp. flour

2 tsp. salt
½ tsp. pepper
oil for frying

Blend potatoes with eggs in blender, a little at a time.
Place in bowl and mix with rest of ingredients.
Fry, by big tablespoons, in heated oil.
Serve with applesauce or sour cream.

MATZO MEAL PANCAKES

1 cup matzo meal
⅔ cup milk
5 eggs, separated

1 onion, grated
salt and pepper to taste
butter for frying

Mix matzo meal with milk and set aside for half hour.
Beat egg yolks; add onion and seasoning and mix into matzo meal mixture.
In mixer, at high speed, beat egg whites until stiff, but not dry. Fold matzo meal mixture into egg whites.
Heat butter and fry by spoonfuls. Brown on both sides.

CHEESE LATKES

3 eggs
1 cup milk
1 cup pot cheese
1 cup matzo meal

¾ tsp. salt
¼ tsp. pepper
1 tbsp. sugar

Beat together eggs, milk and cheese.
Combine remaining ingredients; add to egg mixture and blend well.
Drop by spoonfuls into well-greased frying pan and brown on both sides.
Serve with sour cream, applesauce or jam.

PESACH NOODLES

1–2 tsp. potato starch
½ cup water

6 eggs
½ tsp. salt
pinch of pepper

Dissolve potato starch in water.
Add eggs, salt and pepper and beat well.
In frying pan heat oil; pour batter in piecemeal to make thin pancakes.
Let cool; roll up and slice into noodles of desired thickness.

MATZO BREI

6 matzos
4 eggs
1 cup milk

1½ tsp. salt
¼ tsp. pepper
1 tsp. sugar

Break up matzos and soak in warm water about 10 minutes. Drain and squeeze out water.

In bowl mix together all ingredients.

In large frying pan heat butter on low flame; increase heat slightly; spread matzo mixture in pan and fry on both sides.

P.S. To turn matzo brei over – place large plate over frying pan and invert matzo brei onto plate. Slide back into pan. It may be necessary to heat a little more butter in the pan before turning over matzo brei.

MATZO STUFFING

2 cups hot chicken soup
9 matzos, crumbled up
¼ cup oil
2 onions, diced
3 cloves garlic, minced

½ green pepper
1 cup mushrooms, sliced
2 stalks celery, diced
2 tsp. salt
¼ tsp. pepper
3 eggs, beaten

In bowl pour hot soup over matzos and let stand until absorbed.

In large frying pan heat oil over medium flame and sauté onions, garlic, green pepper, mushrooms, celery, salt and pepper about 10 minutes.

Add to matzo mixture and mix together; let cool.

Add eggs and mix.

BROWNIES

2 cups oil
4 cups sugar
8 eggs
1 tbsp. vanilla extract

¼ cup flaked coconut
1 cup potato flour
1 cup walnuts, ground
1 cup cocoa

Preheat oven 350° F, 180° C.

In mixer, at medium speed, beat oil and sugar; add eggs one at a time and vanilla extract and beat about 5 minutes. Gradually add coconut, potato flour, walnuts and cocoa.

Pour into greased rectangular baking pan and bake at medium heat about 50 minutes.

BANANA NUT CAKE

8 eggs, separated
1 ¼ cup sugar
pinch of salt
1 ¼ cups mashed bananas
1 tsp. vanilla extract

¾ cup matzo meal
½ cup potato starch
1 ¼ tsp. cinnamon
¼ cup flaked coconut
½ cup walnuts, ground

Preheat oven 325° F, 165° C.

In mixer, at medium speed, beat egg yolks, 1 cup sugar and salt for about 2 minutes. Add mashed bananas and vanilla. With wooden spoon, mix in matzo meal, potato starch, cinnamon and nuts.

In mixer, at high speed, beat egg whites until moderately stiff; gradually add ¼ cup sugar and beat until meringue is formed. Fold meringue into batter.

Pour batter into greased 10″ tube pan and bake in medium-low heat 70–75 minutes.

APPLE CAKE

5 baking applies, peeled and grated
1 tsp. cinnamon
1 tsp. lemon juice
5 eggs
1 ¼ cup sugar
½ cup oil
2 tsp. vanilla extract
½ cup orange juice

1 ½ cup matzo meal
2 tbsp. potato starch
¼ cup flaked coconut

Preheat oven 350° F, 180° C.

In bowl mix apples, cinnamon and lemon juice.

In mixer, at medium speed, beat eggs, one at a time about 1 minute; add sugar, oil and vanilla and beat another 5 minutes. Lower speed to lowest setting. Gradually add juice, matzo meal, potato starch and coconut.

Remove from mixer immediately and continue mixing with wooden spoon. Pour ¾ of batter in greased flat baking pan; spread with apples and add remaining batter.

Bake in moderate oven about 1 hour.

MOTHER'S SPONGE CAKE

Prepare all ingredients before starting

12 eggs, separated
1 ½ cup sugar
⅓ cup lemon juice
1 ⅓ cup matzo meal
⅔ cup potato starch

VARIATIONS
1 cup walnuts, ground
1 cup chocolate, grated

Easy and Elegant

Preheat oven 350° F, 180° C.

In mixer, at high speed, beat egg whites until firm, but not stiff; add sugar slowly and beat until meringue is formed.

With wooden spoon gradually fold in rest of ingredients one at a time.

Pour into ungreased tube pan and bake in moderate oven about 1 hour.

Turn pan over an inverted funnel or bottle neck and let cool.

MATZO MEAL CRUST

1–1¼ cups matzo meal	¼ cup sugar
½ cup butter, room temperature	1 tsp. vanilla extract

Mix all together and spread into pie pan.

Bake for 5 minutes in hot oven.

Add filling and bake according to recipe.

CHEESE CAKE

3 cups cream cheese	3 tbsp. potato flour
2 cups sour cream	1 cup cottage cheese
1¼ cup sugar	1 tsp. vanilla extract
4 eggs	¼ cup flaked coconut

Preheat oven 350° F, 180° C.

Prepare **Crumb Crust** (above) and spread on bottom of spring form pan.

In mixer, mix Filling ingredients together and pour over crust.

Bake in moderate oven about 50 minutes.

DEEP DISH APPLE PIE

6 apples	BATTER
½ cup sugar	½ cup sugar
1 tsp. cinnamon	¾ cup cake meal
½ tsp. ginger	pinch of salt
2 tsp. lemon juice	2 tbsp. flaked coconut
2 tbsp. flaked coconut	⅓ cup (75–80 grams) butter
	OR margarine, room temperature
¼ cup walnuts, chopped	

Preheat oven 350° F, 180° C.

In bowl mix together Filling ingredients and place in 1½ quart casserole dish.

In bowl mix together batter ingredients until crumbly and sprinkle over apple mixture.

Bake in moderate oven about 50 minutes.

Carole's PASSOVER MANDELBROIT *(Almond Cakes)*

1 cup margarine
2 cups sugar
6 eggs
2¾ cups matzo meal

¾ cup potato starch
pinch of salt
200 grams (6½ oz.)
    chocolate chips
1 cup walnuts, ground

Preheat oven 350° F, 180° C.
In mixer, at medium speed, cream margarine and sugar. Add eggs, one at a time and beat well.
Lower speed and add dry ingredients.
With wooden spoon fold in chocolate chips and walnuts.
Form 3 thin loaves (log-shaped) and place on greased cookie sheet.
Bake in moderate oven about 35 minutes.
Slice; turn and place open side up onto cookie sheet and bake another 10 minutes.

MUFFINS

Yield: about 20 muffins

1 cup oil
2 cups water
⅓ cup sugar

3 cups matzo meal
9 eggs

Preheat oven 350° F, 180° C.
Place oil, water and sugar in medium pot and bring to boil. Add matzo meal; remove from flame and let stand 5 minutes.
Place mixture in mixing bowl. Add eggs, two at a time, and beat with electric beater until smooth.
Place batter into greased muffin tins.
With greased finger make hole in center of each one.
Bake in moderate oven 30–40 minutes.

SECRETS for SUCCESS

Taste – the test of success

Perfection – not settling for less than the best

Great Recipes – from books, friends, relatives and other countrymen

Quality Ingredients – obtained in stores and markets

Along with these, the *know-how* and *feel* of cooking can only be achieved through experience and experimentation. Knowing the hints, however, the secrets of good cooking, will go a long way toward cooking success. Read this section carefully and you've got a big headstart.

No recipe is beyond your capabilities, you can make anything you want. Complicated-looking recipes merely mean additional time and patience. Before the age of 18, I hardly knew how to boil an egg – and now the compliments and praises I receive tell a different story.

Cooking Hints

BREAD & ROLLS

Yeast comes from the cells of a certain fungus and is a leavening (rising) agent in the baking of breads, pastries and certain cakes.

Before I began working with yeast, I pictured yeast doughs as the most difficult thing in the world. When I finally got the courage to start, I was surprised how easy it is; now, I can't seem to stop. It's as easy as making any cake (especially with the dough hook. Be sure to read the instructions carefully on how to use it).

The difference between dried and fresh yeast: Since dried yeast is more concentrated a lesser amount is required. Dried yeast needs a higher liquid temperature and a higher room temperature for the process of fermenting. When dissolving dried yeast add one teaspoon sugar to the liquid; sprinkle dried yeast on top and leave in warm spot until frothy (about 10 minutes). Whichever you use the results are usually the same.

When dissolving fresh yeast crumble yeast into a warm liquid; stir once and leave for about 10 minutes. Substituting fresh yeast for dried: dried yeast is more concentrated. If a recipe calls for 15 grams (½ oz.) of dried yeast (one American package), use about 25 grams (about 1 oz.) of fresh (one American package).

Storing yeast: fresh yeast can be stored for a few days in a closed jar in the refrigerator. Dried yeast keep for a couple of months.

The Dough

- Kneading: yeast dough needs a good amount of energetic kneading. The dough should become smooth and satiny. (By hand it takes about 10 minutes and with a dough hook, about 7–8 minutes.) Place dough on floured board for the finishing touch to achieve a smooth-satiny finish. Lightly oil a large bowl in which dough will rise. Place dough in bowl then turn over so that both top and bottom are lightly oiled. Cover with damp cotton dish towel and leave to rise.

- Rising time: dough should double in size. A test for readiness – press surface in with finger about 2", if impression remains, the dough is ready. Rising time depends on sugar content and room temperature. Sweeter dough takes longer. If you want to expedite the process use a little more yeast.

Don't be discouraged if you don't get the knack of it right away. It really takes a bit of practice. Keep trying until it becomes second nature.

The Process of Proving: this is the rising time after the dough has been shaped.

What went wrong

- Yeasty taste: too long fermentation (rising time); too much yeast; stale yeast.
- Crumbly: over fermentation; rising too quickly in too warm a spot.
- Uneven texture and holes: too long or too short fermentation; not sufficient kneading; too long proving time; during first rising time, dough is unoiled and left uncovered.
- Cracked crust: flour too soft; baking pan was too small; underfermentation (too short rising time).
- Streaked: underkneading; uneven kneading.
- Doesn't rise: overkneading; stale yeast; liquid dissolving yeast too hot (heat killed the yeast).
- Porous: overfermentation; too slow oven temperature
- Heavy texture: under kneading; underfermentation; too low oven temperature.

STALE BREAD: make breadcrumbs by cutting up the bread and blending it in the blender. I store breadcrumbs in the freezer. If the bread is not too stale, make **Croutons** (See index).

BROWN SUGAR

- Brown sugar hardens when exposed to air: keep in a tightly closed jar or store in a plastic bag in the freezer.
- To soften brown sugar already hardened: place a slice of fresh bread in jar with the hardened sugar and leave overnight. Discard bread.
- To get rid of lumps: place brown sugar in a plastic bag, let out the air, tie up and roll out with a rolling pin.
- Substituting brown sugar for white in baking – in order to counteract the acidity of brown sugar, you should add baking soda. (Ratio: ¾ teaspoon baking soda per 1 cup brown sugar.)
- Brown sugar measurements should be firmly packed.

BUTTER

- To melt: always use low flame; don't leave it alone lest it should burn.
- When sautéing, wait until butter gets brown (not dark brown) before adding other ingredients.
- Clarified butter – the result of a process of changing solid butter into liquid form. Melt butter over low flame; turn off flame and leave until a clear liquid rises to the top. Skim this off and you have clarified butter. Use for delicate sauces.

CAKES

What's so difficult about baking cakes? It would seem that all you need is a good recipe. So why do I hear "I tried your cake recipe and it didn't look or taste like yours."

SOME BASIC RULES:

- Have all the ingredients ready before beginning.
- Read recipe carefully (e.g., sometimes baking soda is sifted with the flour or dissolved into a liquid or semi-liquid).
- Quality and size of pan are important. For best results use shiny metal pans. If a different size pan is used other than mentioned, adjust timing.
- Preheat oven about 10 minutes before using. Make sure the oven is correctly adjusted and use correct temperature.
- Use unsalted shortening (butter or margarine).
- Shortening and eggs should be at room temperature. If you forgot to take out the eggs beforehand, place them in a bowl of warm water for a little while.
- When preparing a standard batter cake, beat shortening and sugar, add eggs and flavoring; beat a few minutes at medium speed until thick (unless otherwise indicated); lower speed; add flour and liquid and beat just until last of flour is added (Do Not Overbeat). Continue mixing with wooden spoon until just blended. Overbeating after flour is added results in tough-textured cake.

- Grease cake pans with solid shortening only. Sprinkle bottom and sides of pan with flour (for white cakes) and cocoa powder (for chocolate cakes). Shake around and then discard excess (this ensures "even" rising).
- Bake batter immediately upon preparation unless otherwise indicated.
- Bake on center shelf without touching sides of oven.
- Don't depend completely on the time stated in the recipe. Test doneness by inserting toothpick which should come out clean.
- Oven door shouldn't be opened during first ⅓ of baking time.
- Cakes should be left in cake pan about 15–30 minutes before removing. It can then be removed and cooled on a wire rack.
- Cool cakes completely before storing.
- To prevent dried fruit from sinking to bottom of cake make sure it is thoroughly dry, dust fruit lightly with flour and dry out in oven before adding to batter. (Fruit sticks when it is too moist.)
- For a lighter textured cake: add 1 teaspoon lemon juice to shortening and sugar.
- For a velvety texture: add 2 tablespoons boiling water to shortening and sugar.
- To measure solid shortening if using "cups": First put a specific amount of water in a measuring cup *e.g.* ¼, ⅓ or ½ cup. Select the measurement such that water plus shortening equals 1 cup (In other words, if the recipe calls for ⅔ cup shortening, put ⅓ cup water and enough shortening to equal 1 cup; pour off water leaving you with ⅔ cup shortening).
- Recommended pans for baking: shiny metal pans reflect the heat away from the cake. Do NOT use dark metal or enamel pans. If ovenproof glass pans are used, lower oven temperature by 25° F, and bake same amount of time.
- To prevent cake sticking to cake plate: sprinkle plate with confectioner's (powdered) sugar.
- Flour substitutions: 1 cup cake flour = ⅞ cup regular flour, 1 cup regular = ⅞ cup whole wheat
- Frosting: frost cake as soon as it's completely cooled and before the crust hardens.
- Glazing: glazes should be spread on cake while still warm.
- Cutting: To cut frosted cake without breaking the frosting – dip knife into very hot water.
- Freezing: Almost all cakes can be frozen including frosted cakes, cheese cakes and fruit cakes. Fruit pies can be frozen but they become soggy. To eliminate sogginess, defrost pie and bake for a while to dry out. I personally try not to freeze pies, but I do keep the dough for the crust in the freezer for ready use. Cakes which I recommend Not to freeze are those with a whipped cream or meringue topping.
- Dusting cake with confectioner's sugar: put sugar in a small-holed strainer; stir with a spoon gently and spread over cake.

Common mistakes with cakes

- Top sinks: too much raising agent; too much liquid; wrong oven temperature; oven door slammed during baking.
- Coarse texture: inadequate mixing; too much baking powder; too cool oven.
- Yellow spots: insufficient sifting of dry ingredients; too much baking soda; baking soda not well dissolved in liquid.
- Crusty ring around sides: over-greasing of sides of pan.
- Hard crust: pan too large; too hot oven; overbaking; too much sugar.
- Not browning: overloaded oven; underbaking; not enough sugar or eggs.
- Overbrowning on bottom: poor quality pan; inadequate greasing or lining.
- Heavy texture: too much flour; underbeating of shortening, sugar and eggs; wrong oven temperature; insufficient sugar or raising agent.
- Cracked top: (loaf cakes do crack naturally) – too much raising agent; oven too hot; overmixing after adding flour; too much flour or not enough liquid.
- Overflowing: pan too small; oven too cool; too much raising agent; too much sugar.
- Burnt: pan too near side of oven; overloaded oven (heat can not circulate evenly); uneven oven heat

CARAMEL

Foolproof way to make caramel: Combine 1 cup sugar with ⅓ cup water in a saucepan. Bring to boil over moderate heat, shaking pan occasionally, until all the sugar is dissolved. Do Not Stir. Boil over low flame, watching carefully, until the desired shade of caramel is formed. Remove from heat immediately and place in a larger pan of cold water in order to stop the cooking process.

CARAMEL SYRUP: Add ⅓ cup water to the cooled caramel; heat over low flame, stirring continuously, until caramel blends together.

CHEESES

The taste of cheese is greatly varied. Each one gives a unique and interesting flavor. Try experimenting with the vast variety of cheese, using one or a combination. Cheeses are great all by themselves served in blocks, cubes or slices accompanied by black bread, crackers, raw vegetables and fruit (pear and apple slices are especially good); in salads; baked into quiches, casseroles, fish, vegetables etc.

Types of cheeses: Their national names, description and use:

- Blue cheese: English Stilton, French Roquefort, Italian Gorgonzola, Danish Blue. These cheeses have a flaky texture with lines of bluish mold. Fresh blue cheese is ivory colored with blue veins running evenly through it. Take out of refrigerator some time before serving and cut with fork to keep the flaky texture. Excellent by itself or mixed into salads.
- Cheddar: This cheese ranges from a mild to a sharp flavor depending on age. The older the cheese the sharper the flavor. Good by itself and in cooking and baking. Can be combined with Swiss and/or Parmesan.
- Edam and Gouda (mild flavor): Best when eaten by itself. Delicious on a slice of pear.
- Feta (mild salted cheese) and mozzarella can be added to a variety of salads.
- French Camembert and Brie: These are considered winter, dessert cheeses. They have a soft-running interior with a firm crust powdered with mold. Serve at room temperature.
- Italian Ricotta: Similar to cottage cheese but with a smoother consistency. Excellent for baking.
- Parmesan: This is a dry cheese, usually grated and used in baking, for pies, pizza, and quiches. Can be combined with Swiss and/or cheddar.
- Swiss: French Beaufort, Ementhal (large holed), Gruyère (small holed). Quality swiss cheese is even-holed, firm and slightly shiny. These cheeses are especially good for melting and puffing. Combine it with Parmesan cheese for a more delectable taste. Good combined with cheddar and Parmesan for quiches, pizza, food pies, etc.

FREEZING hard cheeses: freezing will cause dryness, flakiness and some loss of flavor. Use frozen cheese for cooking and baking. I personally feel it's worth freezing for this convenience. Freeze either in block or grated form. Grate a few kinds, put each one in a separate plastic bag and mark them, then use either individually or combined. Frozen cheese is easier to grate.

GRATING hard cheeses: Use shredder attachment of food processor or mixer. It's beautiful to watch how it comes out. If the cheese is a little soft, freeze it for about 30 minutes before grating. To prevent cheese from sticking to grater, oil grater lightly.

CUTTING: Use a dull knife which has been warmed up.

GARNISHES: I usually serve three cheeses in blocks with cut up raw vegetables, olives, pickles, sliced pears and apples (sprinkle with a little lemon juice to preserve whiteness) and crackers.

TIPS ON DIPS: For a base, I use cream cheese combined with a little sour cream to make it spreading consistency. Add any combination of the following: scallions, olives, dill, parsley, chives, radishes, fresh or granulated garlic, paprika, a little salt and pepper, sardines (with a little lemon juice) etc.

CHOCOLATE

Actually, my favorite chocolate is rich milk chocolate eaten straight from the bar, but right now let's talk about the other possibilities.

- Bittersweet and unsweetened chocolate are not interchangeable, but cocoa powder can be used in lieu of unsweetened chocolate:
    1 square unsweetened = ¼ cup cocoa plus 1 teaspoon shortening.

- Melting chocolate over a double boiler: a bowl over a pot of water is adequate. If it is being melted by itself (without shortening or liquid) grease bowl before adding chocolate to prevent sticking. Melt over hot, not boiling, water. To speed up the process, cut chocolate into pieces. For mousses and cream pies, chill melted chocolate mixture before adding beaten egg whites and whipped cream. This will keep the mixture firm. To chill either place filling container in refrigerator for a while or place bowl in a larger bowl of ice water, stirring occasionally, to prevent lumps.
- Homemade chocolate chips made in the food processor comes out unevenly, so I do it the old fashioned way. Use a 100 grams (3½ oz.) bar; freeze for a while; remove paper wrapper; open foil; place on board; turn bar over; and with sharp long knife cut horizontally and then vertically. The chips will remain in the wrapper. Lift wrapper carefully and slide chips into bowl.
- To prevent chocolate chips from sinking to bottom of cake when baking: mix chocolate chips with a little flour before adding to batter.
- To make chocolate shavings: use potato peeler or grater.

COCOA

- Substituting cocoa for unsweetened baking chocolate:
    1 square unsweetened chocolate = ¼ cup cocoa plus 1 teaspoon butter or margarine.
- Velvety hot chocolate: boil unsweetened cocoa in a little water a few minutes before adding milk and sugar (this breaks down the starch and gives a velvety texture).

COFFEE

- To retain freshness: keep coffee in a tightly closed jar and store in refrigerator or freezer.
- To prevent freshly brewed coffee from having a bitter taste: remove "grinds" within 5 minutes after coffee is ready. Do *not* rewarm coffee more than once and Do *not* allow coffee to boil.
- ICED COFFEE: To retain full strength of coffee, prepare coffee ice cubes.

COOKIES

Do you consider cookies kid stuff? I know lots of adults who love them (me included). Cookies freeze beautifully. (Actually my children prefer them frozen; so much for freshly baked cookies.) Always have them in the freezer ready for expected or unexpected company, but periodically review the situation. The family may have gotten to them once too many times before the guests have a chance to arrive. Just be prepared to have them gobbled up by the family even before you have time to wash the pans.

What To Know
- It's easier to roll out cookie dough which has been refrigerated for a while.
- Bake on center rack only.
- First batch may take a little longer.
- To prevent bottoms from becoming burnt, cool baking pans before reusing.
- Remove cookies with the help of a metal spatula immediately upon taking out of oven.
- Cool cookies completely before storing.

Common mistakes with cookies
- Too crisp: too little fat or too much sugar
- Too soft: too much fat; under-kneading (after preparing dough in mixer some cookie doughs need some extra hand-kneading)
- To preserve freshness: Store cookies either in a tightly closed glass jar or in a tin container (bottom lined with waxed paper).
- If cookies are to be frozen, a plastic container may be used.

CORN SYRUP/MOLASSES

To keep corn syrup and molasses from sticking when measuring: rinse spoon and cup in cold water or grease cup lightly. See EQUIVALENTS/SUBSTITUTIONS.

CREPES

Crêpes are really not difficult to prepare and you can have such fun with the thousand and one different varieties: sweet and salty.

An idea for a fast crêpe dessert: Prepare sweet crêpes and serve with maple syrup or fill first with ice cream, fold up and cover with maple syrup.

Basic batter preparation directions: Sift dry ingredients into a bowl; blend liquid ingredients in a blender or whisk by hand in a large bowl and fold in flour mixture slowly. Do not overmix. Mix until just blended. Batter could even be a little lumpy. If possible let stand ½−1 hour before frying.

Basic frying directions: Lightly grease frying pan (this has to be done only the first time); heat over medium flame; pour in (or use large spoon) an amount of batter to make thin crêpes; tilt pan (or use back of large spoon) to spread batter all around. If there are a couple of small empty spaces, a drop of batter can be placed to fill it. You have to learn how to play around with the batter (experience is the only teacher). Don't be afraid to use your hands to turn crêpe over or to remove from pan (the crêpe is not too hot). Crêpes to be turned over should be turned over as soon as it looks a bit dry (do not wait for the sides to brown). Crêpes are fried on the second side for a shorter period of time). The entire process takes about 15−20 seconds and requires full attention, so don't expect to do anything else while making crêpes.

To store unfilled crêpes: separate crepes by waxed paper. A sheet of waxed paper between each crêpe will keep them from sticking together. Put in a plastic bag and seal. Crêpes can be refrigerated or frozen. If frozen, thaw before separating.

Common mistakes with crêpes

- Sticks to pan: too low heat; too thin batter; pan not oiled correctly; pan not clean
- Becomes brittle and cracks: overfrying; pan too hot
- Tough texture: overmixing of batter
- Not browning: too cool pan

CREAM

Whipping: For best results:
- Cream should be a day or two old.
- Mixing bowl and blade should be cold−either (a) refrigerate bowl and blade for about ½ hour; (b) fill bowl (with blade inside) with ice water and leave a few minutes; or, (c) pour cream in bowl and freeze for 15 minutes (freeze beater separately).
- Start beating cream on low speed then increase to medium-high (not high) speed for 2−3 minutes. Overbeating will result in butter.
- Beat cream with 2 teaspoons powdered sugar, 1−2 teaspoons vanilla extract and lemon juice or rum.
- Cream doubles in bulk when whipped.
- To preserve freshness for a day or two: It's best not to whip cream in advance, but if necessary, beat cream with a little corn syrup (ratio: one teaspoon corn syrup to one cup cream) and refrigerate. Whipped cream can keep in refrigerator for several hours.
- To retain firmness: Whip cream with ¼ teaspoon unflavored gelatin and when refrigerating place whipped cream in a sieve over a bowl (this will drain liquid).

CREAM PIES

Cream pies will keep about two days if refrigerated immediately. If possible, prepare and spread whipped cream the same day that you plan to serve the pie.

EGGS

My family can always tell how much baking and cooking I did by counting the amount of eggs used. I always have eggs in the house for cakes, quiches, muffins, bread, meat loaf etc.
- For best results, have eggs at room temperature. If you forgot to take them out of the refrigerator beforehand, it's possible to speed up the process by placing them in a bowl of warm water for a little while.
- Use stainless steel utensils when beating eggs or when eating soft boiled eggs (the sulfur in the egg will tarnish silver and silverplate).

TO BOIL EGGS

What's there to boiling an egg? You'd be surprised! For one, have eggs at room temperature. You can also add a few drops of lemon juice or vinegar to cooking water or rub a cut lemon over surface of egg (if egg is slightly cracked this process will prevent it from cracking wider).

- 3 MINUTE EGG: place egg into boiling water carefully (you can lower egg into water with spoon); reduce flame and simmer for three minutes (larger eggs take a bit longer). Remove from hot water immediately
- HARD BOILED EGG: place eggs in pot, cover with water; bring to boil; remove from flame; cover and leave for 20 minutes. Rinse under cold water. If slicing, to prevent crumbly yolks dip knife or egg slicer in ice water. I found out the hard way that in high altitude areas eggs take longer to cook. Generally all cooking takes longer in these areas.
- POACHED: crack egg open into a small bowl (if yolk breaks use another egg); add a bit of vinegar or lemon juice to water in shallow saucepan (to prevent whites from spreading); boil water; insert egg carefully. Poach 3–4 minutes over very low flame. Carefully remove with slotted spatula and place on buttered toast, spinach, potato etc.
- CODDLED EGG: quite similar to poached, but after placing egg in rapidly boiling water turn off flame and let eggs stand for 10–15 minutes (whites and yolks will have the same degree of jellied firmness).
- SHIRRED (baked) EGGS: crack egg open into a buttered custard cup; sprinkle with salt and pepper and bake at 325° F (165° C), 15–20 minutes. Serve in cup on saucer.

When adding eggs to hot sauces or puddings: first beat lightly in separate bowl; mix in about 2 tablespoons of sauce or pudding and then add to saucepan. 4–6 eggs = 1 cup

Egg Whites

When beating:

- Make sure there is not even a drop of egg yolk.
- Eggs should be room temperature
- Bowl and beater should be completely clean
- Break each egg separately and place egg whites in bowl
- To increase volume when beating, add about 2 teaspoons water for every egg white after the beaten whites start becoming firm
- For extra fluffiness, add ¼ teaspoon white vinegar to every 3 egg whites.
- Adding flavoring/sugar: whip whites until peaks form; add flavoring/sugar and whip until stiff.
- When folding beaten egg whites into batter, fold gently with wooden spoon to retain as much air as possible
- Optional: add ½ teaspoon cream of tartar to every 6 eggs.
- Egg whites can be frozen for future use. Thaw before using.
        8–10 egg whites = 1 cup

Egg Yolks

To store whole egg yolks: refrigerate in slightly salted water
        10–12 egg yolks = 1 cup.

EQUIVALENTS/SUBSTITUTIONS

Equivalents

Beans, dried 1 cup raw = 2½ cups cooked
Cheese, hard ½ kilo (1 lb.) = 4 cups grated
Chocolate, semisweet 200 grams (7½ oz) = 1 cup
Cream, whipping 1 cup (unwhipped) = 2 cups whipped
Coconut 250 grams (½ lb.) = 3 cups shredded
Cornflakes 3 cups = 1 cups crushed
Dates, pitted 250 grams (½ lb.) = 1¼ cups
1 cup, pitted = 1½ cups chopped

Eggs 4–6 = 1 cup

Egg whites 8–10 = 1 cup

Egg yolks 12–14 = 1 cup

Flour 250 grams (½ lb.) = almost 2 cups

Macaroni 250 grams (½ lb.) raw = 4 cups cooked

Nuts, shelled 250 grams (½ lb.) = 2 cups

Peaches 8 medium = about 4 cups, sliced

Rice 1 cup, raw = about 3 cups cooked

Raisins 500 grams (1 lb.) = 2 cups

Sugar, powdered 500 grams (1 lb.) = 3½ cups sifted

regular 500 grams (1 lb.) = 2¼ cups

Substitutions

Baking powder – 1 tablespoon = 1 tsp. baking soda plus 2 tsp. cream of tartar

Chocolate, unsweetened – 30 grams (1 oz.; 1 sq.) = ¼ cup cocoa plus ½ tsp. fat

Cornstarch – 1 tablespoon = 2 tbsp. flour

Cream, heavy – 1 cup = ¾ cup whole milk plus ⅓ cup melted butter

Cream, light – 1 cup = ¾ cup whole milk plus
1 tbsp. vinegar or lemon juice

Flour, 1 cup regular = ⅞ cup whole wheat

Milk – 1 cup = ½ cup non-dairy cream plus ½ cup water

Buttermilk – 1 cup = 1 cup sweet milk plus
1 tbsp. vinegar or lemon juice

Corn syrup – 1 cup = 1¼ cup sugar dissolved in ¼ cup liquid

Mustard – 1 teaspoon dry = 1 tbsp. prepared mustard

Yeast – 30 grams (1 oz.) frest = 15 grams (½ oz.) dried

VEGETABLES:

bamboo shoots = turnip, zucchini, cauliflower, celery

bean sprouts = turnip, cabbage, zucchini

chives = scallions

water chestnuts = celery, kohlrabi, radishes

mushrooms = prepared eggplant (salted, soaked and drained)

Temperature equivalents

Farenheit	Centigrade	British Marks
325	165	2-3
350	180	4
375	190	5
400	200	6
425	220	7
450	230	8

FISH

Fish is high in protein, low in calories and very versatile. It can be boiled, poached, fried, baked, broiled or barbecued. Hot and cold fish dishes can be served with lemon slices only, or some of a vast variety of sauces and dressings.

- FINDING FRESH FISH: eyes are bright, clear and slightly protruding. Scales will be shiny and snug against the skin.
- TO SCALE: sprinkle salt on wooden board to prevent slipping. Cut off fins; rub fish with vinegar, then scale with a dull knife.
- ELIMINATING ODOR: before cooking marinate in a pan of lemon juice for about an hour in the refrigerator, turning once; rinse under cold water and pat dry.

- KEEPING FISH WHOLE: Fish falls apart easily after cooking. To keep fish sections together, allow fish to cool in pot then move with metal spatula into a lipped serving dish. Pour fish stock into dish and refrigerate.
- DEODORIZING HANDS: Wash hands in heavily salted water or with vinegar.
- CLEANING THE PAN: pour about ½ cup vinegar or salted water into pan; bring to boil; let stand a while and wash in soapy water.
- BAKING: Suggested fish for baking – blue fish, mackerel, salmon, trout, white fish, flounder fillet.
- FRYING: To prevent splattering, fish should be dry. Pat dry with paper towel or dish towel.

FREEZING

Knowing how to freeze foods is the biggest life-saver in the world. The list of foods (raw or cooked) which can be frozen is endless. *e.g.* soups, gravies, sauces, meat balls, stuffed cabbage, quiches, cookies, cakes, breads, crêpes, pancakes, pastry doughs, nuts, egg whites etc.

FREEZING CHEESES: I always keep grated hard cheese in the freezer for immediate use. Frozen cheeses become a bit dry and flaky so I use them only in cooking and baking. They will lose a little of their flavor, but the convenience is worth it. A combination of Swiss, cheddar and Parmesan is great for quiches, food pies, vegetable and fish crêpes etc.

A few things to keep in mind:

- Liquids (soups, sauces) must have room for expansion
- Freeze in air tight containers or bags
- Foods frozen in pyrex dishes should be thawed out slowly before rewarming. Quick heating of frozen pyrex dishes may cause them to crack.
- Don't freeze prepared foods for a long period of time
- Freezing vegetables: use quality produce; wash well; cut into desired pieces; blanch to retain flavor (blanch ½ kilogram (1 lb.) at a time), drain, cool thoroughly, wrap in paper toweling or dish towel and place in refrigerator until completely cold. Sprinkle with a little cornflour (to retain color), place in containers (leaving room for expansion) and place in freezer.
- To defrost vegetables: vegetables cooked with other ingredients do not have to be thawed out. Cook them less than you would fresh vegetables. Note: Defrost and cook only the amount needed.
- Cabbage: to be used for stuffing. Place cabbage in freezer a few days before using. Allow to thaw overnight in a bowl (since water will come out). Cabbage will be then ready for stuffing.

FROSTINGS, ICINGS & GLAZES

Dress up the cake. A pretty party cake can be simply a two-tier layer cake, filled and frosted.

- To frost a layer cake: place one layer upside down on a serving plate (so that the top is flat). Either use a special filling for this layer or use a frosting for both layers (a glaze should not be used for this layer). After spreading frosting or filling place the second layer right side up. If frosting sides, first frost sides and then top.
- To achieve a thick, uncooked frosting: a lot depends on the recipe of course, but also uncooked frosting takes up to ten minutes of fast beating to become thick. If it doesn't thicken adequately, add some powdered sugar and refrigerate for a while before using.
- To prevent frosting from penetrating into cake: wait until cake cools and sprinkle some powdered sugar before frosting.
- If frosting becomes too thick while beating add a little lemon juice.
- Glazes should be made when ready to use (if left standing it will dry up and crack). Glazes are easy and take about a minute to prepare.

Listed below are several examples of quick glazes. The first, Mocha Glaze, is a simple example of the most common form of glaze: combining confectioner's sugar with a little liquid flavoring.

MOCHA GLAZE Melt a little margarine, add a little liquid flavoring, a drop of water, cocoa and coffee (if desired) and confectioner's sugar. Spread or pour on warm cake immediately.

QUICK CUPCAKE ICING place a small square of bittersweet chocolate on each hot cupcake; allow about one minute to melt and spread around with small metal spatula.

QUICK FRUIT TART GLAZE heat jelly with a little water (ratio: 1 tablespoon water to ¼ cup jelly). Use currant jelly for dark fruit tarts (berries) and apricot jam for light colored fruit tarts (peaches, apricots).

FRUITS

Avocado
A ripe avocado 'gives' when pressed gently and has a slight bronze discoloration. It shouldn't be too soft or too brown.

To prevent discoloration after cutting: peel avocado by hand and only use wooden utensils; sprinkle open avocado with lemon juice.

Bananas
Suggestions for overripe bananas – mash, sprinkle with lemon juice and freeze. Can be used for baking; (thaw out before using. Proces can be done in a few seconds in the microwave.)

Dates (dried)
To cut, freeze dates a few hours before. Dip knife in hot water occasionally while cutting. To prevent sinking to bottom of cake: dust with flour before adding to the batter or dry out in slow oven.

Kiwi   Also known as "Chinese Gooseberry," it is native to New Zealand.
- to test for ripeness: a ripe kiwi will "give" a litle under pressure.
- to ripen: wrap each in newspaper; leave in a dark place and check each day for ripeness.

DELIGHTFUL FRUIT SALAD Make a day in advance. Include grapefruit, oranges (both without membrane), persimmons, kiwi, strawberries, bananas, dried dates, flaked coconut, raisins, cointreau, sweet red wine (a little sugar and lemon juice if desired). Sprinkle individual cups with coarsely chopped nuts.

Lemons
One of the most versatile fruits. It's used to eliminate fishy odors, gives a most delicate flavor to foods, keeps fruit from discoloring, removes food stains from hands, cleans brass (use with mild steel wool), and makes a refreshing pitcher of lemonade.
- To get maximum juice – refrigerate in a tightly closed glass jar (keeps for a few days). Freeze in a tightly closed container, allow room for expansion (keeps for a few months).
- To prevent lemon wedges from squirting – prick lemon with fork before cutting wedges.
- To peel – rinse lemon in cold water and grate only the thin yellow skin.
- To store – dry out peel in slow oven; store in freezer in closed container. Can be frozen for a few months.

Oranges
- Orange rind: rinse orange under cold water; grate only thin orange portion.
- To freeze – dry out in slow oven; store in closed jar (keeps for a couple of months).

Peaches
- To skin – drop into boiling water (completely immerse fruit); turn off flame; leave 1-2 minutes; drain; rinse in cold water; peirce sking gently with knife and peel down. Skin should come off easily.
- To ripen – place in brown paper bag with a ripe apple and make a few holes in bag. Leave in a cool dark place.

Pears   To ripen – follow same technique as for peaches, above.

Pineapple   To test for ripeness – inner leaf should pull out easily.

Strawberries
To retain firmness – buy firm strawberries; they will keep for a few days by refrigerating them unwashed in a colander (this allows the cold air to circulate around them.)

Tomatoes
"Slicing" tomatoes should be firm and "cooking" tomatoes soft.
- To ripen tomatoes – place in basket in a dark place.
- To skin – drop tomatoes into boiling water (completely immersed; let boil for about 10 seconds; plunge into a pan of cold water to stop cookng process; drain and peel off skin. Skin may have to be pierced gently to start peeling.

- To prepare tomatoes for stuffing – use small firm tomatoes; cut off about ½″ from top and cut out center stem. If making cold salad stuffing, set aside tops. With grapefruit knife cut around inner circumference; scoop out insides with a spoon; sprinkle cavity with salt; invert and refrigerate about ½ hour.
- Suggestions for cold stuffing: egg tuna, chicken, avocado or rice salad, vegetarian or regular chopped liver. Use reserved tops as hats and place an olive in the middle.
- For hot baked stuffed tomatoes – bake in greased muffin tins to retain shape, or place close together in baking pan.

FRYING & SAUTEING

Frying: quick cooking of whole food in heated oil or other fat in uncovered pan.; *e.g.* fish, croquettes
Sautéing: quick cooking of diced or sliced foods in heated oil or other fat in uncovered pan: *e.g.* onions, garlic, vegetable, nuts.

- Heat oil or other fat before adding food. Be careful not to overheat.
- Melt butter over low flame. Afterwards flame can be increased. (High heat when melting butter will cause burning).
- After frying, drain food on paper towel or paper bag.
- To prevent food from splattering, pat food dry whenever possible before frying and place a flat round strainer over pan.
- To retain crispiness of food after frying, preheat platter. After draining, place fried food on preheated platter and leave uncovered.

GELATIN MOLDS

- To attain firm mold: add one teaspoon of white vinegar to the ingredients
- To unmold:

  Method I – run a knife around the mold; prepare a bowl of hot water bigger than the mold, have the serving platter at hand and dip the mold into hot water for a few seconds (be careful the water doesn't go over the top).Place the serving platter over mold and invert. If mold doesn't drop tap with a knife. If necessary, repeat the process. Refrigerate immediately.

  Method II: Run a knife around mold; invert onto serving platter; wet a towel with hot water and place over mold. If necessary, wet towel again and repeat process. Refrigerate immediately.

GRAINS

Grains include wheat, rye, rice, flour, oats, barley, wheat germ, bran
- To store grains, either store in freezer (which is what I do) or remove from original packaging and store in pantry in tightly closed glass jar. With the latter method grains have a shorter life span, and whole grain products (e.g. whole wheat flour, natural rice) have an even shorter life span.

Flour
- When substituting regular flour for cake flour use about one teaspoon less.
- When substituting whole wheat flour for regular, reduce amount by about one tablespoon. Regular flour is heavier than cake flour and whole wheat is heavier than regular.
- To use flour for thickening sauces, soups, and gravies: first stir the flour into a small amount of melted fat or hot liquid in a separate dish. Mix into a smooth paste and add slowly to the pot or saucepan.
- To give substance to meat loaf, fish cakes, vegetable croquettes, etc., use raw oats, wheat germ and bran instead of bread crumbs; it's healthier and tastier.

HIGH ALTITUDE AREAS

Cooking takes longer in high altitude areas since the boiling point of water is lower. Baking is not affected by high altitude.
- Deep frying: the temperature of fat should be lower. Try using a lower flame.

- Yeast doughs: dough tends to rise more rapidly, thus allow for shorter rising time (check when size of dough doubles) or use a little less yeast.

HONEY

To reliquify crystallized honey, place jar in very hot water (not boiling) and leave until honey thins out.

ICE CUBES

- To prevent air bubbles: boil water; let cool; fill ice cube trays and freeze.
- To retain maximum strength of iced coffee, freeze coffee cubes.

LEGUMES

Dried beans (kidney, navy, lima, pinto, black, and soy), peas (black-eyed, fresh, and split), soy bean curd (tofu), soy flour, peanuts (including peanut butter)

To cut down cooking time of dried beans: soak in cold water (ratio 1 cup beans to 4 cups water) for a few hours or overnight; drain, rinse and cook. Or bring beans and water to a boil; cover and leave two hours. Drain, rinse and cook. Exact cooking time depends on consistency desired, but for pre-soaked beans it is about 2 hours.

MEAT

Meat loaf
- To prevent top from cracking, moisten top with cold water before baking.
- For an added touch: 15 minutes before meat loaf is done spread cooked mashed potatoes on top; smear with melted margarine; return to oven and finish baking

Tongue
- If tongue becomes over-salty from pickling process: to eliminate the extra saltiness, cover tongue completely with water; bring to boil; pour off water; add fresh water and boil 2½ – 3 hours.
- To test for doneness: insert a two-pronged fork into tongue. If it goes in easily, the tongue is done.
- Skinning is easier when the tongue is still warm, but slicing is easier when cold. So cook tongue ahead of time (even a day before). Slice cold and serve as is or place in sauce and rewarm.
  See recipe: **Sweet & Sour Tongue Sauce**

MILK

- To prevent milk from scorching and sticking to sides of pot when scalding: before placing milk into pot rinse pot with cold water.
- If recipe calls for sour milk or buttermilk: you can use whole milk by adding vinegar or lemon juice (ratio: 1 cup milk to 1 tablespoon vinegar or lemon juice).

MUFFINS

There's nothing like muffins with that morning coffee. They're so easy to prepare: just a few stirs with the spoon; pop them into the oven and, before you know it, they're ready.

- When preparing batter, keep mixing to a minimum. Too much mixing will result in tough-textured muffins.
- If you don't fill all the muffin tins, pour a little water into the empty ones (this will prevent the muffins from becoming dry).
- To reheat muffins: preheat oven at 450° F; wrap muffins up loosely in aluminum foil and bake about 5 minutes.

NUTS

Good source of vegetable protein — almonds, brazil, cashews, hazelnuts (filberts) peanuts, pecans, pine nuts, walnuts. To roast all nuts, preheat oven at 200° F; spread nuts on baking sheet and roast until delicately brown. Sprinkle with salt if desired.

Brazilnuts To shell brazil nuts: roast nuts in oven at 400° F about 20 minutes. Remove from oven; cool, crack lengthwise and shell.

Hazelnuts To improve flavor of hazelnuts: bake nuts at 400° F until lightly toasted.

Almonds
- Blanching (skinning): boil water; throw in almonds (completely immersed); remove from flame; leave about one minute; drain; rinse under cold water; squeeze between fingers (or slit with knife if completely closed) and skin will pop off. Dry out on baking sheet in moderate oven (350° F) about 5 minutes.
- Toasting blanched almonds: roast in moderate oven (350° F) about 10 minutes, stirring frequently.
- Sautéing blanched almonds: heat butter in saucepan on low flame; add almonds and sauté a few minutes. When almonds become brown transfer to bowl immediately in order to stop cooking process (otherwise almonds may burn). Great on broiled or fried fish.

PASTA

- To cook pasta (noodles, macaroni, spaghetti) place in rapidly boiling water; mix with fork and cook uncovered over medium-high flame (water should bubble).
- One tablespoon oil added to water will prevent pasta from sticking together and water from boiling over pot.

PASTRY

Homemade pastry doughs are so much better than store-bought ones and with the aid of the food processor, so easy to prepare. See recipe for **Plain Pastry Dough**.
- Using ice water makes the pastry dough flakier.
- Handling pastry dough (plain or short crust): One key to good pastry dough is handling it *as little as possible*. The more you handle the dough, the harder and heavier the finished crust will be. Do not knead the dough. Just mix the ingredients until they hold together.
- Rolling out: For best results, refrigerate pastry dough 20 minutes before rolling. Roll out in one direction at a time to a size a little bigger than the pie plate so that you will be able to flute the edges with the overlap.
- To place dough in pie plate, fold in half; lift carefully; place in plate and unfold. If dough overlaps too much in one place and is missing in another, you can cut off the excess and with floured fingers fill in empty places. Double the overlap onto the edge of the pie plate and flute.
- Freezing: all pastry doughs can be frozen for future use. Allow time for thawing out. One third of the **Plain Pastry Dough** is good for a 9" (23 cm) pie, so before freezing I divide the pastry dough into thirds and freeze separately.
- To prepare pre-baked pastry crust, place pastry dough in pie plate, overlapping and fluting edges; and with fork prick pastry dough on bottom and sides in quite a few places. Spread a piece of aluminum foil on bottom; spread one cup dried beans on aluminum foil and bake as directed. Beans can be stored in jar for further use.
- To achieve a flakier upper pie crust: brush crust lightly with cold water.

Different kinds of fluting
- With fork, press down dough around the edges. Dip fork in flour occasionally to prevent sticking.
- With index and middle fingers of one hand: Spread fingers slightly and hold down crust edge (tips of fingers facing outward from pie) and with the index finger of your other hand push the dough between fingers towards center of pie.

PIES

Sweet, Fruit, Vegetable, Fish, Meat pies and quiches. Pies are great family and company favorites. I use sweet fruit pies as desserts. The pastry dough is almost as important as the filling. Unless otherwise indicated the crust should be rolled out pretty thin.

- To make the pie attractive: finish off (flute) the circumference in a decorative manner.
- Read recipe carefully if pastry crust is to be prebaked, semi-baked or unbaked.
- To attain a shiny upper crust: a few minutes before pie is done, brush the top with a little white (or cider) vinegar and finish baking.

Juicy Fruit Pies
- To prevent a soggy bottom crust: before pouring filling into crust, brush bottom crust with beaten egg white, and allow to dry.
- To prevent juice from running over top crust of pie: For lattice top pies, stick a few pieces of raw macaroni into top crust – macaroni abosrbs the extra juice. (Remove macaroni before serving.) For solid crust top pies, prick top crust with fork in a few places. If juices manage to run over onto floor of oven, sprinkle coarse salt on the spill (this will prevent smoking). Avoid potentially messy cleaning problems by placing a piece of aluminum foil on bottom of oven, underneath pie.

POULTRY

Chicken, turkey, duck, cornish hens, squab, capon.

Chicken
I find chicken to be one of the most versatile foods. It can be roasted, broiled, boiled, stewed, fried or barbecued.
- To prevent unpleasant odors: do not keep raw poultry in plastic bags in the refrigerator. If there is a smell, wash chicken with lemon juice, then rub it with salt and lemon juice.
- To broil chicken: chickens should be broiled at a distance from the flame (broiling too close to flame with cause burnt, unfinished chicken). Broil skin side down 20–25 minutes; turn over and broil 10–15 minutes.
- To roast chicken: to prevent dryness tie up wings and drumsticks (dental floss can be used for this purpose).
- To test chicken for doneness: insert a skewer into the thickest part of the leg. If the oozing liquid is clear, the chicken is done.
- To thicken pan gravy: place some gravy in small pot; dissolve a little cornstarch or flour in a small amount of cold water and mix until smooth; heat together with gravy over low flame.
- To roast frozen poultry: Don't Do It! Roasting poultry which is not completely thawed out will cause stringiness. It's best to defrost chickens slowly (in refrigerator), thus retaining maximum flavor and juiciness.
- Stuffing poultry: stuff poultry when ready to roast. Bread or rice stuffing should be packed loosely to allow room for expansion. If the cavity opening is too large, place an end-piece (heel) of bread at the opening in order to hold the stuffing in place (discard bread before serving). To close up cavity, use either small skewers, toothpicks, or sew up with dental floss. Stuffed poultry requires a longer roasting time than unstuffed poultry.
- To fry coated chicken pieces: after coating pieces with flour it's good to refrigerate for about one hour in order to allow flour to stick to the chicken.
- VARIATION: rub raw chicken with a paste made of fresh crushed garlic, pepper, paprika, mustard and a little wine vinegar. Place sliced onion and a little water in roasting pan. Place chicken in pan breast side down; roast 30 minutes; cover with a mixture of orange juice and dry wine (or other sauce mixture); bake another ½ hour; turn chicken over; then baste every 30 minutes with pan gravy until done. Roasting time depends on size of chicken. Try different basting sauces (orange juice and wine is the simplest one). Try **Apricot Chicken Sauce.**

Cornish Hens
Time table at 400° F, 200° for hen weight of 500 grams: Time = about 1½ hours

Duck
For my family, a roast duck is something special, and since I don't make it too often, I guess it will always be a treat.
- Best duck for roasting is young duck weighing about 2 kilograms (4 lbs.).
- To eliminate smell: rub inside cavity with salt and lemon juice.
- To eliminate that fatty taste: be sure to prick the skin in a few places before roasting to allow the fat to escape.
- Do not use pan gravy for basting. Prepare enough basting sauce and baste with fresh sauce each time.
- Duck feeds fewer people than chicken of the same weight.
- Duck is done when the oozing liquid is a pale yellow color.

- If you want to roast duck on a rotary spit, be sure to pierce the skin in a few places, tie up wings and drumsticks (dental floss can be used); and roast on medium heat. Last fifteen minutes turn heat to high for browning. No basting is necessary and timing is the same as for oven roasting.

TIMETABLE FOR UNSTUFFED DUCK

Temperature to use for all sizes: 450° F, 230° C: first ½ hour
350° F, 180° C for remaining time

WEIGHT	TOT TIME
3½ lbs	1 hr. and 15–25 minutes
4½ lbs	1 hr and 25–35 minutes
5½ lbs	1 hr and 35–45 minutes

Turkey

- To stuff: See Poultry recipe section
- To test for doneness: move drumstick gently. If it moves easily or breaks away, the turkey is done. Don't depend completely on timetable.

Timetable for stuffed turkey at 325° F, 160° C)

WEIGHT	TIME
3½–4½ kilo (7½–8½ lbs.)	4½ –4¾ hours
5 – 6½ kilo (10½–14 lbs)	5 – 5½ hours
7–9 kilo (15–19 lbs)	5¾–6¼ hours
9½–11 kilo (20–23 lbs)	6¼–7 hours

(For unstuffed turkey reduce roasting time by ¾ hours).

QUICHES

Don't be afraid of quiches. They're easier to prepare than you think. Before I began creating quiches, they I was convinced that they were impossibly complicated. Once the initial attempt was made, I found them "easy as pie."

A quiche is a pie-like dish made up of 5 layers with a variable filling layer. Layers include pastry dough, grated or cubed hard cheese (Swiss, cheddar and Parmesan: a mixture of two or three), filling (suggestions: mushroom, tuna and sautéed onion; sautéed scallion; sautéed onion and tomatoes, all with seasoning of salt, pepper, basil, parsley etc.), another layer of grated or cubed cheese, and custard topping (1 cup sweet cream, 2–3 eggs, ¼ cup white dry wine, salt, pepper and pinch of nutmeg – nutmeg is optional).

Tips for making quiches easy: the pastry dough, grated cheese mixture and sweet cream can be kept in the freezer. Just be sure to allow time for thawing out the pastry dough. To grate cheese easily, use the vegetable shredder attachment to your food processor or mixer.

Types of pans: round pyrex pie plate, flan ring or a false bottom straight-sided cake tin.

- When using a flan ring, grease the ring and place on an unlipped greased cookie sheet. Roll out pastry dough and place in flan ring overlapping on sides. Double sides under and flute (allowing ring to be removed after baking). Fill with quiche layers, bake, leave at least 20 minutes to allow for settling. Remove flan ring and slide quiche off baking sheet onto serving platter.
- Quiches made in a false-bottom cake tin should be prepared as for a flan ring. When ready to unmold, place cake tin carefully over a jar or can (smaller than the ring) and remove ring downward. Quiche can then be pushed off with the aid of a long-bladed metal spatula onto a serving plate.
- When to serve quiches: as a side dish with the main course; part of a buffet; as a main luncheon course served with black bread or garlic bread and a salad.

SALADS & DRESSINGS

Whatever else you eat, a salad is always delicious and refreshing when made with fresh, quality vegetables. The salad dressing is even more important than the combination of vegetables used. A salad can even be made with lettuce alone.

The standard tossed salad includes any combination of lettuce, cucumber, red and green pepper, tomatoes, scallions and parsley. Variations can include: red cabbage, radishes, carrots, raisins, sunflower seeds, Roquefort cheese, feta cheese, croutons, avocado, walnuts etc.

Dressings

Mix the dressing ingredients separately in a jar or food processor and then pour over salad. If using food processor, process garlic with metal blade, add rest of ingredients and process until smooth.

- Most dressings will keep in the refrigerator for a couple of weeks.
- For a creamier-extra-smooth dressing, place all ingredients except oil in blender, blend and then add oil slowly. For extra smoothness, place blender dressing in jar, add ice cubes, close jar and shake vigorously. Discard ice cubes and pour over salad.
- When using tuna fish, hard boiled eggs, and/or avocado add a little lemon juice to the dressing.

A good ratio for a standard Vinaigrette Dressing (adjust amount to size of salad):

¼ cup salad or olive oil
2 tbsp. cider or wine vinegar
¼ tsp. salt
7⅛ tsp. pepper

½ tsp. sugar
1 tsp. prepared mustard
2 cloves garlic, crushed
1 tbsp. water (or, if using cider: dry white wine)

A good ratio for Mayonnaise Dressing:

¼ cup mayonnaise
2 tsp. lemon juice

1 tsp. prepared mustard
salt & pepper to taste

These two dressings can be used together in one salad.

Lettuce

- Lettuce should be torn apart by hand (cutting with a knife will cause edges to blacken quickly).
- To core iceberg lettuce: bang bottom hard on counter and remove core.

Tomatoes

To prevent the salad from getting soggy, toss salad without tomatoes. Then place tomato slices or wedges on top just before serving.

- To prevent sogginess of leftover salad: place an inverted saucer on bottom of bowl before putting in the salad.
- When to prepare salads: salads with dressing made with lettuce and/or tomatoes should be prepared just before serving. Other salads should be prepared, dressed and refrigerated a few hours or a day in advance to allow them to marinate.

SOUPS

Soups have many advantages, the main one being that everyone seems to love them. What's better on a cold wintry day than a hot bowl of delicious soup, or a refreshing cold soup in the heat of summer? Soups are also filling. If you serve soup, you can bet few will go away from the table hungry, especially if they ask for a second bowlful.

- A little white wine or sherry added to the soup at the end gives it extra taste.
- To remove fat from soup: place a lettuce leaf on top of the soup, then remove the fat-absorbed lettuce leaf. Or wrap an ice cube in a piece of cheese cloth or paper towel and run it across the top of the soup. The fat will cling to the cold material.
- If soup is too salty, try placing a potato in the soup; boil for 10 minutes, then discard the potato.

Garnishes

- Croutons: especially if they are mixed with melted butter and crushed garlic cloves.
- Grated cheese: one or a combination may be used: Swiss, cheddar, Parmesan. Croutons and cheeses can be used together.
- A slice of French or plain white bread: especially in onion soup. See **Onion Soup**.

TEMPERATURES

- To convert Fahrenheit into Centigrade: subtract 32; multiply by 5; divide by 9 (($F° - 32$) x $5/9$)
- To convert Centigrade into Fahrenheit: multiply by 9; divide by 5 and add 32.

For a chart of temperature equivalents see 'Equivalents'.

THICKENING

FLOUR: gives an opaque color for sauces, gravies, soups. Before adding flour, blend with a small amount of melted fat or with 2–3 tablespoons of hot sauce, gravy or soup. Mix until smooth, then add slowly and stir until blended in and thickened (if left alone after preparing, it will thicken by itself).

CORNSTARCH: retains a clear color for sauces, gravies and soups. Since cornflour is more concentrated than flour use half the amount when substituting. Mix the cornstarch in a small amount of cold liquid before adding to sauce, gravy or soup.

Suggestion: Try blending ¼ cup cornstarch with ¼ cup sherry as a thickening for a 10-cup soup.

EGG YOLK: before adding to sauces, blend with 2 tablespoons hot sauce to prevent yolk from hardening.

OATS: for vegetable soups, chopped meat, fish cakes

BARLEY: for soups

PUREED, COOKED ONIONS or vegetables: for sauces and soups

BREADCRUMBS, WHEAT GERM and flaked bran: for chopped meat, fish cakes

VEGETABLES

Quality, fresh vegetables will ensure tastier dishes.
Check recipe carefully to see if firm or soft produce is required.

To retain freshness when refrigerating

- Don't wash produce before refrigerating; instead, wrap in paper towels, or line vegetable bin with absorbent paper to draw off any excess water on vegetables. (See the following sections on individual vegetables)
- Root vegetables (beets, turnips, carrots): Cut off any excess green, leafy tops before refrigerating to prevent juices from being drawn into the leaves.
- Leafy vegetables and herbs (lettuce, Swiss chard, spinach, leeks, dill, parsley): To clean, soak in salted water for about ½ hour, rinse under cold water, dry in salad spinner or over toweling, wrap in cotton or paper towel, place in plastic bag and refrigerate. Parsley, dill and celery leaves can be frozen for future use in cooking only.

To retain maximum vitamin value when cooking vegetables

- Cut or shred vegetables just before cooking.
- Don't soak vegetables too long prior to cooking.
- To retain the greatest nutritional value of vegetables, cook vegetables whole or in large chunks. The longer vegetables are cooked the more nutrients they lose to the cooking process.
- Steaming vegetables is the most nutritionally advisable method of cooking them – the vegetables are not immersed in the water but rather are cooked in a strainer-like basket over the boiling water. Special steamer baskets and pots are easily available. Remember: don't overcook.
- If cooking in water, use as little water as possible and cook over a low flame. Don't overcrowd: vegetables need breathing space.

THE WOK METHOD: vegetables are sautéed in a small amount of oil for a minimum amount of time. The vegetables retain their crunchiness, taste and nutrition.

BLANCHING: This process is used when vegetables (cauliflower, zucchini) are to be used in other dishes, e.g., salads, frying, baking, etc. To blanch, cover vegetables completely with water, bring to boil, lower flame and cook a few minutes. Drain and rinse under cold water in order to stop the cooking process.

Other variations on vegetables

Dehydrated vegetables: these vegetables are used for quick flavoring of soups and stews. For maximum flavor, quicker and more even cooking soak in a little water for about 10 minutes. Add to soup or stew together with the water.

Revitalizing wilted vegetables: remove brown spots, soak for an hour in cold water in which lemon juice or vinegar was added.

Artichokes

They're a conversation piece. Artichokes are odd looking, but well worth learning how to cook and eat. My family got so carried away with them that I now possess a dozen artichoke plates.

- Fresh artichokes: leaves are close together.
- Size doesn't affect the taste. Feel free to buy the larger, meatier artichokes.

- Preparation and cooking: fill a large bowl with water, a little lemon juice or vinegar, and salt. Cut stem of artichoke with a knife or remove by bending and twisting. If you like, clip artichoke leaves about one inch from top (for esthetic reasons only). With scissors, snip off a little from each leaf. Soak artichokes in the prepared water for about ½ hour. Rinse well under cold water. Place in pot, cover with water, bring to boil and add a drop of oil, some salt, pepper and a few bay leaves. Cook over medium flame, partially or completely covered, 35-45 minutes, depending on size. When they're done the leaves should come off easily. Remove artichokes from pot with slotted spoon and drain upside down. Serve at room temperature with either melted garlic butter, **Vinaigrette Dressing**, or **Tartar Sauce Dressing** (see index).
- To eat: place artichoke upside down on plate; peel off each leaf; dip in desired dressing and eat as much as you can from the bottom of each leaf (only the soft part). Discard the rest. As you get close to the heart remove more than one leaf at a time (otherwise it will take you until tomorrow). When only a few pointy leaves are left, pull off altogether. With a spoon, knife or fingers, remove the hairy choke. What is left is the "heart of the matter." You may eat the whole thing either with fingers or fork and knife (I prefer using the latter). Don't forget to dip each piece into the dressing.
- Artichoke plates: if you become a great fan of artichokes, look into buying artichoke plates. I had no idea what they looked like, but when I saw them in a store window I knew I had found them.
- Artichoke hearts: freshly cooked and served at room temperature, artichoke hearts are the most elegant and delicious dish as an appetizer or at a buffet. Place desired dressing in the center and surround them with colorful vegetables. Serve extra dressing for extra helpings.
- Artichokes can keep for a few days before cooking by refrigerating them unwashed in a damp towel in a plastic bag.

Beets

When buying beets, look for a smooth skin and firm beet. The smaller the better (larger beets tend to be "woody" and stringier in flavor). The condition of the green tops is no indication of freshness since they wither very quickly.

- If raw beets are to be refrigerated a few days, cut off leaves since the leaves will continue to draw out the moisture from the beets.
- To peel beets: cooked beets are easier to peel. Wash beets well with vegetable brush. Cook completely immersed in water until tender, plunge in cold water and drain. With a knife, gently cut into peel and peel off. If recipe calls for cooking grated raw beets, peel off skin with a vegetable peeler.
- To prevent discoloration: cook beets with skin and a little of the stem. If beets must be cooked unpeeled add a little lemon juice or vinegar to the cooking water.
- To remove beet stains from hands: rub hands with a piece of lemon.

Cabbage

I find this to be one of the most versatile vegetables. It can be used as a salad, stuffed, sautéed (along or with other vegetables) and mixed with noodles, in egg rolls, vegetable strudel, on rice, in soups, in corned beef, cooked "sweet & sour" etc.

To prepare for stuffing: place entire cabbage in freezer a few days before using. Allow enough time to defrost (sometimes I leave it overnight). Defrosting time depends on the temperature in the room. When defrosting, place in some sort of bowl since water will run out. When defrosted, squeeze gently to eliminate excess water. Cut around core bottom and remove leaves carefully.

Cauliflower

- To buy: select a firm white one.
- To clean: soak cauliflower in salted water for about ½ hour in order to remove dirt and any foreign matter.
- To eliminate gassiness: boil for five minutes in a little water; drain; rinse under cold water and cook with fresh water.
- To eliminate odor: place a slice of stale bread in the second cooking water. Remove before serving.
- To retain whiteness: place a slice of lemon peel in the second cooking water.

Corn

- To buy: select those with a light or medium yellow color.
- To boil: remove silk and husks, place in pot, cover with water, bring to boil, lower flame and cook covered for five minutes. For added flavor place inner green husks on bottom of pot.

- To roast: remove silk carefully while leaving on husks. Roast at 325° F (160° C) about 25 minutes. Remove husks before serving.
- An easy way to butter corn: melt butter over a low flame and brush on corn with pastry brush.
- Uses for leftover cooked corn: cold corn kernels are a nice addition to salads, e.g., **rice, tuna, Niçoise, Chef.** (see index)
- It's easier to strip kernels from corn if corn was frozen and then thawed out. To strip: hold cob upright and with a sharp knife cut downward. If necessary separate kernels by hand.

Cucumber
When pickling: use non-iodized salt only. Be sure to leave a little room for expansion.

Eggplants
- To buy: the eggplant should feel heavier than its size. Also smaller eggplants are tastier.
- To prepare: in order to get rid of excess water and the bitter taste, slice the eggplant, sprinkle each slice with salt, let stand about ½, hour, rinse under cold water and pat dry.

Garlic
Oh for the flavor of garlic — how divine!
Whenever possible I use fresh garlic. The food processor or garlic press does the job of mincing all my garlic.
- To store: wrap the heads of garlic in a piece of waxed paper and store in vegetable draw of the refrigerator. They can keep for a couple of weeks.
- To make garlic oil or vinegar: Garlic oil – peel off skin from garlic, cut garlic in half, place in oil and leave overnight at room temperature. Remove garlic. Garlic vinegar – peel off skin, cut in half, place in vinegar and leave for a few weeks.
- If skin is difficult to remove, either pound each clove with the side of a knife or soak cloves in warm water for a little while.

Green Beans
To retain maximum flavor and preserve vitamins when cooking: sauté green beans in a little oil before cooking in a little salted water. Only cook ½ kilogram (1 lb.) at a time and use minimum amount of water (slightly salted). It is best to use a steamer.

Mushrooms (One of my favorite vegetables.)
Use raw mushrooms in salads, soups. Sauté for sauces, stews, chicken and meat dishes, scrambled eggs, etc. If you use the caps for salads keep stems for cooked dishes. (See Recipe **Marinated Mushroom Caps**).
- To buy: fresh mushrooms are white and have closed undersides.
- To prepare: fresh white mushrooms do not have to be peeled. Clean them in a bowl of water (do not soak); rinse under cold water and pat dry.
- To store: mushrooms can be refrigerated for a few days. To retain whiteness, try sprinkling with lemon juice before refrigerating. If they get brownish they must be peeled.
- To freeze (although I prefer not doing this): wash mushrooms, dry, place in an airtight container or plastic bag.
- To attain uniform slices: slice with mushroom or egg slicer.

Onions
I never seem to have enough onions. I am forever sautéing onions as a base for so many dishes.
- About sautéing: always preheat oil before adding onion and garlic. Beware not to overheat oil (this may be detrimental to your health). If you're sautéing the onions with other vegetables sauté the onions and garlic a few minutes alone before adding other ingredients.
- For a more "tender" sautéed onion, cover the pan the first few minutes.
- To avoid tears when peeling: Sometimes nothing helps. Try peeling near cold running water or refrigerate them overnight and peel while still cold.

Potatoes
Rules for FRENCH FRIED POTATOES:
1) deep fry in preheated oil (be careful not to overheat oil)
2) pat dry potato strips before adding to oil (this will keep the heat constant and prevent splattering)
3) don't overcrowd. Not heeding these few rules will result in soggy, oily French fries.

POTATO SALAD: prepare the dressing separately in a jar or food processor and mix into warm potatoes. This will cause the dressing to be absorbed better. (See index for **Potato Salad**).

WINES (dry and semi-dry)

Specific times to serve white or red wines: I was once told to serve white wine at fish dinners and red with meat, but actually I prefer offering both at all times. Serving wine adds an elegant and delicious touch to any dinner.

- To store closed corked wines: store on a tilt or completely lying down (if your cabinet shelves are adjustable you may be able to tilt a shelf for the wines). This will keep the cork wet and expanded, thus preventing air from penetrating. A dry cork will split when corking.
- To serve: refrigerate about 2 hours before serving.
- Uses: soups (add at the end of cooking time and heat through), sauces (add and cook uncovered until alcohol smell boils off), meat (brown meat before adding wine, otherwise meat will become wine-soaked).

A Kitchen Dictionary

A la creole: cooked with tomatoes and olives

A la dente (el dente): (slight resistance to the teeth) referring to pasta cooked but not too soft – so that it is still capable of absorbing sauce added to the pasta.

A la mode: (in fashion) usually referring to a dessert pie topped with ice cream

Amandine: containing almonds

Antipasto: an appetizer or buffet platter of finger tidbits (not pasta)

Au gratin: a casserole baked with grated cheese and breadcrumbs

Au jus: usually referring to meat served in its natural juices

Bake: cooking by dry heat in oven

Blanch: (parboil) to scald briefly then drain in order to facilitate removal of skin: e.g. tomatoes, peaches, almonds. Blanching also is a method of preserving flavor in certain vegetables.

Barbecue: to cook over coals on a spit or rack

Bechamel: a thick white sauce

Baste: to pour pan liquid over food while baking for flavoring and preventing dryness

Blini: unsweetened small pancake

Bouillabaisse: fish chowder

Bouquet garni: a combination of herbs tied together in a cheese cloth used as flavoring in cooking (then discarded)

Brisée: (short crust pastry) a crust which is buttery, tender and crunchy

Caramelize: method of melting sugar slowly over low flame until golden brown

Canapés: hors d'oeuvres of bread squares or crackers topped with cheese, smoked salmon, smoked meat, etc., with garnishes

Casserole: (a) a baking pan with or without cover made of earthenware or glass (b) name used for the actual food baked in a casserole dish

Castor sugar: finely granulated sugar

Coat: to cover all sides of food with a dry ingredient

Cobbler: a deep dish fruit pie with top crust

Coddle: method of cooking (usually referring to egg) in hot water just below boiling point

Compote: stewed fruit in syrup

Condiment: relish (e.g. mustard, sauce, ketchup) pickled or spicy food accompaniment

Consommé: clear soup

Coupe: a dish of ice cream

Crêpe suzette: thin rolled crêpe in brandy sauce

Croquette: a firm food cake dried until browned (usually made from fish, poultry or vegetables)

Croutons: crisp browned bread cubes (sometimes stirred into melted garlic butter) usually served with soup or salad

Crumpets: disc shaped yeast muffins

Cube: cutting into small squares

Cut in: combining flour and shortening

Deep fry: food fried completely immersed in heated oil

Diable: a brown sauce usually including white wine, vinegar and herbs

Dissolve: to melt or liquify

Dot: to sprinkle food with small pieces of butter or fat

Dredge: to coat food thickly with dry ingredient

Dust: to sprinkle lightly

Dutch oven: a heavy cooking pot with cover

Entrée: main course

Escalop: to bake with crumbs or cream sauce

Fillet: (a) a boneless lean piece of meat or fish (b) the process of boning

Flake: to separate into small pieces with a fork

Flan ring: bottomless ring for formed pastry crust

Fondant: a soft creamy paste mainly made of sugar usually used as candy filling

> Fondue: A dish which focuses on dipping a food into hot liquid before eating.
> A fondue usually consists of cubes of bread dipped in melted cheese, cubes of meat dropped into and cooked in hot oil, or pieces of fruit dipped in melted chocolate.

Garnish: (a) decorating food dishes with pieces of food (e.g. parsley, olives, pimiento, egg yolk
> (b) a specific decorative food

Glacé: glazed or iced

Glaze: (a) to cover with a sweet syrup (e.g. cakes, meat, poultry) (b) (noun) sweet syrup

Gnocchi: Italian potato dumplings

Grate: shred

Grease: to spread a piece of solid fat over surface of pan (for baking or frying) to prevent sticking

Jambalaya: a rice dish with meat or fish and/or vegetables

Jardiniére: served with diced vegetables

Julienne: cut into long thin strips

Knead: work dough by hand or with dough hook

Lyonnaise: served with thinly sliced fried onions (e.g., potatoes, steak).

Marinade: a prepared sauce or dressing for soaking food for flavor and/or tenderness

Moussaka: a mid-eastern dish made of chopped lamb and eggplant

Mousse: a dessert made of separated eggs, sugar, flavoring and sometimes whipped cream

Panboil: cook in skillet uncovered with or without fat

Panfry: cook in skillet with small amount of fat

Parboil: (blanch) method of partial cooking of food by dropping in boiling water and cooking a
> few minutes, then draining in cold water to stop the cooking process. Used to whiten,
> loosen skin (for removal), eliminate odor or to prepare for cooking by other methods

Pare: peel

Paste: a smooth mixture

Paté: a smooth paste

Paté de foie gras: a paté made from goose livers

Petit fours: small frosted cakes

Pièce de resistance: the best dish or specialty of the chef

Pilaf: a spiced rice dish with meat, poultry or fish

Pit: to remove pit or seed

Pizza: an Italian dish made of pastry dough base with tomato sauce-cheese-garnish topping

Plack: to boil and serve on wooden board (usually fish)

Poach: to cook slowly in boiling water

Pot au feu: beef stew with vegetables

Praline: candy made of nuts browned in boiling sugar

Preheat: to heat oven before baking food

Purée: (a) to strain cooked food through a sieve (b) Noun – sieved food

Quiche: a food pie made of a pastry dough base, filled with an egg mixture, flavored with cheese, vegetables or meat.

Ragout: (haricot) a thick seasoned stew

Ramekins: individual baking dishes

Reconstitute: returning food to its natural form with water

Render: to melt fat over very low heat

Sauté: to fry in solid or liquid fat, stirring occasionally

Scald: to heat liquid just below boiling point (usually referring to milk)

Scallop: to slice food (potatoes, meat, etc.) for baking, in sauce, en casserole

Score: to cut slits on surface of food
Scones: tea cakes
Sear: to brown meat quickly over intense heat
Shard: to cut into thin strips
Shirr: to bake eggs with crumb topping in individual buttered baking dishes
Simmer: to cook, covered, in a little water over low heat
Skewer: to fasten to thin wooden or metal rods
Soufflé: a fluffy baked food
Spumoni: an Italian frozen dessert
Steam: to cook, covered, over boiling water
Steam bake: to bake in oven with pan set in a larger pan of water
Stew: ingredients simmered, covered, in a little liquid
Stock: flavored water from cooking poultry, meat, fish or vegetables
Tamari sauce: soy sauce made of soy beans, wheat and salt
Torte: a rich cake dessert made from crumbs, nuts and eggs
Tortilla: a flat unleavened Mexican bread
Trifle: a dessert made from sponge cake soaked in fruit juices, wine and garnishes
Truss: to secure the wings and legs of poultry to the bird before roasting (with thread, skewers, etc.)
Welsh rabbit (rarebit): a dish of melted cheese and ale

Hints for Using Seasonings

HERBS

HERBS: Derived from the leaves of annual and perennial shrubs.

Bay leaves: pickling, stews (remove before serving), tomato sauce, artichokes, bouquet garni
Basil: tomato dishes, fish, soup, eggplant, zucchini, tomato sauces
Bouquet Garni: a mixture of fresh and dried herbs (marjoram, parsley, bay leaf, rosemary) wrapped in cheese cloth to enhance flavoring of soup, stews, etc.
Chervil: (parsley family) salads, soup, poultry, fish, vegetables. (Can be combined with chives and parsley)
Chives: (onion family) salads, soup, poultry, stuffing, sauces, stews
Dill: salads, soup, pickling, cream cheese
Fennel: fish, poultry, lentils
Garlic: (member of the lily family) almost everything
Marjoram: salads, vegetables, meat, sauces, omelettes, poultry, stuffings, bouquet garni, potatoes, soup, stews
Oregano: (wild marjoram) barbecue sauce, eggplant, tomatoes, soup, stews, zucchini
Rosemary: barbecue sauce, fish, poultry, spinach, stuffings, bouquet garni
Sage: (use sparingly) gravies, stews, stuffing
Savory: barbecue sauces, fish, omelettes, salads, stews
Tarragon: eggs, fish, mushrooms, poultry, salads, sauces, spinach
Thyme: cheese dishes, fish, meats, onion, potatoes, sauces, soups, stews, stuffings
Turmeric: (from the lily family) curries (rice), pickling

OTHER SEASONINGS

Capers: (green hyssop buds) salads, fish, sauces, Tartar sauce dressing
Cream of Tartar: (derived from grape juice after fermentation) reacts with baking soda to produce carbon dioxide to assist in rising process of dough
Salt: In baking a 'pinch of salt' enhances taste, reduces acidity and increases the sweetness of sugar. Additional sugar reduces saltiness and visa versa

SPICES & SEEDS

Derived from the bark, fruits, and berries of perennial plants

Allspice: (berry of the pimiento tree) pickling (its scent resembles that of a combination of cloves, cinnamon and nutmeg)

Caraway seeds: breads, cabbage, cheeses, sour cream, sauces, chopped meat

Cardamon Seeds: (from the ginger family) Turkish coffee (it has a pungent taste and varies in color, black, green and white. The lighter the color the better the flavor).

Cayenne Pepper: (sharp ground red pepper. Use sparingly) cheeses, seasoned sauces, barbecue sauce, meat, soups, stews

Cinnamon: desserts, cakes, meat, sweet rolls

Cloves: (dried buds. Use sparingly) broth, meat, stock, sweet rolls

Coriander: (Chinese parsley) pot roast, cheddar cheese, cream cheese, pickling

Cumin: (member of the carrot family) cheeses, chili dishes, eggs, barbecue sauce, chopped meat, soups, stews, pickling

Curry (mixture of herbs and spices. Variety of blends): Oriental dishes, rice

Ginger: cakes, cookies, fish, Oriental dishes, puddings, soups

Mace: (outer nutmeg covering) cakes, cookies, fish, meat, stews

Mustard seed: appetizers, dressings, fish, meat, sauces, pickling

Nutmeg: garnish to sweet milk drinks, desserts, meat puddings, quiche topping, soups

Paprika: (Hungarian pepper) poultry, meat, sauces, soups, stews, onions, dressings, garlic bread

Pepper: almost everything

Poppy seeds: breads, cakes, cookies, pastries, fish, meats

Saffron: (stigmas of a crocus plant. Gives a yellowish tint. Use sparingly) rice, fish, veal, chicken, certain cakes and breads

Sesame seeds: breads, garnish for soup and vegetable dishes, chicken

Hints on Entertaining

With a little bit of organization and planning the party can also be enjoyed by the host and hostess.

Decide what type of entertaining is best for the evening: A) sitting around the living room. B) full dinner party. C) buffet. D) barbecue (weather permitting) – lots of fun especially if the men take care of the barbecueing.

Sitting around the living room – have everything prepared before the guests arrive, including coffee cups, cake plates, cake servers, etc. The coffee table should be full and colorful – nuts, fruit, candies, dried fruit, hard cheese blocks, chunks or slices, cut-up fresh vegetables, dips, spreads, olives. A hot dish (e.g., quiche) is always a treat – a 9" (23 cm) quiche serves about 6 people. Don't forget small napkins.

Although its traditional to serve the coffee and cake around the dining room table, I find a buffet of cake and coffee works just as well, especially with a large group of people. A buffet lets the guests move around a little and it stimulates the conversation.

As far as setting up a bar – if there is no built-in bar, cover a square table with a cloth and arrange bottles, glasses, lemon wedges, olives, peanuts, and ice cubes in advance.

Dinner parties – occasionally a small formal dinner party is more fun and more successful than any other form of entertaining. The guests should be seated about ½ hour after arrival. Serve cordials, brandy and little tidbits while waiting for all the guests to arrive. Guests for dinner should come relatively on time.

Menu – Don't be afraid to tailor your menu to your mood and time requirements, with the exception of the following basic elements of good menu planning:

Variety and Color – For initial color try individual grapefruit halves, topped with a maraschino cherry or strawberry, placed on the table before the guests sit down.

Nibblers – There's always slack time between courses for nibblers. Refrigerate carrot sticks, celery stalks and radishes in water a day in advance, or the same day in ice water. Prepare plates of olives and pickles.

With more and more people becoming vegetarians be sure to have one or two vegetarian items. Don't have too many starchy side dishes and use one dark green or orange side dish.

Setting the table—two glasses for soft drinks and wine are placed on the upper right side (the wine glass to the right of the drinking glass.) Offer a choice of red or white wine. Using place settings eliminates chaos, and will make the evening more fun and successful. Use bread and butter plates placed at upper right (this can also be used for the nibblers). Prepare coffee cups, cake plates, sugarer, creamer, etc., before guests arrive. Besides soda, place a pitcher of cold water on the table. Serve wine French style, going around the table individually. Plan the logistics of serving and who is to help (if all the women get up at the same time—what then?) Do not remove plates until everyone is finished. If serving fruit salad, use underplates.

The Main Course — Prepare each plate individually and serve. Place the remaining food on platters or bowls (take into kitchen and rearrange size of platters and bowls so that they are full. Use two bowls at both ends of the table and one placed in center of table for seconds (or go around with seconds).

Put up coffee and water while everyone is enjoying seconds. When you feel that everyone has eaten as much as they can, clear the table of everything from the main course before serving dessert and coffee. Besides fruit and a rich cake, have crunchy cookies on the table. If there's time you may bring your guests into the living room for after-dinner drinks and mints.

Warming up — If a few dishes require time in the oven, be sure to take their cooking needs into account. If there's not enough room to warm everything up at one time use a hot plate.

Keeping cold dishes cool in hot weather—Place a serving bowl in a larger flatter bowl filled with water and freeze. When ready to serve, fill the inner bowl and serve as one unit.

Buffet — Create a table full of color and variety. Mix salads just before eating time so that they don't look like they have been sitting on the table all day. Do not wait for bowls and platters to be empty before refilling them. Clear table of main course completely before setting up for dessert and coffee.

Barbecue — This form of entertaining I enjoy the most since it requires the simplest foods and everything is put on the table together. My basic menu: salad and/or cole slaw, humus-tahina spread, pita bread and rolls, hot dogs, hamburgers, one or more of the following — French fried potatoes, corn, cabbage-noodle mix, sweet & sour red cabbage and spaghetti, watermelon, melon, coffee (hot or iced), cake or fruit pie and cookies. Everyone has a good time, especially if the men do the barbecueing.

Hints—Around the Kitchen

BURNS

SKIN BURNS: immediately pour over or douse burnt area in very cold water. When skin dries, wipe with tea bag a few times. (Home remedy—make a paste of baking powder and cold water. Apply to burn and cover with gauze.)

BURNT FOOD ON POT BOTTOM: Try sprinkling with a liberal amount of baking soda or some lemon juice, add water, bring to boil, simmer for a while and let stand a few hours. Lift out burnt food.

GREASE FIRE: if still possible, try sprinkling baking soda over the fire.

OVEN FIRE: immediately turn off heat and close oven door (lack of air will smother the fire).

CANDLES

- To prevent candles from melting quickly: keep candles in freezer and remove just before using.
- Removing candle wax from clothes or rugs: place a paper bag over the wax and iron it with a hot iron.

CLEANING

Like any cleaning guidelines these are not foolproof, only possible suggestions.

BROILER TRAYS: discard excess oil and remains, sprinkle pan with salt or detergent, cover with wet paper towel and leave for a while.

POTS: blackened aluminum pots — try cooking tomatoes in the pot.

ENAMEL POTS: mix bleach with water and boil until stain disappears.

OR make a paste of salt, flour and vinegar, spread on a thick layer, let dry, rinse and wipe. OR use a piece of fine steel wool with furniture polish or lemon juice.

COPPER: clean with a mixture of vinegar or lemon juice and salt. OR make a paste by adding flour.

GLASS: make a solution of ½ cup ammonia, ½ cup white distilled vinegar, 2 tablespoons cornstarch and water.

STAINLESS STEEL SINKS: baking soda with a little water or vinegar. The vinegar will also shine it up.

STAINED FORMICA COUNTERS: scrub with a paste of baking soda and water, leave ½ hour and wash off with a wet rag.

UNCLOGGING KITCHEN SINK: pour one cup of baking soda and a cup of vinegar down the drain. When it foams up, add cups of boiling water. If this doesn't work, call the plumber.

REFRIGERATORS

- Remedy to remove wall stains: wash with a paste of baking soda and water.
- General refrigerator cleaning: add a little baking soda to soapy water.
- To prevent mildew from forming: smear vinegar all over inside of refrigerator.

STOVES

- Small removable parts can be washed in the dishwasher; or soak in a solution of detergent, bleach and water and then wash with steel wool.
- Small stubborn spots on outer chrome, stainless steel or glass: use nail polish remover with a piece of cotton, or spread surface with vinegar, leave about one minute and wipe clean.
- Uneven gas stove flames: may be due to clogged burners. Clean burners with a soapy toothbrush; rinse and pierce holes with a toothpick.

OVENS: Warm up oven, place a glassful of ammonia on upper rack, place a large bowl of water on lower rack, close door and leave overnight. Wash with soapy water.

TEA KETTLES: To get rid of lime deposits, first fill kettle with water, bring water to a boil and discard. Then fill kettle with equal parts of vinegar and water; bring water to boil; leave overnight and wash out.

SCENTS AND ODORS

- Fresh-smelling refrigerators: after cleaning thoroughly with warm soapy water or paste of baking soda and water, rinse with a solution of vinegar and water. Afterwards place an open container of vinegar in the refrigerator to preserve a fresh smell. If there is a specific unpleasant smell, try placing a piece of charcoal or open baking soda package in the refrigerator for a few days.
- Picnic ice chest or cooler: during storage place an open container of baking soda inside.
- Getting rid of fishy fish smells: marinate the fish in a pan with lemon juice for about an hour, turning once. Rinse under cold water and pat dry.
- Fishy smelling hands: wash hands in heavily salted water.
- Fishy odor and grease from pan: pour ½ cup of vinegar in pan; bring to boil and wash regularly.
- Garbage pails: place a few mothballs on the bottom.

JARS

- To prevent cracking glass jar with hot liquid: rinse jar in hot water, place either a spoon (for a small jar) or knife in the jar before pouring the liquid. Allow to cool slightly before removing spoon or knife from jar.
- To open stubborn covers: turn jar completely upside down and tap lightly on the floor. There are also great gadgets available for this purpose.

PYREX: do not transfer a pyrex pan straight from the oven to a marble slab or counter (the shock of the cold marble may crack the pyrex).

SHINING UP

CRYSTAL: wash in a basin of water with a little ammonia.

CHROME & STAINLESS STEEL: wipe with a solution of ammonia or vinegar and water.

VINYL FLOOR: after washing, go over with a mixture of ½ cup vinegar to 4 quarts of water.

STAINLESS STEEL FLATWARE: soak in a solution of ammonia or vinegar and hot water. Rinse and dry.

WINDOWS AND TILES: add ½ cup ammonia, ½ cup vinegar, 2 tablespoons baking soda to a half-bucketful of warm water.

TABLECLOTHS

To keep tablecloth from flying away outdoors: sew pockets on the underside of the tablecloth in four corners; place tablecloth on table and fill pockets with a few marbles.

STAINS

No method of stain-removal is foolproof, but these are good bets to try.

- Red wine stains: put stained area in pot, cover with milk, bring to boil and then remove cloth from pot.
- Ball point pen: sponge with milk.
- Mustard: rub detergent into dampened stain and rinse.

WOODEN BOARDS AND BOWLS

Wooden boards and bowls should be replaced periodically (especially if used for meat) due to the possibility of bacteria retention in the wood.

Wooden boards are ideal for cutting, kneading and rolling out dough (if you do a lot of kneading, rolling and shaping yeast dough etc., it's worth investing in a large wooden board with a lip going up and down in front and back. If you can't find it have a carpenter make it.

Wooden bowls

They are ideal for chopping and for tossing salads.

- How to treat wooden boards and bowls: if you're not careful, your boards and bowls will crack within a short time. Don't leave the wooden board on a counter near a sink (if water is left under the board it will cause cracking).
- Treatment: thoroughly rub mineral oil over the boards and bowls—especially during the first year of use.
- To prevent bowls from becoming sticky: wash and dry thoroughly, then rub bowl inside and out with a piece of waxed paper.
- To remove sticky dough from wooden boards: sprinkle salt on a wet sponge and rub board. If you have to scrape the wooden board or butcher block, use a plastic windshield scraper (it's not as sharp as a knife so it won't damage the wood as much.)

Wooden Spoons

Treatment: scrub spoon clean, place in hot water for about one minute, dry with towel and leave to dry a few hours. Heat cooking oil in pot, dip spoon for a few seconds in hot oil, leave to cool and wipe dry. This process will prevent cracking and keep spoon from absorbing food odors.

INDEX